THE CREATIVE COUNSELOR

THE CREATIVE COUNSELOR

James A. Nicholson, Ph.D.
Northwestern State University
Gordon Golsan, Ed.D.
Adams State College

McGRAW-HILL BOOK COMPANY

New York St. Louis San Francisco Auckland Bogotá
Hamburg Johannesburg London Madrid Mexico Montreal New Delhi
Panama Paris São Paulo Singapore Sydney Tokyo Toronto

This book was set in Optima by J.M. Post Graphics Corp.
The editor was Christina Mediate;
the production supervisor was John Mancia.
Project supervision was done by The Total Book.
Halliday Lithograph Corporation was printer and binder.

THE CREATIVE COUNSELOR

1 2 3 4 5 6 7 8 9 0 HALHAL 8 9 8 7 6 5 4 3

ISBN 0-07-046490-1

Library of Congress Cataloging in Publication Data

Nicholson, James A.
The creative counselor.

Includes bibliographies and index.
1. Counseling. I. Golsan, Gordon. II. Title.
BF637.C6N53 1983 158′.3 82-13959
ISBN 0-07-046490-1

TO OUR WIVES
SUSAN AND WANDA

AND OUR CHILDREN
HEIDI, HEATHER, AND BRETT
BILL AND KRIS

CONTENTS

PREFACE

Creativity is more than a high level of personal and intellectual functioning. It involves a process of preparation, insight, and revision. It is set in motion through risk—the risk of moving beyond preset patterns of problem solving. It occurs consistently only within individuals who risk thinking independently and who see complexity as challenge. The creative individual thrives on translating distortion and confusion into solutions. Such is the case with creative counseling. It represents counseling at its very best—firmly founded in the basic principles of helping, but never tied to any rigid system of intervention techniques. It flows with the client's needs and draws upon whatever resources are needed to meet them. It is an ideal in the sense that it reflects the peak performance of the most effective counselors. But it is a reachable ideal—one that can be reached more frequently when counselors actively cultivate their own creative potentials. The primary purpose of our book is to help the reader reach this potential on a consistent basis.

We are extremely excited about the ideas we are sharing in *The Creative Counselor.* The enthusiasm generated between us has been worth the effort in itself and has made us more effective with our clients and students. We hope that the reader picks up on our optimism and translates the concepts and strategies we present into increased personal and client benefits. However, we do not want to oversell our ideas. They are not earthshaking and basically reflect a good bit of common sense. Ideas at best can never be more than stimuli for reflection, self-evaluation, and constructive change. In a real sense, no one can tell anyone how to become creative. Our ideas have to become personalized before any real value is realized.

While writing does not come easy for us, we have enjoyed the process of organizing and presenting our ideas. This process was stimulated most directly by our students and clients, but was nurtured by hundreds of intense discussions we shared in between classes, racquetball games, and fishing trips. We also owe a large debt to our colleagues and our wives for their suggestions and support. Many of our ideas are borrowed, and we appreciate the stimulus provided by the wide range of resources reflected in our production. It has been an evolving process and continues to change even as we near publication. But that is the essence of creativity and the thing that keeps counseling alive and challenging.

James A. Nicholson

Gordon Golsan

PART ONE

DIRECTIONS AND FOUNDATIONS OF A MATURING PROFESSION

While creativity in counseling is the basic theme of our book, it seems unlikely that creative counseling will occur without a sound foundation in philosophy, theory, technique, and the counselor's own high level of functioning. This high-functioning individual, armed with a broad repertoire of intervention strategies, then meets the prerequisites for entering the client's frame of reference and creatively developing an individualized program of counseling designed to meet the client's unique needs. Since preparation in fundamentals precedes creativity, we will focus on the foundations for creative counseling in Part One.

The theme of creative counseling is an extension of several emerging trends within our profession. Consequently, Chapter 1 will set the stage for creative counseling within the framework of changes which have occurred in our profession within the past three decades and have led to a growing acceptance of eclecticism. But creative counseling moves beyond eclecticism and finds its niche in an interdisciplinary movement the roots of which are presented in Chapter 2. Once the historical context for creative counseling has been established, our energies will be directed at its philosophical and theoretical foundations. Chapter 3 will focus on a broad-based philosophy upon which creative counseling can be founded, whereas the final chapter in Part One will delineate an open eclectic model to serve as a starting point for the creative counselor. The second part of our book will then move beyond foundational basics toward the principles and techniques of the creative counselor.

CHAPTER **1**

TAKING CHARGE OF CHANGE

Change: for better or worse? The helping profession has come through a dramatic period of redirection in the 1970s. There is no question regarding the reality of this transition—it has become a genuine movement and is reflected by the rapidity of change in counselor roles during the preceding decade. This reformulation has been critical to the very survival of our profession and has moved us from stagnation into an era of tremendous excitement and renewed potential for positively impacting the lives of our clients and society in general. Our emerging professional direction reflects the courage of choosing change (for better) and provides a model which can be paralleled by individual counselors who ultimately decide on their own course toward growth or stagnation. While the current *Zeitgeist* (atmosphere of the times) favors a positive direction, the choice is still up to each of us. One road (for worse) is followed by all too many pseudo helpers and leads to nonproductivity, low satisfaction, and dwindling commitment. The other choice (for better) necessitates personal risk and extraordinary dedication but is the only way to reap the exciting benefits inherent in helping others. These are truly exciting times for those who enthusiastically maintain an openness to expanding their personal/professional lives. For those willing to take on the challenge of a changing profession, change is a friendly catalyst and stimulus for continual reassessment of our expanding levels of competence.

Change should be a familiar word to counselors and psychotherapists. It is perhaps the most fundamental concept underlying our efforts to help others (Srebalus, 1975). Transferring increased understanding of our needs and related barriers into constructive action lies at the very core of the counseling process, positive human development, and the growth of an entire profession. As with our clients, however, our personal/professional development must evolve from a rationally based decision-making process which enables us to extend innovation into our existing structure. Change promoted by rational risk taking is what we are talking about. Gerber (1974) suggests that the very essence of enthusiasm and satisfaction among counselors derives from their commitment to the risk taking necessitated by continual self-expansion. Defensive practitioners stagnate as they bemoan the loads of paperwork and administrative junk. Perhaps they gain security from the mundane and in reality are afraid of taking the risk of broadening their approaches to counseling. They are no longer at the center of control of their professional lives and only watch change from the security of their counseling offices.

Robert Carkhuff, the militant humanist, has set a good example for helping professionals through his proactive involvement in promoting our professional redirection. He offers some valuable guidelines for us in his discussion of the three R's of helping (1976)—right, role, and responsibility. He states that only individuals who are functioning at a high level themselves have the *right* to intervene in the lives of others. Further, effective helping is an all-encompassing way of life that is only mimicked in a fake manner by those who operate out of a *role*. Finally, the effective helper must assume the *responsibility* of ongoing revitalization at both personal and professional levels. There is simply no room in our changing profession for anyone who lacks this kind of responsibility, commitment, and high level of energy. We would like to extend this challenge to the readers of this book and assert that its reading is definitely not for complacent professionals who are too afraid to take control of producing an upgrading cycle of change in their lives, let alone in the lives of their clients. We already have too much deadwood in our profession. This book is designed for dedicated helpers who are not afraid of paying the price of personal commitment and professional development.

PROFESSIONAL TRANSITION: FROM CHALLENGE TO CREATIVITY

The change we have alluded to in our initial comments can be seen as part of a cycle which reflects the history of the counseling profession during the past three decades. During this era, our profession has not only chosen to take on the attacks directed at ineffectiveness but has emerged as a dramatically different profession with a broader scope. This period of change may now give way to a time of high productivity and further growth for those who choose the difficult and rewarding road of integrating the wide range of innovative materials generated during this change period. Entering a new decade provides both a time for reflection and the opportunity for setting new goals.

The 1950s: Challenge

Most undergraduate psychology majors are familiar with the classic report presented by Eysenck (1952) which inspired nearly two decades of debate concerning the effectiveness of psychotherapy. The findings challenged the very core of the helping professions by suggesting that neurotics are as likely to improve by being left alone as when treated by trained psychotherapists. Similar findings were also presented by Levitt (1957) and a variety of other research reports. A more sophisticated follow-up analysis a decade later (Eysenck, 1965) continued to stir the controversy with this conclusion: ". . . It seems that psychologists and psychiatrists would have to acknowledge the fact that current psychotherapeutic procedures have not lived up to the hopes which greeted their emergence fifty years ago." The challenge was clear and the response during the 1960s was resounding.

Ironically, a statement by the American Psychological Association (APA) in 1956 that was designed to expand the role of counselors toward prevention through resource mobilization and societal intervention (McGowan and Schmidt, 1962) fell on deaf ears as many sought to make counseling and psychotherapy indistinguishable. We were still enamored with the therapeutic model. The primary response during the 1950s to Eysenck's challenge was a defensive retreat to our laboratories in an effort to prove him wrong. With all of this effort being directed toward saving our sacred cow and preserving existing territories, little creative energy could be released toward redefining priorities.

The 1960s: Choice

The nearly unanimous choice by researchers and practitioners in responding to Eysenck's challenge was to fight back. The first choice, however, was to respond with additional outcome research which generated even more nonproductive fuel for the fire. Literally dozens of such studies followed during the first half of the decade. After attacking the design problems of earlier research on psychotherapy, the reactionary investigations of the early 1960s (with improved methodology) continued to yield the somewhat discouraging conclusion that psychotherapy produces modestly positive benefits. After summarizing most of the studies of this decade, Bergin (1971) expressed the need to "call a moratorium on classical psychotherapy outcome studies and upon a large proportion of the traditional therapy currently practiced." He offered a new direction to the earlier challenge by suggesting that our efforts should concentrate on process research designed to "isolate and define those persons and methods that are most effective." He concluded that "there is little reason to reinforce or reassure the ordinary practitioner of psychotherapy, for we expect future research to show that his labors must be revised toward matching the behavior of a few successful peers who actually obtain most of the therapeutic results."

Fortunately, a number of researchers had already chosen to make their stand along the more productive lines of process research. Subsequent research uncovered a *deterioration effect* in psychotherapy which implied that some therapists consistently produced improvement among their clients whereas others promoted deterioration (Bergin, 1966). These findings opened the door for related studies designed to explore the specific ingredients which tended to yield positive results in psychotherapy. Robert Carkhuff and his associates championed this new direction in research and pioneered the translation of their findings into a more comprehensive picture of the effective counseling process as a guideline for theory and practice which set the tone for improving the effectiveness of counselors [many publications could be cited, but Carkhuff and Berenson (1967) is the most significant]. This group of researchers identified the dimensions of effective helping and stimulated dozens of studies to further clarify the basic core conditions which have become familiar to many of us. This critical choice of putting understanding into action is still making an impact on the direction of the profession.

Drawing energy and encouragement from those who chose to take on Eysenck's challenge, the work of the psychotherapist seemed to take on renewed promise toward the end of this decade, but new challenges were to emerge. Even if psychotherapy could produce benefits and could be taught to high-functioning individuals, its application as our primary professional direction was being questioned, and a dramatic change in priorities appeared to be in order. Dissatisfaction with the narrow therapeutic role was growing but would not be solidified into a movement of change until the next decade. In retrospect, Wrenn (1962) was a prophet of the change that was to come in his call for expanding the counselor's role to include consultation, community involvement, and resource coordination. Questions regarding the most fundamental values and directions of the profession could only come out of a growing edge of healthy confidence, and these concerns would provide the impetus for the upcoming decade of change.

The 1970s: Change

The *Zeitgeist* of the late 1960s, with its demands on credibility and attacks on traditionalism in the schools, paved the way for a moratorium against the impotence of an all too narrowly defined counseling profession. The mandate for change forced by school-oriented counselors was also being echoed by many agency psychotherapists. Society in general became sensitized to change as a key factor in this new decade through the writing of Alvin Toffler in *Future Shock* (1970). The scientist/practitioner model (Raimy, 1950) which had become the guiding light (or perhaps shadow) for clinical and counseling psychology over the two preceding decades was in jeopardy. In his presidential address in 1969, George A. Miller (APA) challenged his colleagues to move the body of psychological knowledge out of the laboratory and into the mainstream of social problems. Birdie (1972) suggested that the counseling profession had evolved to meet the real needs of individuals, but had borrowed its theories and methods from other related disciplines and had "improvised modes of operating." As president of The American Personnel and Guidance Association, he asserted that the responses to social problems were neither carefully thought out nor planned and that its rationale was developed after the fact. It appears that this decade had brought with it the demand for change toward the development of new and more effective directions.

Growing concern with the viability of the structure of the counseling profession was primarily directed toward the limited confines of an inherited direct service model which was essentially passive and marginally effective. In a key publication, Drum and Figler (1973) indicated that counselor ineffectiveness had its historical roots imbedded in its adoption of therapeutic, psychometric, and stop-gap administrative functions. While concentrating on a limited range of safe, visible problems, i.e., eliminating maladaptive behavior and identification of underachievers and college material with all of the related testing and book-keeping details, counselors had systematically removed themselves from the main-stream of the educational scene. They had become negatively oriented and largely impotent whereas counselor educators had continued to provide a supportive base for noninvolvement. Comfortable peacemaking tasks kept counselors so busy that an immunity to more creative and active involvements with their clients had been built and served as a defense against meaningful redefinition of relatively nonproductive, reactive, passive roles. Ralph Birdie (1972) offered the challenge for change in the 1970s:

> Counseling as we know it is a profession of the 20th Century. But in spite of its youth and vigor, we can raise serious questions about its survival possibilities. Unlike the oldest professions, this younger one has failed to incorporate itself into the fabric of society and to demonstrate that it satisfies basic and continuing needs of individuals. Counselors have done much good and have helped many individuals, but their occupation has not been widely acknowledged as a profession, nor have its roots extended deep into our supporting economic and social state. The survival of counseling as it now exists is doubtful (p. 451).

Clearly, we were at the crossroads: Change or die a comfortable death, without being noticed, within the privacy of our offices. With the increased disenchantment concerning the profession's basic structure and the emergence of many laudable yet disconnected programs, i.e., outreach, prevention, and peer counseling, the *Zeitgeist* now favored the development of organizational models which would integrate recent changes and provide a future direction. Subsequently, several multimodel systems were proposed as vehicles for the delivery of diverse counseling services. These models provided both the structure and further impetus for change. Drum and Figler (1973) presented a "seven-dimensional model of outreach potential" designed to facilitate the release of counseling services previously untapped by the direct service model. This system emphasized the potential for revitalizing our profession through a renewed emphasis upon growth and prevention.

Both authors can recall the feeling of exhilaration as we became exposed to the Vail Conference "cube model which was bursting with stimulating ideas" (Goldman, 1974). Based on earlier efforts by Morrell, Oetting, and Hurst (1972), this brainchild was formally introduced in a special issue of the *Personnel and Guidance Journal* in February 1974. This model became the symbol of "change and new direction but also reflected an 'integration' of much that has been happening over the past 25 years." As editor of this special issue, Parker (1974) describes the model as a metatheory capable of integrating a variety of innovative trends within the profession. After presenting the 36 faces of counseling contained in the cube (see Figure 1-1), Morrell, Oetting, and Hurst (1974) concluded:

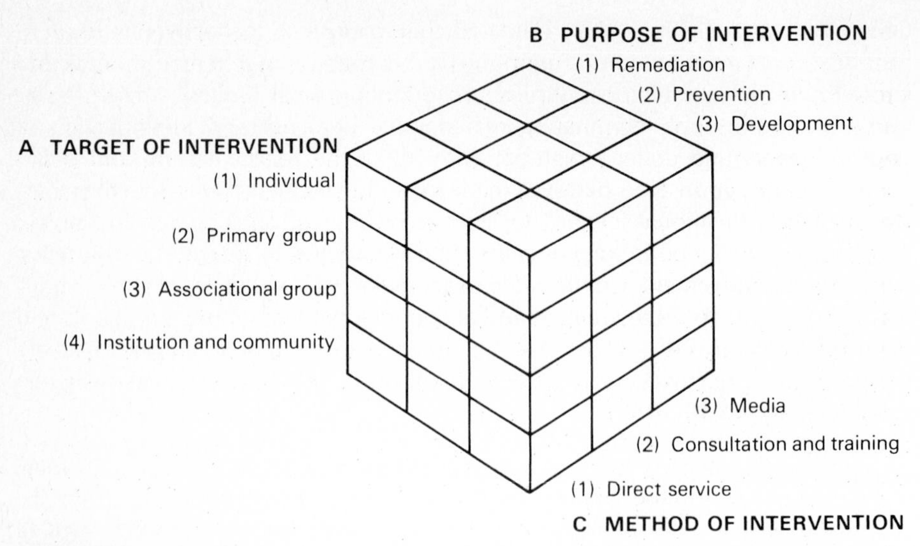

FIGURE 1-1
Thirty-six faces of counseling.

> Counseling as a profession simply cannot afford to function in the comparatively ineffective ways of the past. Utilizing a comprehensive intervention model can lead to new and meaningful programs that really meet the human needs of our society (p. 359).

In examining the potential impact of this model 1 year later, Ivey and Leppaluoto (1975) asserted:

> The recommendations of this conference are staggering in their complexity and scope. Depending on the reader's point of view, the recommendations may appear to represent the future direction of helping, may seem naively optimistic, or may even seem destructive. Nonetheless, after the initial reactions have been recorded, those who seek to change their existing patterns of training will for the first time have a serious set of recommendations that endorse, even demand change (p. 748).

These authors suggested that psychologists must recognize themselves as political beings who must explore their impact on society. We must likewise stop the avoidance of tough issues while soliciting greater consumer participation in the utilization of psychological services. They concluded the article by calling for greater interdependence between professional helpers and their representative organizations.

The catalytic value of this cube model is reflected in the proliferation of meaningful programs which have symbolized a decade of change. The development of more productive means of counselor intervention within the context of this innovative structure has injected our profession with renewed viability. Evidence for these developments abound in the interrelated trends toward paraprofessional training, self-help literature, the adaption of numerous therapeutic models within preventative contexts, and dozens of related innovations. After examining the political and social conditions which allowed these seeds of change to flourish, Herr (1980) concludes that the decade of the 1970s witnessed the maturing of a profession. Change has been the hallmark of a transition from identity (even survival) crisis to renewed viability. A recent survey of this maturing process by several counselor leaders (Pinson, Herr, Gysbers, Hoyt, and Wrenn, 1980) further identifies many of the accomplishments of the past decade—professional reform, demystification of counseling, developmental theory, team approaches, holistic models, and so forth. These strides toward maturity also reflect a positive dynamism for the profession's movement into the current decade. Whereas this growth has brought about a broader definition of helping, the next decade will see a demand for even further expansion of the multimodel intervention theme. Unfortunately, many of our colleagues, engulfed by traditional agency structure, still operate within the narrow confines of a direct service orientation. They are reluctant to risk involvement in the exciting pace of change we are experiencing and may continue to be left behind in their discontent as we move into the 1980s.

The 1980s: Creativity

The rapidity of change that hallmarked our previous decade continues into the 1980s and will precipitate crises among many counselors who are not prepared to meet the challenge. Some will undoubtedly withdraw in the face of change-mitigated stress into the safety of their past skills training or the rigidity of unidimensional systems of counselor intervention. Others will take charge of change by using the principles and techniques previously generated within the profession as a foundation for effectively interacting in our helping efforts with others. The creative counselors will be those who successfully integrate a wide variety of skills within a broad-based and positive philosophical orientation toward their clients. With this as a foundation, they will then be free to take the risks inherent in the intensity of counseling. They will be able to see their clients in their true complexity and engage themselves [as Otto Rank put it some 50 years ago (Rank, 1929)] in creative interchanges guided by internal standards.

Gysbers (1980) suggests, "The challenge of the 1980's is to empower those we serve to become all they can become." We see counselors as the pivotal ingredient in the human development equation and, thus, would focus Gysbers's challenge directly toward the counselors' efforts at becoming their own potential. Counseling at its most effective level, then, can become a highly creative endeavor in which counselors are totally involved in facilitating a problem-solving process with those who seek their assistance. The counseling process itself can become creative (even going beyond the intended limits of its creator) in capitalizing on seemingly accidental combinations of its basic ingredients. But we contend that creativity in the counseling context will not occur consistently without the prerequisite skills and attitudes. Consequently, our book focuses initially upon the basic foundational ingredients of effective counseling before moving on to consider some of the fundamental elements of creative counseling.

Specifically, the remainder of Part One attempts to identify these fundamentals and provides a context for the remaining chapters which delineate some of the key variables relevant to creative counseling. Chapter 2 provides a broad perspective of the historical roots of our profession and builds a case for the merging of the divergent branches of the helping profession in the 1980s. Just as the creative counselor must be relatively free from internal turmoil, so must the counseling profession move beyond issues of territoriality toward interdependence with the spiritual, medical, and psychosocial views of helping. We are optimistic about the potential of further professional maturity in the present decade as we continue to expand professional boundaries.

Chapter 3 presents a philosophical orientation and some considerations regarding basic human nature and development. A series of principles defining human movement in deteriorative and constructive directions is delineated and serves as a basis for consideration of the counseling process in the following chapter. Chapter 4 presents existing insights into the counseling process and identifies the contributions and limitations of current models before pointing toward future areas of expansion to be developed in Part Two. Our goal is to critique and integrate existing knowledge as a basis for new directions. Consequently, a thorough review of critical resources regarding the counseling process is beyond the intent of this book, and readers who are unfamiliar with this extensive background literature are encouraged to supplement their reading with a guided review of related key publications which we recommend. The creative counselor must be firmly based in fundamentals and that only comes from a basically healthy outlook on life supplemented with extensive reading and experience.

The past two decades witnessed revolutionary progress in the identification of critical counseling skills and the development of unifying process systems. In fact, without these foundational efforts there would be little basis for the highly effective and creative kind of counseling which is the basic theme of our book. However, there are many pieces to the counseling puzzle which remain to be explored. These are the variables which move the counselor from the fundamental to the creative. Part Two of this book focuses on these relatively uncharted directions.

Whereas a wealth of knowledge surrounding the actual counseling process has been generated, we have largely ignored the context out of which any helping effort must emerge. Chapter 5, therefore, explores the critical contextual variables which set the stage for a highly creative and productive interchange during counseling. Much of the work of counseling takes place outside of the actual therapeutic encounter—this applies to the counselor as well as the client. Consequently, we develop pre- and postsession strategies which can maximize the release of the counselor's creative energies. Chapter 6 explores risk as a key variable in the creative counseling process. Risk moves the counselor beyond the seeming security of the structure provided by schemes and eclectic models and into a primary focus on the client's needs—out of theoretical confines and into creative involvement. In Chapter 7, we extend the concept of risk into the context of preventive/developmental counseling. We believe that the process of creative counseling reaches its maximum potential when dealing with relatively healthy people who are grappling with developmental issues. We provide specific guidelines for moving beyond the remedial confines of creative counseling. In Chapter 8, we expand on the current interest of multidimensional counseling as a basis for further extending the counselor's boundaries of intervention. The creative counselor must be able to move beyond the client's psychological concerns into the spiritual and physical arenas in order to stay with the complexity of client needs, and we develop some guidelines to help the counselor meet this challenge. Our final chapter focuses on creative counselors themselves. They are the most critical ingredients in creative counseling and have to take good care of themselves by nurturing their own strength through a constructive lifestyle. Therefore, we conclude by offering a scheme for counselor renewal designed to keep us at the kind of peak functioning necessary for creative counseling.

SUMMARY

In Chapter 1, we have identified some of the historical changes within the counseling profession. The positive flow of the profession has occurred as follows: Responding to the challenge for effectiveness in the 1950s; making an assertive choice to improve its effectiveness through more specific outcome studies in the 1960s; and developing a professional identity characterized by a broader role definition (prevention, developmental counseling, and a growing acceptance of an eclectic framework) during the 1970s. During the 1980s, the authors believe that additional positive movement will occur for our profession. An eclectic orientation will become increasingly accepted and serve as a foundation for counselors to interact in highly creative ways as they seek to meet client needs. High levels of personal functioning and a wide range of intervention techniques serve as a basis for creatively entering the client's personal perspective. The perceived limits of eclectic counseling will be expanded in several directions as the creative counselor develops additional areas of expertise. These extensions of contemporary eclecticism will serve as the major focus of our book.

REFERENCES

Bergin, A. E. Some implications of psychotherapy research for therapeutic practice. *Journal of Abnormal Psychology,* 1966, *71,*235–246.

Bergin, A. E. The evaluation of therapeutic outcomes. In A. E. Bergin and S. C. Garfield (Eds.), *Handbook of psychotherapy and behavior change.* New York: Wiley, 1971.

Birdie, R. 1980 counselor: Applied behavioral scientist. *Personnel and Guidance Journal,* 1972, 50(6),451–456.

Carkhuff, R. R. *Constructive and destructive living.* Presentation of the Colorado Personnel and Guidance Association Convention, Denver, Fall 1976.

Carkhuff, R. R. and Berenson, B. G. *Beyond counseling and therapy.* New York: Holt, 1967.

Drum, D. J. and Figler, H. E. *Outreach in counseling.* New York: Intext Educational Publishers, 1973.

Eysenck, H. J. The effects of psychotherapy. *International Journal of Psychiatry,* 1965, *1,*97–178.

Eysenck, H. J. The effects of psychotherapy: An evaluation. *Journal of Consulting Psychology,* 1952, *18,*319–324.

Gerber, E. R. Toward professional commitment through risking and sharing. *Personnel and Guidance Journal,* 1974, *53*(3),187–191.

Goldman, L. Introduction: How this issue came to be. *Personnel and Guidance Journal,* 1974, *52*(6),346.

Gysbers, N. C. Profession matures during the '70s. *Guidepost,* January 1980, p. 8.

Herr, E. L. Profession matures during the '70s. *Guidepost,* January 1980, 8.

Ivey, A. E. and Leppaluoto, J. R. Changes ahead! Implications of the Vail conference. *Personnel and Guidance Journal,* 1975, *53*(10),747–752.

Levitt, E. G. The results of psychotherapy with children. *Journal of Consulting Psychology,* 1957, *21,*189–196.

McGowan, J. F. and Schmidt, L. D. *Counseling: Readings in theory and practice.* New York: Holt, 1962.

Morrell, W. H., Oetting, E. R., and Hurst, J. C. *Technical report number 1: Dimensions of counseling intervention.* Fort Collins, Colo.: Rocky Mountain Behavioral Science Institute, 1972.

Morrell, W. H., Oetting, E. R., and Hurst, J. C. Dimensions of counselor functioning. *Personnel and Guidance Journal,* 1974, *52*(6),355–359.

Parker, C. A. The new scope of counseling. *Personnel and Guidance Journal,* 1974, *52*(6),348–350.

Pinson, N. M., Herr, E. L., Gysbers, N. C., Hoyt, K. B., and Wrenn, C. G. Profession matures during the '70s. *Guidepost,* January 1980, p. 8.

Poser, E. The effects of therapist's training on group's therapeutic outcome. *Journal of Consulting Psychology,* 1966, *30,*383–389.

Raimy, V. (Ed.). *Training in clinical psychology.* Englewood Cliffs, N.J.: Prentice-Hall, 1950.

Rank, O. *The birth trauma.* New York: Harcourt, Brace, 1929.

Srebalus, D. J. Rethinking change in counseling. *Personnel and Guidance Journal,* 1975, *53*(6),415–421.

Toffler, A. *Future shock.* New York: Bantam, 1970.

Wrenn, C. G. *The counselor in a changing world.* Washington, D.C.: American Personnel and Guidance Association, 1962.

CHAPTER 2

INFANCY TO INTERDEPENDENCE

Unity within the helping professions is still more the reflection of the emerging edge of an exciting direction than a tested reality. This glimmer of resolution is tempered by centuries of conflict. The remaining limits to the counselor's growing impact are, in part, products of the rigidness of past theories and practices. Graduate training programs are still too often seen as divided into opposing camps (the behaviorists versus the humanists, for example) fighting for territorial rights. At times, the only united front among some psychologists seems to be in their mutual resistance to medical or spiritual explanations of human dysfunction and treatment.

It is typical during the graduate training experience to become seduced by the charismatic Freudian or Rogerian therapist on the staff into a discipleshiplike adherence to their orientation. Many of us have experienced the schizoidlike fluctuation from identifying with one school of psychotherapy and then another. Some students even become discouraged from the ambiguity created by facing a bewildering variety of competing theories and their exuberant proponents. Seeming simplicity becomes more seductive as we become more insecure, and anxiety is reduced among novice clinicians by enthusiastic devotion to narrow systems. Premature identification with specialized methods not only relieves insecurity and enables us to feel unique and knowledgeable, but removes the responsibility, risk, and energy investment necessary to develop a broad-based philosophy and repertoire of techniques.

We think that Ungersma (1961) has made a reasonable assessment of the kind of confusion which existed in the previous two or three decades and still betrays our movement toward unity within the helping professions. He stated:

> The present situation [during the 1960's] in psychotherapy is not unlike the man who mounted his horse and rode off in all directions. The theoretical orientations of therapists are based upon widely divergent hypotheses, theories, and ideologies. . . . Individual practitioners of any art are expected to vary, but some well-organized schools of therapy seem to be at cross-purposes with other equally well organized schools. Nevertheless, all schools, given favorable conditions, achieve favorable results: the patient or client gets relief and is often enough cured of his difficulties. (p.55).

Allport (1962) suggested that the problem with divergent "current theories rests in their incompleteness (rather than inaccuracy) of describing the nature of man and the corresponding modalities of therapeutic intervention." In speculating about the future of our field nearly two decades ago, Carl Rogers (1963) stated that "the field of psychotherapy is in a mess" but was optimistic in viewing the turmoil of the 1960s as a healthy climate for the development of a new comprehensive paradigm for theory and practice.

In presenting his philosophy of science, Sinnott (1958) suggested that the struggle of psychotherapy to find an exclusive niche within a unique body of knowledge has been paralleled by most fields at their infancy stage. We believe that a valid analogy may further exist between the stages of human development and the growth of the helping professions. Erikson (1963) has outlined a series of critical periods, with the struggle against mistrust of infancy and the defensive adolescent battle for unique identity gradually moving toward the healthy productivity that comes with maturity. The following discussion will relate this process (dependence to independence to interdependence) to the historical roots of our profession and suggest that we have largely resolved our professional identity crisis and are moving toward a more mature holistic status within the counseling profession.

A HISTORICAL PERSPECTIVE: RADICAL TO RECEPTIVE

Our philosophical view of human nature has paralleled our methods of therapeutic intervention throughout history. From psychosurgery to free association, the precursors of contemporary therapeutic modalities can be traced back thousands of years. This dynamic movement has been characterized by the ebb and flow transition from periods of progressive reform to regressive steps backwards, with the predominant view of any particular time reflecting the *Zeitgeist* (tenor of the times) of that period.

In ancient history (Bach, 1977), human beings were seen holistically as an integration of body, mind, and spirit. An Egyptian priest/physician named Imhotep (circa, 3000 B.C.) founded a school for healing based on the precepts of sensible diet (physical), alert mind (mental), and adherence to cosmic law (spiritual) while emphasizing the triadic interaction as inseparable and in constant need of balance. Bach states that "Imhotep, physician, teacher, minister within his time, first combined within himself and then inspired within others the concept of holism as a practical approach to total health." He points out, however, that the passage of time was marked with fragmentation as religious, medical, and psychosocial views became separated. Conflicting positions emerged during the infant and adolescent stages of our profession which rested on defensiveness and dualistic thinking, but established a necessary foundation for a contemporary movement toward the interdependence of spiritual, physical, and psychosocial orientations. Centuries of radicalism are only now giving way to an era of receptivity.

The Spiritual Domain: Humans as Moral Beings

Coleman, Butcher, and Carson (1980) report that one of the earliest treatments of mental disorders has been associated with the stone-age people's use of crude stone instruments to chip away a portion of the skull. This procedure (now called *trephining*) provides a classic example of the logical consistency between the conceptualization of human misery and its treatment. If an evil spirit is seen as the cause of anguish, then the local shaman's efforts to release the demon through this process seem to fit quite rationally. Early Chinese, Hebrew, and Greek thought concerning human misery involved variations of exorcism. These tactics were supplemented by some of the Grecian priests (circa, 800 B.C.) with the use of music, prayer, walking, riding, and other recreational measures.

Jesus (the "Great Physician") was heavily invested in healing and represented a dramatic break from the narrow demonological position even though he included the casting out of evil spirits within his healing repertoire. Although his primary interest was within the spiritual domain, Christ was concerned with the human's wholeness and still represents our highest possible model for integrating body, mind, and spirit.

Unfortunately, much of Christ's teaching was ignored, whereas the deterministic bias toward humanity with its concomitant use of exorcism was carried into the thinking of the Middle Ages following the period of medical/scientific advance which dwindled with the collapse of Roman and Greek civilizations. The Middle Ages brought on a revival of superstition and demonology mediated through the organized church with the clergy being primarily responsible for the treatment of disturbed individuals. Again, prevailing philosophy was extended into treatment, and people with problems during this era were subjected to the most horrendous interventions. By the end of the fifteenth century, the dysfunctioning individual was generally considered to be a witch, and several official church documents paved the way to years of witch hunting, burning, beheading, and countless examples of sanctioned inhumanities. The view of disorders as representing God's punishment continued to dominate well into the nineteenth century. It is still common for the authors (perhaps because of our location in the rural southwest) to see highly religious clients who perceive their problems as stemming from spells and witchcraft directed at them. We illustrate our approach to this kind of situation in Chapter 8 as we discuss spiritual aspects of counseling.

The contemporary humanitarian view held by most of today's spiritually oriented healers had its roots in Christ's ministry and later, in isolated cases, of progressive reform in Europe (Coleman et al., 1980). The colony of Gheel in Belgium was originally developed in the thirteenth century out of a more humane Christian tradition. It still exists today as a refuge for mental patients and rests on a treatment model which emphasizes prayer, kindness, and love within a community setting. The York Retreat established by William Tuke (an English Quaker) in the late eighteenth century allowed patients to work and rest in a benevolent religious atmosphere and set the tone for the humanitarian reform of the nineteenth century in America. Unfortunately, the application of moral therapy based on the belief that the insane were essentially normal people reacting to stress overload saw a decline with the growing popularity of an illness model of human misery which emerged in the late nineteenth century in response to medical advances. Ironically, however, more recent times have seen the renewed advocacy of the moral treatment approach by several prominent scientists (Mowrer, 1969; Szasz, 1961). We think that part of the spiritualistic movement of the past decade (with resurgence of both ends of this dimension, from devil worship and black magic to meditation and fasting) can be seen as a reaction to rationalism and a grasping for a more meaningful inner life.

Contemporary thinking among spiritually oriented psychotherapists seems to reflect a transition from narrowly focused victim/sin theory to a more holistic paradigm of human functioning. As a biologist and theologian, E. W. Sinnott (1958) has suggested that we are beginning to reconcile our view of man by bringing his diverse qualities together into a unity and thereby fitting man into the universe an integration of matter, mind, and spirit. He went on to conclude that man's developmental power is not limited by mind and body but can transcend bodily development through contact with a higher, external reality inaccessible to reason and based on faith. Gordon Allport (1950) has indicated that in the 1940s the subject of religion was a source of embarrassment to scholars and that the topic had gone into hiding among intellectuals. However, he noted a growing concern with the relationship between psychology and religion that has developed with modern psychologists, and points out an inherent absurdity in keeping these two interacting fields at odds. More recently, Progoff (1980) has reintroduced the mystical/spiritual themes of Jung, Buber, and Tillich as a legitimate part of psychotherapy. This time it appears that a lot of people are listening. Collins (1976) also represents this new breed of spiritually oriented psychologists who attempt to break down dichotomous thinking and emphasize the constant interaction of human beings' various domains of existence during the counseling process. He states, "Feeling, thinking, and acting—all three are important in the Scriptures and each must be considered in counseling." In teaching counseling skills to a wide range of clergy over the past several years, the authors have truly sensed an emerging openness toward seeing humanity in its totality of functions. We further define the importance of integrating spiritual considerations into creative counseling as a major theme later in this book.

The Physical Domain: Humans as Organic Beings

The organic paradigm has been espoused by scientifically oriented therapists at various points in history in opposition to the spiritual viewpoint. Again, this perspective on human nature has produced therapeutic techniques that have paralleled its philosophy. As a precursor to modern medicine, Hippocrates (460–370 B.C.) rejected a supernatural explanation of human inadequacies in favor of a disease theory which suggested that behavior was determined by physical substances in the body. According to Davison and Neale (1978), "Hippocrates regarded the brain as the organ of intellectual life, and it followed accordingly that if someone's thinking and behavior were deviant, there was some kind of brain pathology." In contrast to the use of exorcism during that era, Hippocrates prescribed drugless healing, bleeding, exercise, sobriety, and vegetable diets as primary modalities of treatment. Prior to the eclipse of the medical viewpoint with the collapse of Roman and Greek civilization, medical practices flourished and treatment for mental patients took on a variety of physical forms involving walking, hydrotherapy, gymnastics, and hypnotism. Unfortunately, this period of progressive reform ended around 200 A.D. with a return to a demonological viewpoint and was not revitalized until the sixteenth century with Johann Weyer who believed that those who were being burned and tortured for witchcraft were really mentally sick (Coleman et al., 1980). Weyer's notion was met with great skepticism (the *Zeitgeist* was not ripe for antispiritual thinking), but his efforts gradually led the way to more humane patient care in hospital-like asylum settings. Many of these institutions, however, proved to be little better than prisons, and many patients through the nineteenth century were treated with straitjackets, purgative agents, starvation, and cold baths.

According to Davison and Neale (1978), the organic view was revived in Europe during the nineteenth century along with the emergence of modern medical science. In 1883, Emil Kraepelin published the forerunner of our modern diagnostic classification system and promoted the notion that brain pathology was the cause of mental disorders. During this period of time, much energy was focused on developing a medical explanation of human abnormalities, and the underlying organic bases for many forms of pathology were uncovered. Thus, the stage was set for the dominance of the medical model which still serves as a major paradigm for explaining and treating human problems. The medical model, with its emphasis on the disturbed person as sick, draws an analogy between physical disease and a disease base of abnormal behavior. Although the organic viewpoint is still popular today, there are some signs that its narrow focus is opening toward a broader-based conceptual framework of human functioning.

In *The Myth of Mental Illness* (1961) and numerous related publications, Thomas Szasz has led an attack against the narrow organic view which has had a tremendous effect on the profession. He not only criticizes the destructiveness of psychiatric labels and the view of the individual as an involuntary victim of a disease process, but rejects the idea of mental illness as primarily biologically based. Likewise, in their attack of the medical focus of community mental health centers, Chu and Trotter (1974) proposed that aside from an organic component in virtually all psychosocial problems most disorders fall outside the realm of any strictly definable disease categories. They indicated that whereas most of the federally funded services offered through the National Institute of Mental Health are tied to an outdated disease model, there is growing concern among prominent professionals regarding the validity of this thinking (Albee, 1968; Braginsky, Braginski, and Ring, 1969; Rosenhan, 1973).

The revision of the official diagnostic manual of the American Psychiatric Association (*DSM* III) brings the mind/body issue into contemporary controversy and reveals that the debate over the organic basis of human misery is still burning among diverse groups of practicing psychotherapists (Goleman, 1978). Whereas it allows for increased diagnostic flexibility and precision, the *DSM III* appears to encompass even more forms of mental illnesses as biologically caused. Coleman et al. (1980) have focused the center of the controversy on the definition of "mental disorder" and suggest that the pervasive emphasis on organic causation has created a strongly negative reaction from clinical psychologists and psychiatric social workers. Perhaps there is some validity in George Albee's (past president of the APA) assertion that this expanded disease focus is a power play by psychiatry for a larger piece of the insurance-supported treatment reimbursement "pie" (1968). A similar argument has been presented regarding physician overuse of psychoactive drugs. Rogers (1971) believes that many physicians are "wedded to an obsolete model of human behavior—the concept that psychological problems have medical causes." He further asserts that this viewpoint expands the physician's jurisdiction by identifying increasing numbers of individuals as potential medical patients, and even draws an analogy between physician abuse of chemotherapy to the street "pusher" peddling illegal drugs. He concludes that many people are being seduced by the simplistic belief that everyday problems of living have quick chemical solutions.

There is also evidence of growing dissatisfaction with the narrow organic view from within the medical profession as indicated by the increasing number of psychotherapeutic approaches being developed by physicians which break both from the strictly biological and orthodox psychoanalytic traditions. Masserman (1973) represented this expanded position in his book *Dynamic Therapy*. He has recognized the importance of the patient's personal faith and belief in life's purpose, meaning, and values. He states that "medicine as a humanitarian science can never be in conflict with philosophy and religion. All three seem to have been designed by a beneficient providence to preserve, console, and comfort man." This trend toward a more interdisciplinary perspective among medical healers is further associated with the holistic healing movement which recognizes the inseparability of body, mind, and spirit. The expanded awareness of physical functioning is also reflected by the increasing popularity of lifelong physical activities such as running, racquetball, aerobics programs, and many other recently renewed areas of physical involvement. Antimedicalism among psychologists appears to be giving way to a new appreciation of the organic aspects of psychological function. We are seeing growing support for a more open viewpoint which implicates psychological factors in the cause and treatment of virtually all physical disorders (Pelletier, 1979). We believe that counselors cannot afford to ignore the physical aspects of client concerns. In fact, we offer specific guidelines for the creative counselor's involvement within the physical domain in Chapter 8 of this book.

The Psychosocial Domain

Whereas the psychosocial view of human beings as a function of their affective, cognitive, and behavioral interaction with their environment is a relatively recent phenomenon, its precursors go back to ancient Roman and Greek thinking. According to Reiss, Peterson, Eron, and Reiss (1977), Plato emphasized the sociocultural aspects of cognitive and behavioral development, whereas Aristotle believed that adjustment problems were caused by pent-up emotions which could be released through cultural activities. Cicero introduced the notion that bodily dysfunction is caused by emotional factors and emphasized the relevance of fear, rage, and grief. Pinel (1745–1826) made significant contributions to the psychosocial viewpoint by proposing a classification system that precluded both the biological and demonological positions. Nevertheless, controversy surrounding the nature/nuture issue has remained prominent throughout psychology's short history.

Among twentieth-century psychosocially oriented theorists of psychotherapy, we have seen an ongoing struggle for supremacy among advocates of affective, cognitive, and behavioral schools of thought which has stimulated tremendous divergency of opinions regarding the relative importance of these three domains of existence. Proponents of each of these viewpoints have pointed to the inconsistencies and contradictions inherent in the other approaches. In recognizing these divergencies, Carl Rogers (1951) suggested that they "seem irreconcilable because we have not yet developed a larger frame of reference that would contain them." However, much of the identity crisis antagonism between conflicting schools of psychotherapy has been resolved recently as support has gathered for an eclectic point of view. Even so, some antagonism remains.

The issue of territoriality has been put into the professional limelight during the last few years with the tremendous energy invested in dealing with the issue of licensure. This area of concern has brought divergent orientation out of the ivory tower and onto the political and financial battlefield. In addressing a national meeting of counselor educators in 1979, Pete Havens [past president, American Counselor Educators and Supervisors (ACES)] indicated that this is the most pressing issue facing counselors in America (Havens, 1979). The "sunset review" issue, which deals with professional standards, professional rights, and third-party payments, is the hottest one facing state boards of psychological examiners as we enter the 1980s. Chaotic results have already stemmed from the disbanding of licensure boards in South Dakota and Florida, whereas Virginia psychologists now operate under a "superboard" which regulates several professions within one structure. In Arkansas, licensure for counselors has become state law preempting a ruling by the state board that all providers of counseling services must be licensed, which would have affected the employment of counselors in a wide variety of settings (*Guidepost,* 1979). This same issue of the *Guidepost* also included an article which indicated that a Senate bill has been proposed to require licensure for all psychology positions in the Veterans Administration. In an *ACES Newsletter,* David Tiedeman (1979) stated his opposition to licensure of counselors and identified the issue as "anti-ethical to the purposes we seek to achieve." The controversy goes on in nearly every professional conference we attend and seems to be the hallmark of our professional identity crisis. We remain optimistic, and predict that this will become one of the issues which will rally a maturing profession in the 1980s toward a richer appreciation of the interrelatedness of apparent divergencies of thinking within the field of helping. The kind of radicalism critical to the emergence of various orientations in their adolescence must be replaced by openness in order for those positions to experience continuing growth.

The Human as an Affective Being Whereas acknowledgment of internal processes and subjective experience can be traced to classical humanists like Plato and Aristotle, the extension of humanistic philosophy into treatment has its direct origins in the late eighteenth century when Pinel replaced chains with kindness among patients in LaBicetre, a hospital in Paris for the insane (Coleman et al., 1980). As the humanitarian movement gained impetus, treatment methods, in spite of notable exceptions, became more humane throughout Europe and the United States. Modern humanism emerged as the "third force" in psychology in reaction to the deterministic pessimism of psychoanalysis and behaviorism and asserted that man has the potential for self-direction and fulfillment through internal forces which guide experience (Wandersman, Poppen, and Ricks, 1976).

Whereas Freud based his model on observations of neurotics and behavioristic theory evolved out of the laboratory, affective models of therapy were based on the unique experience of fully functioning individuals. Humanists argue against the radical behavioral view that only observable data should be included in the counseling process and tend to emphasize the affective factors as primary (Smith, 1974). The person is seen as possessing the potential for self-fulfillment with the self-concept as the organizing component of human development. The individual is viewed as inherently good with functioning placed on a continuum from high-level actualization to extreme nonadaptive patterns. The infectious disease model has been rejected by traditional phenomenologists and replaced by defining maladjustment as an incongruence between feelings and their overt expression. The focus is on the affective with behavior viewed as tangential to inner experience.

Whereas several affectively oriented approaches to psychotherapy have been developed, the client-centered approach clearly is most representative of this position. The early works of Carl Rogers (1951) concentrated on feelings and placed little credence in the analysis of cognitive aspects of the client's concerns. Therapy encouraged a catharsis of feelings, but allowed the client to assume responsibility for the extension of insight into action. The relationship was seen as primary as illustrated by the identification of "the necessary and sufficient conditions of therapeutic personality change."

1. Two persons are in psychological contact.
2. The first. . . . The client, is in a state of incongruence, being vulnerable or anxious.
3. The second. . . . the therapist, is congruent or integrated in the relationship.
4. The therapist experiences unconditioned positive regard for the client.

5 The therapist experiences an empathetic understanding of the client's internal frame of reference and endeavors to communicate this experience to the client.
6 The communication to the client of the therapist's empathetic understanding is to a minimal degree achieved (Rogers, 1957, pp. 95–96).

The specific techniques generated from this position were all directed toward freeing clients toward growth and allowing them to experience previously denied feelings. Listening and nonverbal communication of unconditionality became the channels through which client potential could be unleashed.

As with other schools of psychotherapy, the affective model has been attacked for its incompleteness and has served a catalytic function for the development of more comprehensive approaches. Carkhuff and Berenson (1977) suggest that the client-centered model actually limits the range and intensity of client affect and fails to allow for more directive therapist interventions. They further critique the phenomenological framework in terms of its lack of provision for translating insight into action. Their updated version of humanistic psychotherapy moves beyond an exclusive feeling focus toward a more holistic view of humanity. This brand of contemporary humanism recognizes the importance of cognitive and behavioral components of helping which flow out of a relational base. Likewise, Gestalt therapy (Passons, 1975) has extended its humanism to a holistic inclusion of mind and body processes as they interact with feelings. While seeing human beings as proactive, capable of choice, and responsible for their behavior, this model has generated a wide range of techniques directed at integrating human beings' fragmented existence. Behaviorism and humanism may even be in the process of resolving apparent diversity. Patterson (1966) concludes that "There is no necessary contradiction between behavioral therapy and relational therapy." He further states, "It is interesting and significant that both groups are coming to the same conclusions, one from laboratory work in conditioning, the other from experience and research in counseling and psychotherapy." Ironically, Maslow (1969) has voiced disappointment over humanist protest against behaviorism and has proposed its inclusion within a larger psychological perspective. Hosford and Zimmer (1972) argue that behaviorism is humanism. Thoresen (1978) said that the sophomoric dichotomization has yielded a "crude caricature of these positions." He concluded that the real issue is in how to integrate both concepts and methodologies within a single framework.

The Human as a Cognitive Being The cognitive viewpoint has its roots in ancient philosophy, but its development from theory into treatment has evolved primarily as an extension of twentieth-century psychoanalytic theory in which the patients' inherent weaknesses are revealed through a didactic process. In critiquing the Freudian viewpoint, Carkhuff and Berenson (1967) identify its deterministic foundation and negativistic view of humans. Human beings are at the mercy of their instincts and at best can manage a compromise existence between id impulses and societal demands. Psychoanalysis is then a vehicle for gaining insight into the low-level existence through uncovering the unconscious and identifying the patients' irrationality and destructiveness. The therapist is seen as an all-knowing authority figure who uses free association, dream analysis, transference, interpretation, and a variety of related techniques to improve the patients' cognitive perception of their conditions. Whereas this model recognizes the influence of the affective domain, catharsis is seen as a way to get rid of feelings which can then be replaced with a more rational intellectual framework. As with affective orientations, insight preempts action and becomes a potential block to dealing with behavioral change. Representing the humanistic position, Carkhuff and Berenson (1967) suggest that this model offers little to psychotherapy beyond its historical roots and see it as a seductive suicidal game between low-functioning participants.

Whereas the neo-Freudians expanded on Freud's ideas and broke with fragments of his theorizing, several cognitively oriented therapies have more recently emerged with dramatically different philosophical and treatment perspectives. Whereas they emphasize objectivity, reason, logical thinking, and the role of instruction in therapy, these approaches rest on a positive philosophical foundation. Human beings are generally seen by contemporary cognitive psychotherapists as creative and striving beings potentially capable of change and control of their lives through the intellectual control of choice patterns. Most current cognitive psychotherapies identify with Alfred Adler as a precursor who made a clear break from Freud's negativism. Adler's present resurgence in popularity may reflect his holistic view of human beings and acknowledgment of relational as well as interpretive and action aspects of helping. According to Mosak and Driekurs (1973), many of the theoretical assertions made by Albert Ellis in his rational emotive therapy converge with Adler's thinking. Both theories emphasize belief and attitude systems and assume that "emotions are actually a form of thinking, and that people create or control their emotions by their thinking." Therefore, the therapist must promote patient responsibility for feelings and challenge irrational thoughts as the core of ineffective living. Dyer (1977) has further popularized this view with his focus on the individual's control over personal destiny through a rational choice process.

Stemming from this cognitive tradition, three other influential models have emerged in the past two decades which extend the boundaries of the rational focus and suggest an openness to a broader perspective. Ironically, the authors of all three models hold medical degrees. Eric Berne has developed a practical "method for analyzing a person's thoughts, feelings and behavior" (James and Jongeward, 1971). Transactional analysis places a high priority on our freedom to choose and change through logical self-confrontation, while breaking from the vagueness and esoteric jargon of its psychoanalytic foundations. Morality, in the sense of accepting personal responsibility, is central to a related model developed by William Glasser (1965). In reality therapy emotional problems are seen as a product of low performance and failure in interpersonal functioning. Whereas the founders of both of these schools of therapy were trained as physicians, they have rejected the narrow mental illness conceptualization. However, they have certainly not negated the relevance of human beings' physical functioning. Finally, Beck (1976) has emphasized this interrelatedness and stated, "cognitive therapy consists of all the approaches that alleviate psychological distress through the medium of correcting faulty conceptions and self-signals." The emphasis on thinking, however, should not obscure the importance of the emotional reactions which are generally the immediate source of distress. The authors believe that this tone reflects the growing edge of the cognitive therapies, as we see a new openness toward viewing people as they really are—the complex interaction of many factors.

The Human as a Behaving Being In opposition to the infectious disease rationale of the medical model and centrality of the subconscious in psychoanalysis, behaviorists asserted in the 1920s that the only areas of humanity open for objective study were the overt responses emitted by the organism. The radical behaviorism of the Watsonian era rigidly held its position that humans are determined by conditioning principles which operate in their environment. The humanists have strongly reacted to experimental behaviorism which seems to strip away individual autonomy while reducing humans to depersonalized, manipulated objects. Borrowing from learning principles developed in the laboratory, this philosophy was gradually translated into treatment techniques for the clinical setting which have been directed at altering the real life behavior patterns of the client. Early behaviorists saw little need for concern with the clients' inner life or the relational aspects of therapy. Since abnormal behavior is learned, the therapists' job is to help the client unlearn nonadaptive behaviors and establish more effective patterns. Many effective techniques (from systematic desensitization to aversive conditioning) have evolved out of this tradition and have added tremendously to the effective psychotherapist's intervention repertoire. Both authors are heavily invested in both the principles and practice associated with behavior modification, but see behavioral techniques within a broader therapeutic context.

Most contemporary behavior therapists support a more proactive philosophy which states that humans are not only a product of their environment but can also shape their own destiny by controlling environmental forces (Carkhuff and Berenson, 1977). The focus on gaining control is essential to any effective treatment, and behavioral therapists have led the way in their openness towards considering the client's physical domain in psychotherapy. Relaxation techniques and biofeedback training are only a sample of behavioral treatments which pay deference to the physical/behavioral interaction. Although behaviorists have tended to eschew the spiritual domain, a growing number of behaviorally oriented therapists are including cognitive elements in their theories and practices (Meichenbaum, 1976). Bandura (1971) also considers the radical behavioristic position as incomplete and suggests that we can no longer ignore inner causation since cognitive functioning interacts continually with behavior and in fact is its determinant. It is particularly exciting to see that even the traditional behavioral taboo on relational and affective considerations is being lifted. This is evidenced in a publication by Wandersman, Poppen, and Ricks (*Humanism and Behaviorism: Dialogue and Growth,* 1976) which identifies the potential for theoretical synthesis with the possibility of these divergent schools incorporating into a single broader perspective. Redd, Porterfield, and Anderson (1979) suggest that few contemporary behavioral clinicians identify with a single theoretical doctrine. They have coined the phrase "eclectic behaviorism" to characterize modern behavior therapists who pragmatically apply a wide range of empirically validated techniques. As Lazarus (1971) points out, the behavioral therapist should use whatever is effective and not become saddled with rigid theoretical biases. The behaviorist seems to reflect a pervasive professional mood shift from defensive radicalism toward a maturing receptivity.

Toward Maturity: Defensiveness to Interdependence

Our brief historical perspective seems to suggest a growing openness to humanity's true complexity. The dogma of opposing views that once seemed irreconcilable as various schools fought for exclusive territories is giving way to mutual appreciation of divergent contributions and a more holistic picture of humanity. "Niche fighting" has served a growing profession well by providing a catalyst for research and lively debate. Perhaps now we are reaching toward another stage in the development of the helping professions. Erikson's (1963) stage theory asserts that whereas conflict resolution surrounding each crisis period may never be completely resolved, we emerge from each with increased strength, good judgment, and sense of unity. To parallel Erikson, we feel that our profession is progressing from the defensive battles (involving struggles with mistrust, self-absorption, isolation, and identity crisis) of adolescence toward a maturity that entails a renewed capacity for interdependence.

Our present *Zeitgeist* seems to reflect a readiness for what Maslow (1972) has labeled as a "transcendence of dichotomies" or moving from polarities to superordinate wholes. He defines this further as binary separates (such as affective/cognitive, directive/nondirective, insight/action, and so on) which must become integrated. In discussing the transcendence of mutual exclusiveness, he states that we can rise above our differences toward a coordinated unity "which would be more realistic, more true, more in accord with actual reality." This concept is further elucidated by his notion of synergy (cooperative growth). He identifies low-synergy societies as setting up institutions against each other to rival for limited goods, whereas high-synergy groups promote transcendence of dichotomies and fusion of apparent opposites. This is the language of eclecticism at a philosophical level. In counseling practice, the eclectic operates out of a wide base of interventions which can be creatively applied to promote constructive client change.

Whereas the growing edge of our profession is leaning toward synergism, the foundations for interdependence among psychotherapists from religious, medical, and psychosocial orientations have already been laid. Unfortunately, eclecticism prior to the last decade was something of a dirty word among counselors. It was seen as a weak orientation based on contradiction and confusion. The climate was apparently not yet matured enough to foster the incorporation of diversity. The roots of modern eclecticism can be traced back to the organization of the Mayo Clinic in the 1880s which brought together a wide range of medical specialists into a cooperative team approach. Robert S. Woodworth promoted clinical efforts at eclecticism in the 1930s and suggested that none of the schools of psychology at that time provided adequate conceptualizations. Whereas Woodworth's unification endeavors were largely ignored, Frederick Thorne's (1973) brilliant contributions to eclecticism unfolded during the rebellious 1960s and have received only token appreciation and waves of defensive criticism. Rejections by specific schools have unfairly attacked this position as a blindly irrational "shotgun" method which promotes a smattering of proficiency in many areas without corresponding competency in any aspect of treatment. Thorne (1973) says, "In contrast with the 'schools' centering about some prominent authority, eclecticism has never attracted a vocal body of adherents dedicated toward its promotion." This lack of a proselytic following may also reflect the kind of insecurity generated by the requirement of developing global knowledge and competencies associated with this position. It may further be a product of its lack of ideology and systematization. However, the authors would propose that it primarily represents a lack of maturity within the profession which may not be the case as we move into the 1980s.

Carkhuff and Berenson have offered a clearer ideology of eclecticism in their landmark publication, *Beyond Counseling and Therapy* (1967). They have critically reviewed the pros and cons of several major schools of psychotherapy and developed a personalized eclectic model as a means for integrating divergent contributions to the therapeutic process. They have further attacked dichotomous thinking in their second edition (1977) of this book when they characterize the humanistic therapist as "together" physically, intellectually, and emotionally (implicitly incorporating the spiritual and behavioral domains as well). They assert that "functioning on any one of the dimensions is ultimately related to functioning on the others. At the highest levels, these dimensions are integrated in a fully functioning person into more than the sum of these dimensions." This type of open eclecticism was introduced in the 1960s but only began to flourish in the last decade. Borrowing from Carkhuff and his associates, Egan (1975) pushed eclecticism further into professional acceptance through an organizational framework for incorporating the relative contributions of the respective schools of counseling. Even more recently, Palmer (1980) has recognized the complex and changing nature of people through a text on eclectic therapy which combines techniques borrowed from a wide range of resources. It appears that eclecticism is finally being appreciated for what it is—an essential perspective for dealing with the complexity of human problems.

Ironically, just as eclecticism is gaining popularity, its theme of diversity is being pushed even further. Hammond and Stanfield (1977) suggest that we need to expand the limits of psychotherapy toward an even more comprehensive type of eclecticism that is multidimensional (spiritual, physical, and psychological) in nature. Bach (1977) identifies a growing holistic movement which is gaining momentum. He sees interdisciplinary approaches as a product of the times—"the reunion of three indivisible disciplines—dramatically taking place within individuals and society." Perhaps our professional identity crisis is being resolved as we seem to be turning our efforts from competing systems of dogma toward a more productive stage of interdependence. Ironically, we seem to have gone full cycle since Imhotep's time (3000 B.C.) when therapeutic intervention was seen from a triadic perspective. This is where we find the creative counselor. But creativity requires a firm foundation in theory and skills, so we will turn our attention in that direction first.

SUMMARY

We have presented an historical foundation for the current directions of counseling as a more mature and holistic profession. We have traced its spiritual, physical, and psychosocial roots and observed a growing trend toward interdependence among the professional helping groups represented by each of these areas—a necessary foundation for creative counseling. As a result of this growing atmosphere of acceptance, we believe that the tone is set for creative counseling as we approach the last two decades of the twentieth century. We anticipate a shift away from territorial fighting among the various schools of helping and toward a more productive and creative investment of energy into the problems and challenges faced by our clients.

REFERENCES

Albee, G. Models, myths and manpower. *Mental Hygiene,* April 1968, 168–180.
Allport, G. W. Psychological models for guidance. *Harvard Educational Review,* 1962, *32,* 373–381.
Allport, G. W. *The individual and his religion.* New York: Macmillan, 1950.
Bach, M. *The power of total living.* New York: Fawcett Crest, 1977.
Bandura, A. *Social learning theory.* New York: General Learning Press, 1971.
Beck, A. T. *Cognitive therapy and the emotional disorders.* New York: New American Library, 1976.
Braginski, B. M., Braginski, D. D., and Ring, K. *Methods of madness: The mental hospital as a last resort.* New York: Holt, 1969.
Carkhuff, R. R. and Berenson, B. G. *Beyond counseling and therapy.* New York: Holt, 1967.
Carkhuff, R. R. and Berenson, B. G. *Beyond counseling and therapy* (2nd ed.). New York: Holt, 1977.
Chu, F. D. and Trotter, S. *The madness establishment.* New York: Grossman, 1974.
Coleman, J. C., Butcher, J. N., and Carson, R. *Abnormal psychology in modern life* (6th ed.). Glenview, Ill.: Scott, Foresman, 1980.
Collins, G. *How to be a people helper.* New York: Vision House, 1976.
Davison, G. C. and Neale, J. M. *Abnormal psychology* (2nd ed.). New York: Wiley, 1978.
Dyer, W. *Your erroneous zones.* New York: Avon, 1977.
Egan, G. *The skilled helper: A model for systematic helping and interpersonal relations.* Belmont, Calif.: Wadsworth, 1975.
Erikson, E. H. *Childhood and society.* New York: Norton, 1963.
Glasser, W. *Reality therapy.* New York: Harper & Row, 1965.
Glasser, W. *Positive addiction.* New York: Harper & Row, 1976.

Goldman, L. (Ed.). *Research methods for counselors.* New York: Wiley, 1978.
Goleman, D. Who is mentally ill? *Psychology Today,* January 1978, 34–40.
Hammond, D. C. and Stanfield, K. *Multidimensional psychotherapy.* Champaign, Ill.: Institute for Personality and Ability Testing, 1977.
Havens, P. Address to American Counselor Educators and Supervisors Association Annual Meeting, Las Vegas, Nevada, 1979.
Hosford, R. E. and Zimmer, J. Humanism through behaviorism. *Counseling and Values.* 1972, *16,* 162–168.
James, M. and Jongeward, D. *Born to win.* Reading, Mass.: Addison-Wesley, 1971.
Lazarus, A. A. *Behavior therapy and beyond.* New York: McGraw-Hill, 1971.
Maslow, A. H. Toward a humanistic biology. *American Psychologist,* 1969, *24,* 724–735.
Maslow, A. H. *The farther reachers of human nature.* New York: Viking, 1972.
Masserman, J. *Theory and therapy in dynamic psychiatry.* New York: Jason Aronson, 1973.
Meichenbaum, D. Cognitive behavior modification. In J. T. Spence, R. C. Carons, and J. W. Thibaut (Eds.), *Behavioral approaches to therapy.* Morristown, N. J.: General Learning Press, 1976.
Mosak, H. H. and Dreikurs, R. Adlerian psychotherapy. In R. Corsini (Ed.), *Current psychotherapies.* Stasca, Ill.: F. E. Peacock, 1973.
Mowrer, O. H. Sin, the lesser of two evils. *American Psychologist,* 1969, *15,* 301–305.
Palmer, J. O. *A primer of eclectic psychotherapy.* Monterey, Calif.: Brooks/Cole, 1980.
Passons, W. R. *Gestalt approaches in counseling.* New York: Holt, 1975.
Patterson, C. H. *Theories of counseling and psychotherapy.* New York: Harper & Row, 1966.
Pelletier, K. R. *Holistic medicine.* New York: Dell, 1979.
Progoff, I. *The practice of process meditation.* New York: Dialogue House, 1980.
Redd, W. H., Porterfield, A. L., and Anderson, B. L. *Behavior modification: Behavioral approaches to human problems.* New York: Random House, 1979.
Reiss, S., Peterson, R. A., Eron, L. D., and Reiss, M. M. *Abnormality: An experimental and clinical approach.* New York: Macmillan, 1977.
Rogers, C. R. *Client-centered therapy.* New York: Houghton Mifflin, 1951.
Rogers, C. R. Psychotherapy today or where do we go from here? *American Journal of Psychotherapy,* 1963, *17,* 5–16.
Rogers, J. M. Drug abuse—just what the doctor ordered. *Psychology Today,* Sept. 1971, 16–24.
Rosenhan, D. C. Being sane in insane places. *Science,* 1973, 79.
Sinnott, E. W. *Matter, mind, and man.* London: Ruskin House, G. Allen, 1958.
Smith, D. Integrating humanism and behaviorism toward performance. *Personnel and Guidance Journal,* 1974, *52*(8), 513–519.
Szasz, T. W. *The myth of mental illness: Foundations of a theory of personal conduct.* New York: Hoeber-Harper, 1961.
Thoresen, C. W. Behavioral humanism. In C. C. Thoresen (Ed.), *Behavior modification in education.* Chicago: National Society for the Study of Education, 1978.
Thorne, F. C. Eclectic psychotherapy. In R. Corsini (Ed.), *Current psychotherapies.* Stasca, Ill.: F. E. Peacock, 1973.
Tiedeman, D. V. Shame on me! and maybe a little on us. *ACES Newsletter.* December 1979, 6.
Ungersma, A. J. *The search for meaning.* Philadelphia: Westminster Press, 1961.
Wandersman, A., Poppen, P., and Ricks, D. *Humanism and behaviorism: Dialogue and growth.* New York: Pergamon Press, 1976.

CHAPTER 3

PRINCIPLES OF HUMAN FUNCTION

A FOUNDATION FOR CREATIVE COUNSELING

As we have seen, philosophy (view of basic human nature) has paralleled attempts at intervention (counseling and psychotherapy) throughout history. Dichotomous thinking regarding this basic human nature has led to philosophical controversies for centuries and has been translated into divergent human intervention models. The kind of "schoolism" associated with psychotherapeutic models is paralleled by philosophies and personality theories which are reviewed in several excellent texts (Forgus and Shulman, 1979; Mischel, 1981). The mutually exclusive view of humanity as basically evil and its optimistic counterpart in which humanity is good and striving for constructive ends are obviously naive. The kind of holistic treatment of human beings that we have identified as the emerging direction of our profession requires a broad philosophical perspective. The task for counselors is to internalize an integrated system of basic principles which facilitate an understanding of their clients and serve as a philosophical and practical foundation for creative problem solving. Whereas this implies a personal eclectic philosophy unique to each counselor, there are some basic principles which can serve as a foundation. We would like to present some of these fundamentals before developing an eclectic model for counseling itself. In this effort, we will move from general principles in this chapter toward specific techniques of intervention throughout the remainder of the book. Principles in this sense are relevant to many situations, whereas counseling techniques become ways of implementing a principle and vary dramatically from client to client (Heath, 1980). Readers are encouraged to use our coverage as a beginning point toward developing their own model of human functioning—a model that is an evolving guide for organizing insight about client concerns and a reminder of their infinite complexity.

We can see human beings as essentially neutral in their original nature with the potential for moving in a positive or negative direction. These potentials are then manifest within the framework of several general principles of development. Although human beings first enter the world as biological beings within an environmental context, the emerging self has the potential for providing the focus of development. It is this rational decision-making power that allows them to choose to modify their own destiny. They are the pivot point and remain in charge to the degree that this sense of choice is maintained. It is analogous to the bicycler who pedals to produce motion by generating an interaction between the rear (biological) and front (other people, environment) wheels. As self-differentiation continues, the spiritual and psychological (cognitive, affective, behavioral) self gradually merges within its biological framework. The communication process serves as the vehicle upon which the self-structure emerges with every interchange yielding another piece of the individual puzzle as we interpret and incorporate incoming experiences. Our cognitive screening systems translate (decode) incoming messages while our growing behavioral repertoire enables us to respond (encode) to internal needs as we impact the outside world. These outside forces interact with internal states and learned patterns of expression to yield our behavioral responses (Stein, 1972). This perpetual cycle unfolds as a two-way street where cognition shapes behavior and vice versa, while our basic feelings regarding self, God, and world evolve (see Figure 3-1).

FIGURE 3-1
The interaction cycle.

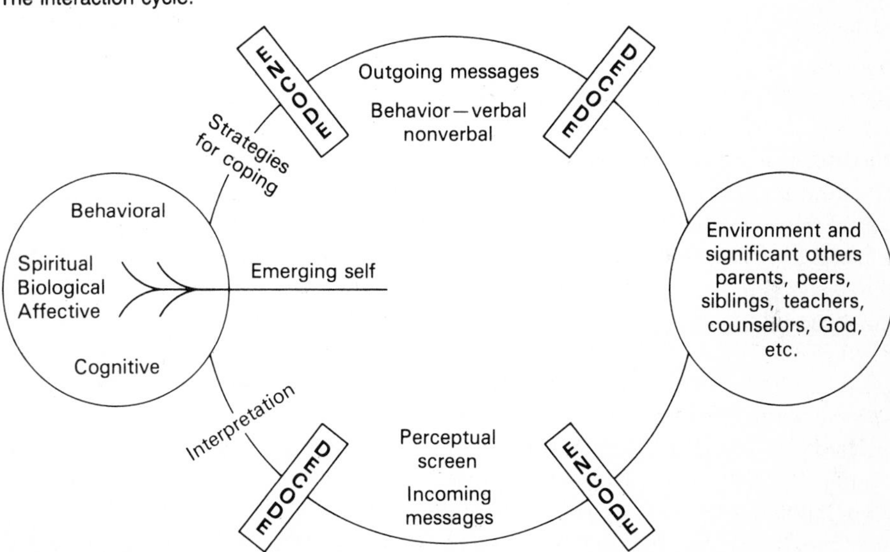

Even our biological makeup is subject to change in response to this cycle. Our entire approach to life takes shape as the cycle is repeated over and over again on a moment-to-moment basis. We have found this scheme to be a practical backdrop for viewing client concerns. In fact, the faces of some of our clients come to mind as we put this conceptual system into practice. We would invite you at this point to place yourself (or a client) into this system as you continue to read. The adage that nothing is as practical as a good theory still holds for the practicing counselor who must facilitate client self-understanding.

This process is for better or worse as each interaction throughout life is translated into a cumulative spiraling movement upward toward growth or downward toward deterioration (Carkhuff, 1969). Understanding (or confusion) leads to action (or inaction) as the consequences of each interchange pave the way for subsequent interactions. Each communication has an impact in a positive or negative direction. Counseling, as all other encounters with significant people, makes a difference. If past experience has been basically positive, the self-picture tends to be healthy and the outside world is viewed with an optimism which generates further successful interactions. If, on the other hand, the emerging self-structure is riddled with negative experiences, then the expectancies for future encounters tend to be pessimistic and the downward spiral is enhanced by self-fulfilling prophecy. As the cycle continues to unfold, individuals plot themselves along a continuum of human effectiveness which may range from the severely disturbed to the fully functioning (see Figure 3-2). Both client and counselor will fit somewhere on this continuum at any given point in time. Obviously, a counselor at the bottom end has little to offer clients in terms of hope for constructive change. Only the high-functioning counselor can consistently yield positive outcomes in counseling (Carkhuff and Berenson, 1967) and become creatively involved in the counseling process.

Perhaps an example will best illustrate our point. This case occurred some years ago when the senior author served as an institutional psychologist in a state penitentiary. The client (call him Marty) was my age, but had been moving downward in terms of self-image and destructive behavior while I was building a strong sense of confidence and esteem. Unfortunately, it was a very typical situation for that particular setting. He was referred because of an assault on a guard in our auto mechanics shop. It was a hot summer day, and he had been pushed to his limit. For years, he had accepted the self-inscription of "dummy" and an entire line of labels from parents, teachers, peers, and a long string of correctional officers. On this occasion he had been asked to fill out an application form for a transfer to the auto mechanics shop—an impossible task for a man who could not read. As his story unfolded, a vivid illustration of a downward spiral emerged through a lifelong history of negative events which had continually pushed this young man down further and further. For a detailed case study illustrating our point and a brief description of my approach to therapy, turn to Appendix One (Part A: Marty and the Downward Spiral).

Whereas the raw materials and quality of interaction may vary tremendously, the complex process of differentiation rests on several universal principles. Growth

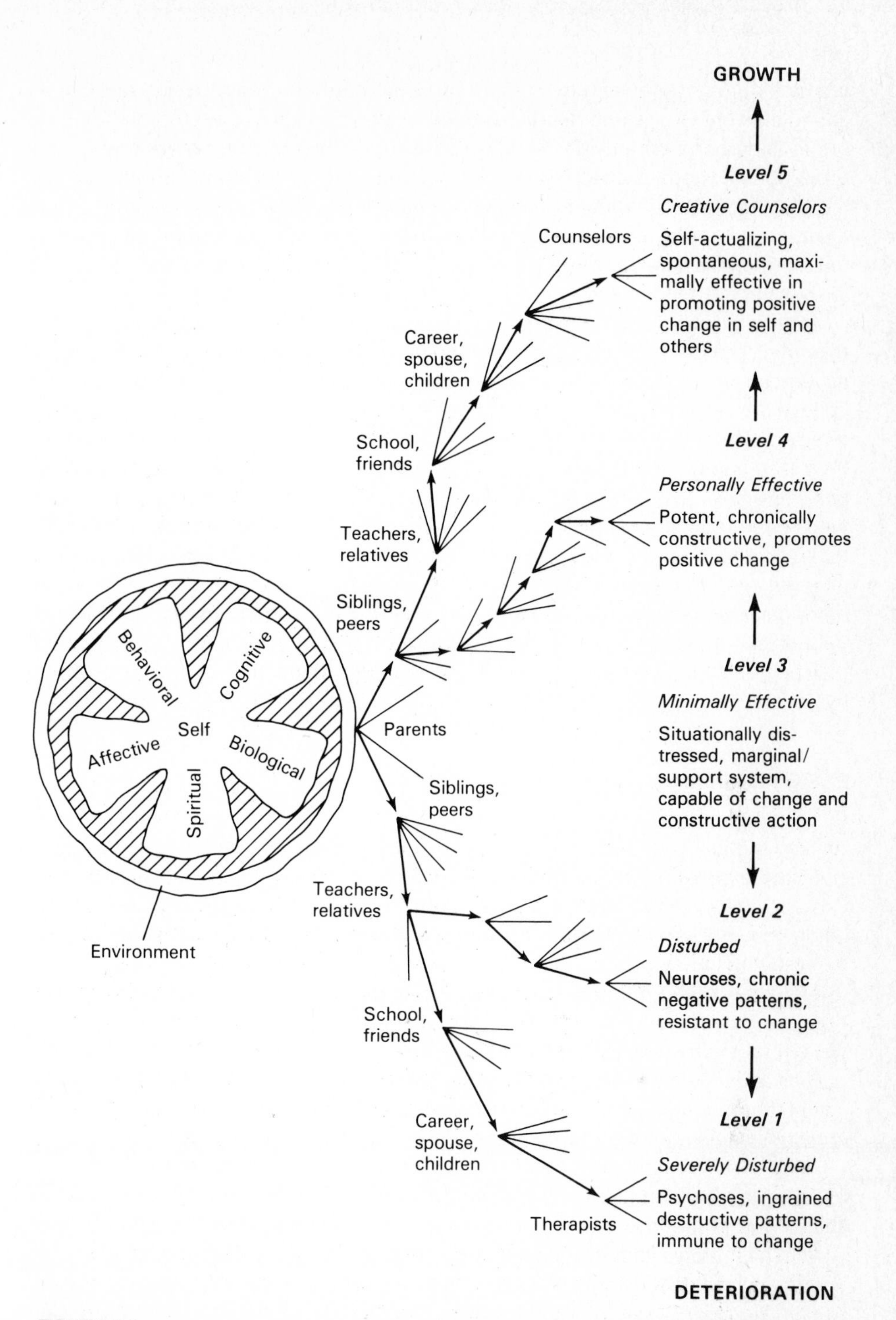

FIGURE 3-2
Growth and deterioration. Cumulative impact of facilitating and retarding experiences as they interact within our major domains of functioning. *(Extended from Carkhuff and Berenson, 1967.)*

and deterioration are seen as lying on a single continuum and based on similar ingredients of human interaction. We will explore some of these commonalities of the underlying dimensions of movement in either direction before identifying some of the unique characteristics of individuals operating along various parts of the continuum. It is critical for counselors and psychotherapists to identify clients as basically similar to themselves with behaviors which are founded on similar basic principles. We are more able to deal with differences when a common base for behavior is recognized.

Traditional diagnostic systems tend to distort our understanding of the client's dilemma. The disease model further removes client responsibility and perpetuates an unrealistic dichotomy between client and counselor. We would prefer to believe that all behavior (healthy and destructive) is reactive, motivated, and goal directed. Thus, even the most deviant behaviors can be seen as tactical devices used to manipulate the interpersonal surroundings as a means to obtain certain goals (Braginski, Braginski, and Ring, 1969). Unfortunately, temporary successes with self-defeating strategies can readily develop into ingrained destructive patterns. Clients then are viewed as humans with reasons for their behaviors and thoughts—qualitatively no different from those who are trying to help them build more constructive approaches to life's problems. It is the counselors' job to see through some of the distortion (tactical devices) and help individuals understand their self-defeating patterns as a first step toward reversing a downwardly destructive cycle.

BASIC PRINCIPLE I: BEHAVIOR IS PURPOSIVE

All behavior is mediated by an arousal system activitated by internal and external stimuli. Motivational factors interact with experiences and performance to generate the expression of internal states toward particular goals (Schlesinger and Groves, 1976). A common dimension of movement toward growth or deterioration lies in its motivational base which provides the intensity and energy for the resulting behavior. Thorne (1967) utilized the concept of integrational milieu to depict the multidimensional, multilevel hierarchies of needs which seek expression. He identified the internal (psychological forces driving the individual toward behavioral expression) and external (perception of environmental stimuli) milieu as constantly changing and requiring frequent revision. The balance of these forces (maintaining homeostasis) is a primary need of all human beings and serves as a drive mechanism for the production of both healthy and self-defeating behaviors.

Adaptation level theory asserts that people develop a reference point for evaluating incoming stimulation based on previous experience and contextual variables. Several theories of personality have been built upon the consistency principle which states that the energy and direction for behavior is produced by discrepancies between internal states and incoming cognitions (Festinger, 1957; Kelly, 1955). The most thorough model of homeostasis has been offered by Fiske and Maddi (1961) who suggested that we strive to maintain a customary level of activation—established neuropsychologically through the interaction of biologically based organismic excitation and past experience—in filtering stimulation. The overall directionality for living then is governed by a constant effort to match customary and actual levels of activation (incoming stimulation). Overstimulation is balanced by impact-decreasing behavior and perceptual defenses, whereas understimulation leads to impact-increasing behavior. The downward spiral toward deterioration can be associated with an increasingly narrow and unrealistic evaluative perspective, whereas healthy functioning is correlated with an openness to a wide range of incoming stimulation. This conceptualization fits neatly into our communication scheme (Figure 3-1) and indicates that encoded responses to people around us and our environment in general are in deference to maintaining balance and rejecting information inconsistent with our basic picture of self and world.

This principle is well illustrated by our depressed clients. Their decoding systems are jammed with negatives (Beck, 1976). They may not only fail to perceive positive therapist comments as such, but actively seek out situations and people consistent with their negative cognitive set. Constructive suggestions are incongruent with their present self-picture and may be actively rejected. Indeed, it is a primary task of the counselor to penetrate the barriers to healthy patterns projected by these clients. It is because some people become so skilled at maintaining their own misery that creative counselors must have a wide repertoire of tactics themselves.

We believe that this consistency principle goes beyond its application with depressed clients, as it seems to support virtually every pattern (constructive or otherwise) of behavior we emit. Anyone who works with young children can see it come to life. Children's behavior is constantly geared toward protecting their perception of themselves and others, even if that perception is quite destructive. Both authors' wives are elementary teachers and have given us a long list of examples. Most first graders respond acceptingly to praise, hugs, or teasing. For some, however, adult affection is foreign to their experience and expectancy. Ruffling such a child's hair may be directed affectionately, but perceived with confusion or even anger by the child.

These stimuli (from a second person and contextual sources, as well as internal) that are continually being evaluated can be categorized into biological and psychological needs in Maslow's (1943) familiar hierarchical system. Lower levels must be satisfied before energy can be released for encoding responses to higher-level needs. The more basic needs (biological, safety) will be particularly germane to our later discussion of deteriorative downward spiral, whereas self-actualization considerations will become relevant to our coverage of the fully functioning individual in the next section. It is the middle-level needs of belonging and esteem that provide the drive force behind most of our everyday patterns of behavior. They are pivotal needs and determine the potential of energy release at other need levels. Although Maslow places love needs as basic to needs of self-esteem, we see the latter as even more primary in some cases. As biological and safety needs become minimally satisfied, the need to establish a consistent self-image emerges. Much of our behavior is then geared toward maintaining adequacy. If adequacy needs are not met, then self-concept distortion may become prominent and fear of rejection inhibits involvement in meaningful relations (Stein, 1972). Resources for risking relational involvements can only be released when the individual feels at least minimally adequate. Conversely, increased relational risks become more likely when we feel the security of interpersonal support. Combs and Snygg (1959) have indicated that the adequacy issue is central to all personality development and subsumes all other sources of motivation. Glasser (1976) sees the needs for worth and support as fundamental to all personality development, and suggests that the first step toward pathology involves giving up the fight for establishing personal adequacy. A person cannot extend love beyond the level of personal self-acceptance. Only when self-esteem needs are minimally achieved can we move toward satisfying needs for belonging, acceptance, and love, and yet these need levels obviously interact and feed on each other.

Once again, there are direct implications for counseling. Some models of counseling place relational concerns as primary, whereas others emphasize the importance of behavior changes which support healthier self-esteem. We believe that both elements are critical to all helping efforts, but that the specific sequence and emphasis can only be determined by the unique need systems our clients present. No lock-step formula will work in all cases, since the confrontation that opens the door with one client may close it with another one who needs gentle support. It is the sensitivity to these needs and their interaction which serve as the basis for creative counseling.

The associational process of linking basic drives with psychosocial motives serves as a platform for the development of an endless array of secondary motives. Some of these motivational forces are involved primarily in pushing the individual toward growth (curiosity, achievement, risk taking, intimacies, self-actualization, creativity), whereas other secondary motivators (fear of failure, frustration, anxiety) become integrally involved with the deterioration process. Since effective counseling is an extension of the counselor's sensitivity to the client's need system, it becomes evident that a solid and yet flexible perspective of these needs and their interaction is fundamental to all efforts at promoting constructive change.

BASIC PRINCIPLE II: GROWTH OR DETERIORATION IS A CUMULATIVE PROCESS

Change (positive or negative) in any domain of functioning (spiritual, physical, affective, cognitive, or behavioral) will produce concomitant change in the other domains. It is a cumulative process.

Once again, we are confronted by the interactiveness of the various sides of our complex existence. It is inescapable. Carkhuff and Berenson (1967) asserts that change in any sphere will yield change in the other spheres in the same direction. Growth in the physical domain, for example, affects the potential for positive change in the remaining domains. Growth or deterioration will have a cumulative stacking-up effect which influences the effectiveness of the entire communication process. Whereas Thorne (1973) suggests that physiological factors provide the substrate for functioning in other areas, he also postulates that no preconceived theoretical model can accurately assign weightings to "the etiological equation underlying specific behavior." In other words, the interaction is obvious, but the sequence and exact consequences can only be specified within ongoing behavioral/interactional dynamics. Obviously, this principle may not apply in all cases, as evidenced by those who undergo spiritual and emotional growth spurts while facing a terminal illness or overcoming a physical hardship.

The experience of emotion provides an excellent example of this interactive process which we will further illustrate in our discussions of growth and deterioration. Despite continuing controversy regarding the exact interactive sequence, virtually all contemporary theories of emotion recognize the interdependence of bodily states and cognitive evaluation in producing emotion. In contrast to early theories which viewed emotion as a direct response to bodily change, Schachter and Singer's (1962) classic research has provided evidence that emotion is an interactive byproduct of physiological arousal and cognitive interpretation. This conceptualization has been borne out through extensive research and can be readily accommodated by our diagram of the communication cycle. Physiological arousal of the autonomic nervous system which has no ready explanation will be labeled (decoded) as an emotion according to available cognitions and in turn serve as a motivator toward encoding a behavioral coping response. Thus, the complex diversity of emotions we experience is a function of our unique decoding systems which screen information and interpret general arousal states.

The implications of this principle for creative counseling are profound. It would suggest that there is no set formula for where (in terms of which domain) to initiate the counseling process or where to invest our primary effort. It will vary tremendously from client to client and depend upon their unique strengths, problems, and support system. Creative counselors totally invest themselves in designing a unique counseling formulation to fit the needs of the particular client. Creative counselors must have skills in facilitating growth in all of these areas, and will inevitably involve (implicitly or directly) all areas of client functioning with the potential for producing a snowballing effect. Even small change in emotional level, insight, beliefs, physical fitness, or behavior can be of great importance. In fact, effective counselors are sensitive to small client changes and strive to use the spiraling process to the client's advantage. They creatively blend client resources from each domain and help the client generate new skills to replace deficiencies.

Using these principles as a foundation (common to both growth and deterioration), we shall now focus on relatively unique characteristics of the continuum. In the following sections, we break our continuum into its two extremes in order to identify some of the basic ingredients of the downward deteriorative spiral and upward movement of growth. It should be apparent, however, that movement in real life along this continuum is neither uniform nor entirely predictable but that a basic grasp of its underlying dimensions is critical for forming a meaningful ı/client interaction. Our coverage here can only serve as a readers are encouraged to expand upon these concepts in pnilosophical base consistent with their approaches to counseling.

HELPLESSNESS: THE DOWNWARD SPIRAL

The deterioration effect mentioned previously within the psychotherapeutic context seems to have general relevance to all human relationships. Involvement with significant others is inevitably for better or worse. The deteriorative process tends to reflect the cumulative impact of retarding encounters (Carkhuff, 1969) and can be represented as a downward spiral with reducing potential to utilize enhancing experiences and increasing vulnerability to destructive encounters (whether physical, spiritual, or psychological). The notion of self-fulfilling prophecies seems particularly germane as readers may testify to in terms of their observations of others. As this negative self/other picture develops, incoming discrepancies (anything positive such as someone reaching out with a helping hand) are systematically avoided in order to maintain internal consistency. Selective screening becomes a primary function of the emerging perceptual systems. These individuals move increasingly toward impotence as they avoid the risks of constructive involvement and withdrawal to the immediacy of reinforcement inherent in the safety, yet miserableness, of their corners.

At various parts of this adjustment continuum, we find the whole range of human misery from the situationally traumatized to the anxiety-ridden neurotic and ineffectual character-disordered. Sometimes our jargonistic labels get in the way of understanding, but there is no denying the reality of the despair experienced by many of the people around us. James and Jongeward (1971) suggest that these are the losers in our society who hang on to destructive manipulative techniques learned in coping with negative experiences. Losers dig their own graves as they distort, repeat mistakes, rationalize, and void themselves of spontaneity and gratification in their relationships with others. Carkhuff and Berenson (1967) have further indicated that many professional counselors function at this low level and cannot promote growth because of their own immunity to constructive change. The retarding therapists (level 1) are not only disturbed themselves, but actually serve as catalysts for destructive processes in their clients.

Several authors (Dyer, 1977; Ellis and Harper, 1975) have pointed to the critical role that cognitive factors play in the deteriorative spiral, and we would identify the pivotal function that our choices serve as a common denominator for the interaction of our various domains of existence. In contrasting people as strong and weak, Glasser (1976) has hypothesized that many people choose misery because they are convinced that they lack the strength to assume the responsibility entailed in the converse choice. He delineates the three fundamental choices of the downward spiral. First, they give up by believing that continuing the struggle will only bring about further failure. They accept life as miserable and avoid people who succeed. "Only a few give up completely but huge numbers settle for a lot less love and worth in their lives than they could if they had the strength to work for more." Unfortunately, the desperate struggle to hurt less blocks them from paths which might bring them more out of life. The fear of failure preempts the risks which might open up successful experiences.

The second choice of the weak involves the movement from transient avoidance of responsibility (the first choice) to the development of chronic symptom patterns (acting out, anxiety, depression, psychosis, or psychophysiological disorder). All of us choose a symptom at times of frustration, but the choice of substituting a symptom for struggling as a permanent pattern involves its value as a shield from failure and enables the weak person to ask for help. As painful as the symptom is, it is "less painful than facing his inadequacy." The symptom comes to represent a substitute for the "love and worth he is convinced he can no longer get in the real world." The final choice in the hierarchy of dysfunction is to relieve the pain through negative addiction. Addicts become locked into their habits. They lose the ability to make constructive choices. To quit means a return to symptom pain plus a process of withdrawal, and they do not have the strength to confront the alternative. The self-defeating pattern becomes an ingrained part of the individual.

Glasser's three-choice model is reminiscent of the three-stage stress-reaction paradigm proposed by Selye (1976) and known as the general adaptation syndrome (alarm, resistance, exhaustion). Through a variety of publications, Selye has established stress as a principal factor in all human behavior and a basis for most physical illness. Once again, the psychological (cognitive screening of stressor events) and physiological (triggering of the hypothalamus and related reaction of the autonomic nervous system and mobilization of endocrine functions) are inextricably intertwined. As suggested by Tanner (1976), stress can pile up and "push behavior over the adaptive range." Concomitantly, stress serves as a central ingredient in the breakdown of physical functioning as evidenced by a wide range of psychophysiological disorders from headaches to heart disease. Hereditary and environmental factors interact to predispose dysfunctioning individuals toward increased stress sensitivity as their related behavior becomes increasingly self-defeating. Maladaptive patterns emerge as protective devices and compound themselves in individuals' attempts to deal with stress over- and underload, and the adaptive range for coping with stimulus input shrinks as a byproduct of this vicious cycle. According to Rotter (1966), the locus of control is perceived as external in these people, and the reinforcements that do occur are seen increasingly as beyond their control. Expectancy becomes the reality in the downward spiral.

A logical extension of the preceding discussion leads us to the concept of learned helplessness as one of the most basic units of all human suffering. Seligman (1975) has utilized this phrase to represent the psychological and physical state that results when events are perceived as uncontrollable. He describes the infant's "dance" with the environment which yields a sense of mastery or, in this case, helplessness. The latter is learned when there is little correlation between responses and outcomes which results in a "lack of response initiative, negative cognitive set, and anxiety and depression." These perceptions in turn serve as a foundation for developing "emotional and motivation structures." Numerous experimental findings are offered in support of the role played by this central element in the development. A whole range of disorders plotted across the negative end of our adjustment continuum suggests that even death may be precipitated by this phenomenon in its most extreme form.

Whereas an image of an institutionalized psychotic may come to mind here, we would remind the reader that even healthy individuals can periodically become drawn into this kind of thinking. Stress overload, lower performance, and perceived loss of control are all too commonly the core of systems among the authors' client caseloads. Situational stress can become chronic, and it is the counselor's job to be sensitive to the early warning signs among potential clients. Catching the spiraling process at its onset can save future misery. As college professors, the authors are in daily contact with the whole range of student functioning. Sensitivity to subtle signs (drops in attendance, comments after class, and so forth) that may be early warning signals may make a critical difference in heading off big problems.

Once again, we are only scratching the surface here as we formulate some of the unifying principles of human misery. Effective counseling is enhanced by a firm foundational understanding of what makes clients hurt. Creative counselors are continually building upon their foundations to add insight into their clients' functioning. This foundation is ever changing as we continue to read, experience, and mature in our efforts to understand and help those caught in downward spirals. There are many excellent resources (Coleman, Butcher, and Carson, 1980; Sue, Sue, and Sue, 1981, to mention only two) which can be of value in expanding the counselor's insight. We would encourage the reader to take up this challenge as truly creative counseling demands a continually expanding philosophical/theoretical foundation.

RELEASING CREATIVE ENERGY: THE UPWARD SPIRAL

We concur with Carkhuff (1969) who conceptualized growth as a cumulative process in which facilitative experiences enhance the potential to employ future positive experiences and decrease vulnerability to destructive encounters. As Glasser (1976) suggests, the strong gets stronger and "uses his extra strength to gain more love and more worth, more pleasure, more meaning, more zest from life in general." Growing individuals spiral upward as they translate insights about themselves and their environment into constructive action. They are free to choose their destiny and the locus of control remains internal. Even negative experiences can be transcended or actively translated into the individuals' benefit.

The recent upsurge of interest in prevention and development with the helping professions has made us more aware of the need to develop a conceptual model of the healthy personality. A comprehensive model of human growth has obvious merit for guiding our work with high-functioning clients, but may also serve as a basis for drawing out the hidden strengths of the more dysfunctional client. Heath (1980) has made an outstanding response to this challenge. He describes a highly flexible model of maturity which offers a way of organizing our knowledge about healthy development and has heuristic potential for the creative counselor. He defines five interdependent dimensions (symbolization, allocentrism, integration, stability, autonomy) which can be assessed across four personality sectors (cognition, self-concept, values, personal relations). The healthy personality is viewed as moving toward more accurate cognitive reflection, empathetic understanding, internal consistency, and self-regulating while becoming less rigid and egocentric. Whereas a detailed presentation of this model is beyond our scope, we think that it has considerable merit and is consistent with the counseling orientation presented in this book. It offers the flexibility essential to serve as a foundation for creative/eclectic counseling, and readers are encouraged to review it for themselves. Heath (1980) has also extended his principles of healthy development, directed into their counseling implications, and offers some excellent suggestions for promoting healthy development along each dimension of maturity.

Several other theorists have added to this basic model of healthy functioning. The humanists suggest that we have an innate predisposition toward developing our potentials and Rogers (1961) conceptualizes human beings as in a process of creating themselves. We feel that such a force is released primarily within the context of facilitative relationships through which more basic needs of love and esteem are being satisfied. Some clients have these needs well met. For others, forming a supportive relationship may become the primary focus of counseling. Maslow provides the classic characterization of the self-actualizing individual, and many others have pushed this concept further. Carkhuff (1969) provides an operational definition of his fully functioning individuals and suggests that they are the only ones who can offer successful psychotherapeutic intervention to others. All of these versions have focused on the upwardly spiraling person as trustworthy, genuine, democratic, autonomous, self-aware, compassionate, spontaneously self-loving, and capable of engaging in intimate empathetic relationships. This person is not constrained by a mechanistic formula for relating, but is able to give to self in the risks of creative involvement. This creativity is the keynote of the growing individual. As Thorne (1967) suggests, ". . . achieving the highest level of integration of which man is capable requires an optimum combination of circumstances in which all lower-level functions are operating perfectly in support of the high-level creative activity representing the highest achievement." Glasser (1976) has conceptualized the release of creative energy as coming during positive addiction states in which "mind and body flow together" while providing optimal conditions for new neural connectives and brain growth. The release of creative energy then receives its impetus from an integrative substrate (a foundation based on basic attitudes and effective skills of living) which frees the person to develop even higher levels. Whereas most people strive continually to maintain strict homeostasis within all areas of their existence, the fully functioning individual can risk and even gain pleasure out of small discrepancies from the balanced state (McClelland, 1951). It is a bit like master downhill skiers who have such a command of the basics that they are freed to attack the slopes with seeming abandon as they creatively negotiate difficult terrain with a fearless sense of confidence (occasional injuries do not keep them from trying again).

Risking becomes a vehicle for expanding self-awareness and building new areas of competence and serves as the learning edge of positive development. The outsider may marvel at their ability to enjoy themselves so much while appearing to be out of control.

Both authors find an analogy to this phenomenon in our teaching experience, and know that our very best classes (peak experiences for us, if not our students) come when we have done our homework and then somehow move beyond the structure of lecture notes and preplanned formats. At these times (which we can learn to maximize), there emerge a free flow of ideas that creatively interact to generate an exciting and productive class. Similarly, creative counseling transcends the boundaries of specific theories and techniques. The high-functioning counselor, backed by extensive awareness of counseling process and technique, is free to risk creative involvement with clients. The focus is shifted toward the client, and away from concern with saying the "right" thing. We think that this integrative foundation of the growing individual is analogous to the blooming of a flower. Heredity provides the roots, environment the nourishment, and emerging self the stem upon which the flower will blossom. Unlike the flower, however, we determine a major share of our own direction through choice, which can enable us to transcend our environment. In drawing a similar analogy, Schafer (1978) points out, "It is important to note that in order to grow, the plant needed stressful conditions—up to a point. It could not grow in a vacuum. Challenges as long as they are not too great, stimulate rather than retard growth." Hans Selye, the eminent stress researcher, has even coined a new term, *eustress,* to represent the beneficial aspects of stress which help us convert potential distress into positive experiences while lending zest to our existence (Selye and Cherry, 1978). It is our expectancies, based on our perception, that become critical. High-functioning people choose to translate their environment in ways that are ultimately constructive for themselves and others. As Miller, Nunnally, and Wackman (1975) point out, ". . . your interpretations are not simply based on the way things are on some 'reality out there.' They are based on what you perceive (sense) plus all the feelings, intentions, and prior interpretations you bring into each situation." Positively spiraling individuals develop the capacity to provide their own impetus for growth (change in one area stimulates change in another) as part of their own self-fulfilling prophecy. It is, therefore, not just the conditions we face but the conceptual framework out of which they are encountered that enables the person to unfold as a beautiful flowering plant. It is this self/world perceptual component of the healthy individual that blends the petals together as a creative unit.

SUMMARY

Creative counseling cannot occur without a sound philosophical foundation and related insight into human functioning. In this chapter, we have developed two principles which are basic to understanding the human condition and translating that understanding into desired change. The first principle focuses on motivational systems which are critical in producing client dysfunctioning as well as providing the energy for constructive change. The second principle takes account of the interactive nature of our various domains of functioning (spiritual, physical, affective, cognitive, behavioral) and assumes that change in any area will produce concomitant change in other domains. Whereas these principles are very simple, they provide a foundation for building an eclectic approach to counseling and provide insight into the basic helping process. These basics, in turn, serve as a backdrop upon which highly creative counseling can occur.

In addition to these unifying principles, we have also provided some guidelines for understanding both the deterioration and growth ends of the human continuum. The creative counselor must have a broad-based understanding of human dysfunction in order to help clients remedy chronic problems. But creative counseling goes beyond helping people break negative cycles, and looks for innovative ways to help high-functioning individuals expand perceived limits. Whereas this chapter builds a foundation for creative counseling around a few unifying concepts, our most fundamental principle is that people are extremely complex and cannot be fitted neatly into any system. Consequently, only a broad-based and continually expanding view of human functioning can serve as a basis for creative counseling, and the reader is encouraged to use this chapter only as a starting point upon which to organize and build a personal view of people.

REFERENCES

Beck, A. T. *Cognitive therapy and the emotional disorders.* New York: New American Library, 1976.

Braginski, B. M., Braginski, D. D., and Ring, K. *Methods of madness: The mental hospital as a last resort.* New York: Holt, 1969.

Carkhuff, R. R. *Helping and human relations* (Vol. 1). New York: Holt, 1969.

Carkhuff, R. R. and Berenson, B. G. *Beyond counseling and therapy.* New York: Holt, 1967.

Coleman, J. C., Butcher, J. N., and Carson, R. C. *Abnormal psychology and modern life* (6th ed.). Glenview, Ill.: Scott, Foresman, 1980.

Combs, A. W. and Snygg, D. *Individual behavior.* New York: Harper, 1959.

Dyer, W. *Your erroneous zones.* New York: Avon, 1977.

Ellis, A. and Harper, R. A. *A new guide to rational living* (Rev. ed.). Hollywood: Wilshire Books, 1975.

Festinger, L. *A theory of cognitive dissonance.* Stanford: Stanford, 1957.

Fiske, D. W. and Maddi, S. R. (Eds.). *Functions of varied experience.* Homewood, Ill.: Dorsey, 1961.

Forgus, R. and Shulman, B. *Personality: A cognitive view.* Englewood Cliffs, N. J.: Prentice-Hall, 1979.

Glasser, W. *Positive addiction.* New York: Harper & Row, 1976.

Gordon, T. *Parent effectiveness training.* New York: Wyden, 1970.

Heath, D. H. Wanted: A comprehension model of healthy personality. *Personnel and Guidance Journal,* 1980, *58*(5), 391–399.

Helson, H. Adaptation level theory. In S. Koch (Ed.), *Psychology: A study of a science.* New York: McGraw-Hill, 1959.

James, M. and Jongeward, D. *Born to win.* Reading, Mass.: 1971.

Kelly, G. A. *The psychology of personal constructs* (Vol. 1). New York: Norton, 1955.

Maslow, A. H. Dynamic theory of human motivation. *Psychological Review,* 1943, *30,* 370–396.

McClelland, D. C. *Personality.* New York: Dryden, 1951.

Miller, S., Nunnally, E. W., and Wackman, D. B. *Alive and aware.* Minneapolis, Minn.: Interpersonal Communication Programs, 1975.

Mischel, W. *Introduction to personality.* New York: Holt, 1981.

Rogers, C. R. *On becoming a person.* Boston: Houghton Mifflin, 1961.

Rotter, J. B. Generalized expectancies for internal vs. external control of reinforcements. *Psychological Monographs,* 1966, *80* (609).

Schachter, S. and Singer, J. W. Cognitive, social and physiological determinants of emotional states. *Psychological Review,* 1962, *69,* 379–399.

Schafer, W. *Stress, distress, and growth.* Davis, Calif.: Responsible Action, 1978.

Schlesinger, K. and Groves, P. M. *Psychology. A dynamic science.* Dubuque, Ia.: Wm. C. Brown, 1976.

Seligman, M. *Helplessness.* San Francisco: Freeman, 1975.

Selye, H. *The stress of life.* New York: McGraw-Hill, 1976.

Selye, H. and Cherry, L. On the real benefits of eustress. *Psychology Today,* March 1978, 60–70.

Stein, J. *Effective personality: A humanistic approach.* Belmont, Calif.: Brooks/Cole, 1972.

Sue, D., Sue, D. W., and Sue, S. *Understanding abnormal behavior.* Boston: Houghton Mifflin, 1981.

Tanner, O. *Stress.* New York: Time-Life, 1976.

Thorne, F. C. Eclectic psychotherapy. In R. Corsini (Ed.), *Current Psychotherapies.* Stasca, Ill.: F. E. Peacock, 1973.

Thorne, F. C. The etiological equation. In R. R. Carkhuff and B. G. Berenson (Eds.), *Beyond counseling and therapy.* New York: Holt, 1967.

CHAPTER 4

TOWARD CREATIVE COUNSELING: AN EMERGING PARADIGM

As we have previously suggested, the foundations for creative counseling in the 1980s were solidified during the two preceding decades. During this period, a framework for effective helping was established and potency added to this basic form through the development of numerous intervention techniques. The narrowness of schoolistic views has increasingly given way to a more open eclectic orientation among professionals. This emerging paradigm (Guiding force, Kuhn, 1970) has allowed for the integration of seemingly divergent thinking and continues to generate hypotheses and solutions. In fact, it is these new directions that extend the previous boundaries of eclecticism and lead to our theme of creativity in counseling. Before moving beyond old territories, however, we would like to take a closer (and critical) look at our invaluable eclectic legacy. It has its limits, but still serves as a foundation for effective counseling as we move through the present decade.

THE CARKHUFFIAN MODEL

Despite the pioneering efforts by Frederick Thorne in paving the way, eclecticism through the 1960s was still denounced as an unsystematic and catchall approach. It took the prolific writing and charisma of Robert Carkhuff ("the radical humanist") to promote personalized eclecticism as a legitimate movement. Through extensive research, Carkhuff and his associates documented a two-phase model as a framework for unifying input from a wide range of therapeutic schools. The model incorporates resources throughout the directive/nondirective continuum and provides a conceptual structure for unifying divergent philosophies and approaches as the two-phase process translates client insight (understanding) into programs for cognitive behavior change (action).

Phase I: Understanding the Client

The first phase of therapy was identified by Carkhuff and Berenson (1967) as a "downward and inward" movement involving the therapist's offering of increasingly higher levels of empathy, respect, and concreteness which enable clients to turn inward and explore themselves and their areas of concern. In this initial focus, the counselor's efforts are aimed at engaging the clients in self-exploration to promote meaningful insight and self-understanding. Extensive empirical documentation was provided for these facilitative conditions which extended the

TABLE 4-1
SUMMARY OF CORE FACILITATIVE CONDITIONS

Scale 1
Empathic understanding in interpersonal processes
Level 1 The verbal and behavioral expressions of the helper either *do not attend to or detract significantly* from the verbal and behavioral expressions of the helpee(s) in that they communicate significantly less of the helpee's feelings and experiences than the helpee has communicated himself.
Level 2 While the helper responds to the expressed feelings of the helpee(s), he does so in such a way that he subtracts noticeable effects from the communication of the helpee.
Level 3 The expressions of the helper in response to the expressions of the helpee(s) are essentially interchangeable with those of the helpee in that they express essentially the same effect and meaning.
Level 4 The responses of the helper add *noticeably* to the expressions of the helpee(s) in such a way as to express feelings a level deeper than the helpee was able to express himself.
Level 5 The helper's responses add *significantly* to the feeling and meaning of the expressions of the helpee(s) in such a way as to accurately express feelings levels below what the helpee himself was able to express or, in the event of ongoing, deep self-exploration on the helpee's part, to be fully with him in his deepest moments.
Scale 2
The communication of respect in interpersonal processes: a scale for measurement
Level 1 The verbal and behavioral expressions of the helper communicate a clear lack of respect (or negative regard) for the helpee(s).
Level 2 The helper responds to the helpee in such a way as to communicate little respect for the feelings, experiences, and potentials of the helpee(s).
Level 3 The helper communicates the minimal acknowledgment of regard for the helpee's position and concern for the helpee's feelings, experiences, and potentials.

TABLE 4-1 *(Continued)*

Scale 2

Level 4
The helper clearly communicates a very deep respect and concern for the helpee.
Level 5
The helper communicates the very deepest respect for the helpee's worth as a person and his potential as a free individual.

Scale 3

Personally relevant concreteness or specificity of expression of interpersonal processes

Level 1
The helper frequently appears to lead or even allow discussions with the helpee(s) to deal only with vague and anonymous generalities.
Level 2
The helper frequently appears to allow or even lead discussions of material personally relevant to the helpee(s) to be dealt with on a vague and abstract level.
Level 3
The helper is open and at times facilitative of the helpee's discussion of personally relevant material in specific and concrete terminology.
Level 4
The helper appears frequently helpful in enabling the helpee(s) to fully develop in concrete and specific terms almost all instances of concern.
Level 5
The helper appears always helpful in guiding the discussions so that the helpee(s) may discuss fluently, directly, and completely specific feelings and experiences.

Source: Adapted from Carkhuff and Berenson, 1967.

earlier statements of Rogers's (1957) "necessary and sufficient conditions for therapeutic personality change." Carkhuff and his associates (1967, 1969, 1971, 1972, 1976) identified core facilitative conditions as integral to the helping process and designed a quantifiable scaling approach to assess the level of therapeutic functioning on each of these dimensions (see Table 4-1). Thus, a technology for training and assessment evolved which was operationalized in the following manner:

> For our own purposes, we have incorporated five levels of functioning with lower levels being essentially commensurate with the description of the distressed client or retarding therapist, and the higher levels commensurate with the facilitative individual, whatever his label. On all of the scales, level 3 constitutes the minimal level of facilitative functioning. Thus, level 1 describes not only the retarding therapist, but also the severely disturbed client who is essentially immune to constructive human encounters. Level 2 describes the more moderately retarding therapist or distressed client who, unlike the level 1 person, lives in a world of distortion but does live in the world and is not

oblivious to his world; level 3 describes the minimally facilitative therapist or the situationally distressed client who for all other purposes, is functioning at a minimally effective level. Level 4 may characterize the more potent individual who relates effectively and "makes things happen," whatever his area of endeavor, but including in particular the facilitation of other persons. The level 5 person, in turn, is involved in a lifelong search for actualization for others as well as for himself, and readily amenable to the sharing of his search with others (Carkhuff and Berenson, 1967, p. 46).

We agree with the authors who concluded that "the implications for a comprehensive model of facilitative processes are profound." The implications remain profound, and we need to continue to build upon it.

Phase II: Moving the Client into Action

The second component of this model was described as "the upward and outward," in which the therapist, in conjunction with the client, seeks to translate insight into constructive life changes. The counselor actively works "to put the picture together" through an integration of divergent "pieces" shared by the client. The counselor supports client exploration of the problem and the translation of understanding into action. The related core action conditions initiated by the counselor were identified as genuineness, self-disclosure, confrontation, and immediacy (see Table 4-2). These conditions hopefully culminate in a specific plan for change ("preferred modes of treatment") for dealing with the identified problem. The authors of this model have recommended that the level of counselor directiveness is determined by the client's insight, motivation, and behavioral skills, but that as much responsibility as is feasible be left with the client throughout the process.

TABLE 4-2
SUMMARY OF CORE ACTION CONDITIONS

Scale 4
Facilitative genuineness in interpersonal processes

Level 1
The helper's verbalizations are clearly unrelated to what he appears otherwise to be feeling at the moment, or his only genuine responses are negative in regard to the helpee(s) and appear to have a totally destructive effect upon the helpee.
Level 2
The helper's verbalizations are slightly unrelated to what he appears otherwise to be feeling at the moment; or when his responses are genuine they are negative in regard to the helpee, and he does not appear to know how to employ his negative reactions constructively as a basis for inquiry to the relationship.
Level 3
The helper provides no negative cues of a discrepancy between what he says and what he appears otherwise to be experiencing, but he provides no positive cues to indicate a really genuine response to the helpee(s).

TABLE 4-2 *(Continued)*

Scale 4

Level 4

The helper presents some positive cues indicating a genuine response (whether positive or negative) in a nondestructive manner to the helpee(s).

Level 5

The helper appears freely and deeply himself in a nonexploitative relationship with the helpee(s).

Scale 5

Facilitative self-disclosure in interpersonal processes

Level 1

The helper appears to attempt actively to remain detached from the helpee(s) and discloses nothing about his own feelings or personality to the helpee(s). If he does disclose himself, he does so in a way that is not tuned into the helpee's interests and may even retard the helpee's general progress.

Level 2

The helper, while not always appearing actively to avoid self-disclosures, never volunteers personal information about himself.

Level 3

The helper communicates an openness to volunteering personal information about himself that may be in keeping with the helpee's interest, but this information is often vague and indicates little about the unique character of the helper.

Level 4

The helper freely volunteers information about his personal ideas, attitudes, and experiences in accord with the helpee's interest and concerns.

Level 5

The helper volunteers very intimate and often detailed material about his own personality, and in keeping with the helpee's needs may express information that might be extremely embarrassing under different circumstances or if revealed to an outsider.

Scale 6

Confrontation in interpersonal processes

Level 1

The verbal and behavioral expressions of the helper disregard the discrepancies in the helpee's behavior (ideal versus real self, insight versus action, helper versus helpee's experiences).

Level 2

The verbal and behavioral expressions of the helper disregard the discrepancies in the helpee's behavior.

Level 3

The verbal and behavioral expressions of the helper, while open to discrepancies in the helpee's behavior, do not relate directly and specifically to these discrepancies.

Level 4

The verbal and behavioral expressions of the helper are keenly and continually attuned to the discrepancies in the helpee's behavior.

Level 5

The verbal and behavioral expressions of the helper reflect a keen and continual awareness of self-defeating patterns of functioning on the part of the helpee.

TABLE 4-2 *(Continued)*

Scale 7
Immediacy of relationship in interpersonal processes
Level 1 The verbal and behavioral expressions of the helper disregard the content and affect of the helpee's expressions that have the potential for relating to the helper.
Level 2 The verbal and behavioral expressions of the helper disregard most of the helpee expressions that have the potential for relating to the helper.
Level 3 The verbal and behavioral expressions of the helper, while open to interpretations of immediacy, do not relate what the helpee is saying to what is going on between the helper and the helpee in the immediate moment.
Level 4 The verbal and behavioral expression of the helper appear continuously to relate the helpee's expressions directly to the helper-helpee relationship.
Level 5 The verbal and behavioral expressions of the helper relate the helpee's expressions directly to the helper-helpee relationship.

Source: Adapted from Carkhuff and Berenson, 1967.

In deference to the underlying complexity inherent in this model, Carkhuff and his associates went on to identify specific modes of intervention to be applied within the basic two-phase structure. They critiqued several of the schools of psychotherapy (Carkhuff and Berenson, 1967) in terms of limitations and contributions to this emerging superstructure. Thus, the counselor's own level of functioning as operationalized in terms of the core conditions served as a foundation through which specific contributions from various approaches could be filtered toward the two phases. This system could operate as a prototype for the objective and personally relevant evaluation of any potentially viable theory or technique and provide the vehicle for a self-generating open eclecticism (see Figure 4-1).

Literally hundreds of studies supporting and extending (to paraprofessional training, educational applications, rating varifications, and so forth) this model emerged during the decade following its first appearance. However, the next major elaboration of the system was a contribution made by Gerard Egan (1975a) in *The Skilled Helper*. In this landmark publication, the two-phase Carkhuffian model is subdivided into a prehelping phase and three stages which shift the focus from affective to cognitive to behavioral as the process unfolds. Each of these components is translated into client/counselor goals with appropriate skills at each stage. [A supplementary training manual has also been published as a guide to skills development (Egan, 1975b).] The prehelping phase is equated with the word "attending" which emphasizes the verbal and nonverbal communication of acceptance as the first goal of counselors. We would add a preattending period in which counselors ready themselves (clearing themselves of tension and distractions while preparing for their meeting with the client—a concept to be expanded later in Chapter 5). Stage I emphasizes the counselors' responding skills (primary empathy, respect, genuineness, concreteness) as a precondition for the client's self-exploration. A feeling of acceptance must be established to allow for the client's sharing. Stage II focuses on counselor integration—pulling together the pieces shared during the client's self-exploration into a more meaningful and workable picture—and increased self-understanding on the part of the client. In addition to the skills associated with stage I, this stage requires higher levels of

FIGURE 4-1
An eclectic framework for integrating divergent views of counseling. The shaded area represents the facilitative conditions essential to counseling and the secondary contributions of various schools of psychotherapy. The nonshaded areas contain limitations implied in these schools which are therefore not incorporated into the counselor's repertoire of responding. Note that all potential approaches may be evaluated within the counselor's personal emerging eclectic framework. *(Adapted from Carkhuff and Berenson, 1967, p. 230.)*

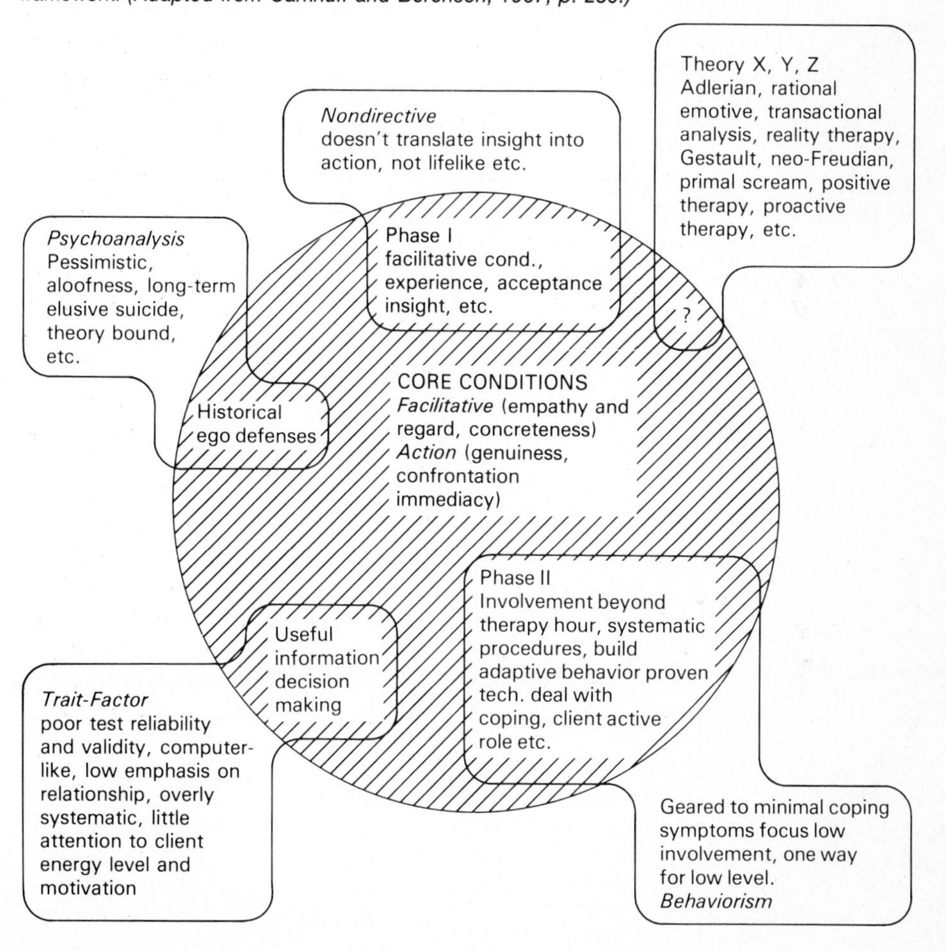

TABLE 4-3
SUMMARY OF THE ECLECTIC SYSTEM PHASE I (RELATIONAL: DOWNWARD AND INWARD)

Pre-helping (Attending) → **Stage I (Responding)**

Helping the client share his concern

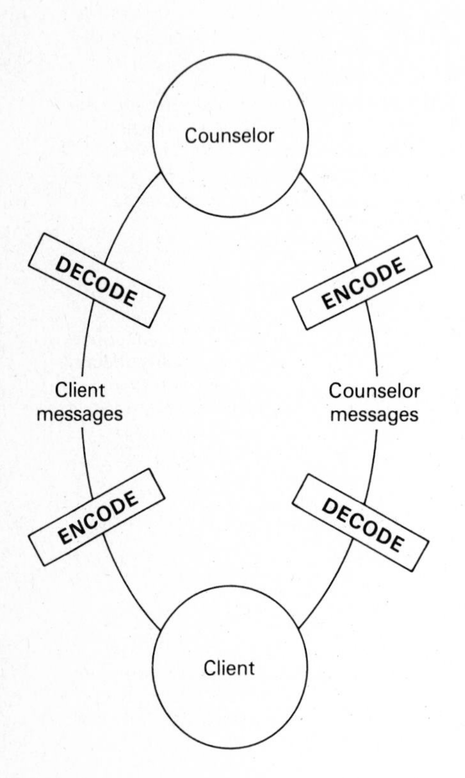

Nonverbally attending:

At intermediate levels
- eye contact
- office arrangement
- body posture
- facial expression
- distraction free

Verbally attending:
- "door openers"
- reflection (level 3)
- simple acknowledgements to convey respect and empathy
- use of intermediate levels of facilitative conditions and remain sensitive to client's decoding system
- define counseling process and expectations with client
- "listen" to client's nonverbal behavior

↓

(Feeling of acceptance and wants help)

TABLE 4-3 *(Continued)*

Stage II (Integration)	Stage III (Facilitating action)	Follow up
	Putting the pieces together	Helping the client change from destructive to constructive patterns.
I. *Primary level empathy* • active listening: listen to intensity and to what is not being said • respond to feelings and content (higher level reflection) • be gentle but don't let client "run" from issues II. *Genuineness* • confrontation in form of "door openers" • escalated gently • nondefensive III. *Respect* • being "for" the client • awareness of uniqueness of client (strengths) • suspend critical judgments until relationship builds IV. *Concreteness* • use of specific "homework" to operationalize the concern • use of clarification summaries to initiate and close sessions	I. *Advanced accurate empathy* • interpretive reflections deal with hidden material • interpretive summaries • generate counseling contract • problem solving (exploring the alternatives) • develop unifying themes (connect islands) II. *Counselor Self-disclosure* • (only in areas of own personal growth) III. *Confrontation* (with inconsistances and needed areas of change) • facilitate client self-confrontation when possible • use lowest level that still gets the job done • confront tentatively • never confront beyond level that relationship can tolerate • be aware of client defenses and readiness to hear confrontation IV. *Immediacy* • interpretation of your relationship with client as analogy to other relationships	I. *Goal setting* - divide outcome into specific goals (concreteness at high level) • establish criteria for success • identify strengths and supports II. *Specific strategies for accomplishing goals* ("Preferred Modes of Treatment") • verbal instruction (i.e., systematic desensitization, application of learning principles, etc.) • modeling and role playing desired behavior III. *Implementation of change strategies* • "in vivo" practice • monitor progress • building "outside" support system • specific homework • integrate new behavior and insight (Stage II) IV. *Follow-up* V. *Recycle* with related issues at higher levels VI. *Deal with dependency and resistance issues* VII. *Recycle or terminate* VIII. *Follow-up*

empathy, self-disclosure, immediacy, and confrontation to be expressed by the counselor and nondefensive listening by the client. The familiar action conditions are employed to facilitate the social influence process made possible by the power base established by counselors in the preceding stage. As clients see the necessity for change, movement into the action conditions of the final stage is initiated. In stage III, counselors rely on all the previous skills in addition to the use of specific action programs and the supportive base already established. Clients are given direction, relevant skill training, and support as they risk the steps proposed to implement the mutually defined therapeutic goals. We feel that the principle of counterconditioning should be adhered to as the risks of behavior change are approached gradually, systematically, and do not extend beyond the limits of the individual's support system.

We believe that the communication model proposed in the preceding chapter (Gordon, 1970) complements Egan's stage system and offers an excellent way to conceptualize the unfolding counseling process. The stages serve as a backdrop for the core conditions which are, in turn, translated into the ongoing bits of interchange between counselor and client. Verbal and nonverbal behaviors are screened through respective decoding systems and then rechanneled to the recipient via encoded message. Table 4-3 represents the culmination of this eclectic system and has the potential to serve as a meaningful guide for navigating through the maze of messages offered by our clients. It should be noted that while the counselor may be functioning at higher levels, the client is represented (through equal-sized circles) as having equal psychological size in this interactional equation, even though the flow of communication may shift its weight and direction as various stages are traversed. Whereas the flow of this process is not necessarily unidirectional, the intensity of interchanges is generally regarded as magnifying (reflected in movement toward level 5 of the core conditions) as more information is shared, and the relationship and concomitant push toward related behavior change occurs. For a more thorough understanding of this model, the reader is invited to investigate the selected resources outlined as an annotated bibliography in Appendix Two.

We want to emphasize that this eclectic system is much more than a philosophy for integrating divergent approaches to counseling. It has served for both authors as a very practical tool for structuring our counseling contacts and guiding us through the moment-by-moment interchanges. It serves as a standard for assessing progress and a guide for pulling various techniques into focus at the appropriate time. Perhaps an example would best illustrate the applicability of this system. We invite the reader to turn to Appendix One (Part B: Alice and the Carkhuffian Model) if an illustration would help. We add here that as invaluable as this system is, it has its limits. Obviously, it is limited by the counselor's own level of functioning—no system can overcome this by itself. In fact, as we have used this system through hundreds of counseling contacts over the years, we have come to see that the only real limits for a high-functioning counselor are in rigid adherence to the system. It can be used as a support and crutch, but is at its best when used only as a starting point. It provides a foundational structure, but creative counselors are not tied to any system. They use the system but also move beyond it. The more the basics of the system become an ingrained part of counselors, the more counselors become free to transcend its boundaries. No system (only highly caring, skilled, and creative counselors) can keep up with the incredible complexity of the counseling process.

In keeping with the eclectic theme and the prototype set by this model, we will now attempt to formalize our assessment of this system. We will use the same format suggested by Carkhuff by first identifying the contributions and then the limitations of this orientation. Finally, we will offer some guidelines for the future direction of this model which will be developed in the remainder of this book.

CONTRIBUTIONS OF THE CARKHUFFIAN MODEL

In contrast to the largely unheralded efforts of Fredrick Thorne during the decade preceding Carkhuff's first major publication, the *Zeitgeist* of the late 1960s was more receptive to a systematic eclecticism. As a reflection of our profession's increased maturity, schoolism started to give way (at least for some) to an emerging openness to diversity. The resulting model has made tremendous impact. Just as Watson brought the findings of Thorndike and Pavlov out of the laboratory, Carkhuff, building from the efforts of Rogers, Thorne, Truax, and others, brought eclecticism out of obscurity into a growing acceptance among professionals. He has championed an emerging trend in our profession and should rightfully be identified as the father of this movement. Beyond its historical significance, the following list provides at least part of the contributions associated with the model we have outlined in this chapter.

1 The philosophy of radical humanism which acknowledges that intervention is for better or worse and that counselors only have the right to intervene when they are functioning at a high level themselves.

2 The research foundations of the model provided renewed credibility in counseling and defined (in researchable, operational terms) the basic skills involved in effective helping. It went beyond outcome research and looked inside of the process of helping.

3 Broad applicability of model. Whereas most schools of psychotherapy were developed out of clinical practice with a narrowly defined population, i.e., neurotics, schizophrenics, this model allows for the incorporation of useful techniques to respond to basically healthy individuals undergoing situational distress as well as to those who are severely and chronically disorganized. The model has served effectively in both educational (Aspy, 1972) and clinical settings and also acknowledges the importance of prevention (Carkhuff, 1976).

4 A teachable system that has didactic value in counselor education (Truax and Carkhuff, 1967). We have found it to be extremely valuable in teaching both practicum and academic courses in our counselor education program.

5 The evaluation scales serve as a valuable tool in rating counselor effectiveness in ongoing interactions which is extremely helpful in providing a framework for feedback in supervision as well as for stimulating further delineation of the counselor/client interaction itself.

6 Like effective counseling, the model provides a safe framework for exploring (with an open mind) various potential contributions of new theories without the risk of being overwhelmed. It not only has the potential for unifying traditional orientations, but serves as a system for ongoing analysis and integration of new knowledge into the counselor's existing personal framework.

7 The system allows for the integration of affective, cognitive, and behavioral components of counseling and provides guidelines for these interactions and relative status throughout the counseling process. It incorporates the relational/action as well as the directive/nondirective continuum of counseling.

8 It encourages high-functioning counselors to develop their own specific skills and personal qualities. Beyond the acquisition of the basic core conditions, counselors are responsible for developing a wide range of techniques and continually expanding their intervention repertoire.

9 The stage structure of the model gives practicing counselors an ongoing check before, after, and during counseling sessions to locate themselves in the process and see what comes next. We find this extremely valuable as a guide for moving from relationship to action and identifying which skills might be appropriately used to implement progress through a particular stage.

10 A "clinically meaningful system based upon the contextual variables. It is the first open eclectic model in which the therapist is shaped by what is effective for the client, and hopefully, in which both will be shaped by what is effective for themselves and others" (Carkhuff and Berenson, 1976, p. 233).

We would summarize by concluding that this model has the potential for offering a profound guiding force to our profession. We would, in fact, elevate it to the status of a paradigm which, according to Kuhn (1970), is a vehicle which directs the development of a profession. A paradigm serves to free the scientific community from the need to constantly reexamine its first principles—in this case, the core conditions which have been thoroughly documented and are essential foundation principles for all effective helping—so that members of that community can concentrate on extensions and ramifications of the paradigm. In keeping with our theme, a thorough knowledge of this paradigm—cognitively, and more importantly, in terms of an internalized framework—can serve as a springboard for truly creative interpersonal facilitation. To maintain its viability, however, any effective paradigm must be extended beyond its current limits. Carkhuff has established a starting point, but the challenge is to move beyond its boundaries through our own creative energy.

LIMITATIONS OF THE CARKHUFFIAN MODEL

We should emphasize that the limitations we will discuss in this section are less inherent in the model itself and more a product of misinterpretation and misapplication. Carkhuff himself has an acute awareness of this problem which follows inevitably from the disparity between the development of a theory and its implementation in practice by its adherents. He had quoted from Kierkegaard to explicate this phenomenon: "In relation to their systems, most systematizers are like a man who builds an enormous castle and lives in a shack beside it" (Farber,

1956). In other words, it is essential to separate what practitioners do from what they say. We all know effective therapists who call themselves psychoanalytic or client-centered. It is our belief, however, that these therapists are probably eclectic in a more real sense than they admit and certainly offer high levels of core conditions to their clients. Fiedler (1951) pointed out that effective therapy transcends specific training and orientation. The same is true of those who espouse the Carkhuffian model. Exposure to the system (or even facility with its structure and concepts) does not assure that the counselor will be effective. Once again, we must separate the man from his system. What works for Carkhuff does not guarantee success for his followers.

It is not enough to have learned a number of skills and a system for tying them together, but the zealousness of the proponents of this system have tainted the model with some of the dogmatism found in the traditional schoolism criticized earlier in our discussion. As with other schools, the flexibility initially promoted by its originator has been transformed into rigidity by many of its proponents. Whereas the security of the model's simplicity is a major contribution, it has also offered a seductive enticement to a would-be counselor looking for an easy road to success. Many of the so-called "Freudians" have succumbed to the same temptation. Freud himself continually revised his paradigm, while many of his disciples caught glimpses of his creative genius and held on. Likewise, many of the Carkhuffians have clung to pieces of the model without really getting inside of the system.

The naive enthusiasm of some of the early followers of this model is somewhat analogous to the struggling we go through during adolescence to establish our identity. The weak succumb and may reflect a mirror image of the indoctrination drilled into them by parent figures. It is a pitiful thing to see individuals clinging to untested principles and dogmatically holding on to the "purity" of their heritage, afraid to question or really look at their own structure. Fortunately, the strong transcend the comfort of their former dependence. The unquestioned loyalty to parents gives way to an even greater appreciation of our inheritance when we can really assess their legitimate contributions. The assessment of contributions and limitations becomes a catalyst for our own growth and self-assessment. We do not throw away the basic structure, but use it as a filter for digesting and incorporating (even changing the structure itself) other viewpoints. It has been all too easy to become a disciple (be it Carkhuffian, Rogerian, Gestalt, or whatever) rather than taking on the hard work of continual expansion. The Carkhuff model is excellent, but we must strive to extend it rather than be strapped to its perceived boundaries. We say "perceived" because the real limits are within us rather than the system.

Perhaps the skill training movement equated with this model has the greatest potential for the seduction of simplicity we have been discussing. It is easy to skip over the basic premise (counseling is a way of life) and go directly to the appealing surface of the system (the skills which only reflect the essential core conditions). Once caught up in the technology of the system (rating scales and step-by-step process), some counselors fail to hear the real value contained in the simple realities presented. It is possible to hide in the security of skill training, even though in reality the skills are *not* simple, which can serve as a barrier to the individual's more basic helping skills. We are reminded of an old manual for bird-dog training which presented a simple truth: Do not force train your dog into specific responses until you have seen how his innate behaviors are manifest in the field (let what is natural develop alongside your training). Maybe the real danger here lies in counselor educators who indoctrinate rather than follow the essense of what Carkhuff said at the most basic level of this model: Understanding (relationship, exploration, integration) should lead to action (a unique formula for behavior change designed specifically with the other person). This is the essence of the creative cycle and the core of the road toward effective helping—creativity based on a foundation in solid principles providing the leading edge for gaining more knowledge (or, the good old scientific method and upward spiral rolled into one). This creative energy can be released only to the extent that counselors are thoroughly competent in terms of prerequisite knowledge, skills, and their own high levels of personal functioning. The development of specific skills provides a necessary foundation, but effective counselors move beyond the mechanics to integrate the skills into a broader framework. They move from transcendence of skills and toward their creative application.

An extension of overcommitment to this or any system is that it may start to speak for itself. Effective counseling must operate from the client's needs rather than out of a system (the model is useful to the extent that it facilitates this process). Unfortunately, it is comforting to define all client concerns in terms of "knowns" of a model rather than risking the exposure of our incompetence. It is a seductive trap, and we have all been there—offering a client *our* special approach only to find out later that what was needed was something else (counselors have defenses, too). This point may remind us of some of the training films we have seen in which the therapist "plugs in" a preprogrammed solution, and we are left with the feeling that the same script would have been offered to anyone who walked in the door.

A related danger which flows directly from overbuying this particular system involves locking into the predictable sequence of stages presented in the model. We must emphasize again that the model's originator intended for the system to increase individual flexibility and, in fact, discusses the interaction of these phases and exceptions to the typical flow in considerable detail (in several of the publications previously mentioned). Once again we are impressed with the model as an outstanding cognitive road map (attending——responding——integration——action), but point out the potential danger in rigidly adhering to a step-by-step approach. We would offer an alternative to this kind of structured unidirectional flow in the form of a highly individualized flowchart which could be visualized as an expanding spiral. This is a highly flexible formula which may be initiated at any point along the spiral, depending on the client's needs.

Before moving on, let us mention that the limitations presented in this section are primarily based on the inadequacies of the model's adherents rather than on any substantive deficiencies inherent in the system itself. Having low-functioning individuals offering themselves as counselors is a problem, no matter what specific orientations they espouse. Carkhuff (1969) identified the core of this problem through his research finding that most psychotherapists function below level 3 in terms of the core conditions. There is simply no substitute (skill training begs the basic issue) for human beings who can genuinely offer themselves to those in need. As Carkhuff puts it:

> The fault, it appears, lies not so much in the system or the organization or the discipline or the profession as it does in people. Some individuals can deliver and some cannot. Those who cannot deliver must be trained; those who cannot be trained nor treated must not hold positions of responsibility in the area of human relations. Those who can deliver must be pushed to the limits of the fourth R of helping—the full realization of their full resources—and raised to positions of responsibility (Carkhuff, 1969, p. 289).

BEYOND LEVEL 5: FURTHER LIMITATIONS AND FUTURE DIRECTIONS (FROM ECLECTIC TO CREATIVE COUNSELING)

Using the previous discussion as a conceptual context, we will consider several limitations which reflect areas in which the eclectic paradigm needs to be expanded. In keeping with the example set by the developers of this paradigm—promoting constructive redirection rather than criticism for the sake of criticizing—we will establish guidelines for pushing the paradigm beyond its present conceptual base and extend its applicability. We will briefly introduce five areas which can serve to expand the existing eclecticism. Each of these areas will then be developed as chapter themes in Part Two of our book and will formulate the major component of creative counseling. Whereas we appreciate the rich heritage of eclecticism, we also see counseling as much more than the application of specific skills within its structural confines.

Beyond the Counseling Hour

The counseling hour emerges out of the context of everyday life for both the client and counselor. Whereas the basic eclectic four-stage model we have outlined provides an excellent foundation for conceptualizing the actual counseling session, it should be extended into meaningful guidelines for what might happen during this contextual time—before, after, and in between the contact with our clients. We develop this theme in Chapter 5 as we explore a variety of concepts which link together the counseling hour and patterns of everyday life. Specific suggestions are also offered for effective use of personal energy in the professional counselor's demanding life as part of our concluding chapter.

Beyond Existing Core Condition

The essence of counseling is wrapped up in breaking out of comfortable, yet nonproductive, patterns and moving toward more effective attitudes and behaviors. This cannot happen without risk which is a key element for both client and counselor in the process of creative counseling. Likewise, a key element of effective risk taking is its rationality and the structured preparation necessary to prevent destructive risking. These themes have been largely ignored in the counseling literature and are developed more fully in Chapter 6 our book. Risk itself is developed as an additional core condition which directs the interaction of the other core dimensions.

Beyond Remediation

Whereas the labels of "treatment and psychotherapy" associated with the initial emergence of eclectic orientation may have been necessary to add impetus to this movement (many therapists would not open the cover of a book with a counseling title), a shift toward a new identity is in order and is represented more clearly by the "helping and counseling" labels. As Thomas Szasz (1978) suggests, labels are the "mirrors of our minds" and that jargonistic terms such as psychotherapy have become metaphorical and inappropriate. He goes on to state that:

> Treatment means, and should only mean, a physiochemical intervention in the structure and function of the body aimed at combating or curing disease. The term psychotherapy insofar as it is used to refer to two or more people speaking and listening to each other, is therefore a misnomer, and misleading category. . . . There is, properly speaking, no such thing as psychotherapy. Like mental illness it is a metaphor and a myth. By calling some types of human encounters "psychotherapy" we only impede our capacity to understand them (Szasz, 1978, p. xvi).

Even more important than a further dissociation with this kind of stigma is the need for expanding our helping orientation to include an increased awareness of people's strengths and the relevance they play in the counseling process. This is not to deny the reality of the problems faced by our clients, but to suggest a renewed emphasis on their positive attributes. In critiquing negative therapies as those which focus essentially on diseases or problems, Wiesen (1977) concludes that:

> Hour after hour of therapy time is negatively oriented, as if a person enters the therapist's office with only a sack of soiled problems to be washed, bleached, and if possible, even ironed out. It is my conservative estimate that negative therapy composes about ninety-nine percent of all that goes on in psychotherapy . . . (Wiesen, 1977, p. 3).

He goes on to endorse Freud's idea of closed mental energy which purports that there is a limited amount of energy available to anyone at a given point in time. When the counseling hour focuses exclusively on the negative, little positive energy is left to be channeled into constructive strength-building efforts: "It is not the amount of psychological energy one possesses that differentiates the habitual winner from the person who has not yet learned to attain meaningful goals, but the manner in which the person expands the energy that is available to him." Preoccupation with "trap circuits" (Wiesen's basic unit of self-destructive thinking, feeling, and behaving) can divert energy from building new resources and make the client more dependent, more anxious, and worse off than before. Since our energy reservoirs are limited, we would suggest that the focus on the positive energy available during the counseling process take two relatively untapped directions. First, as strengths are developed the problem areas can be seen from a different perspective. The goals become growth directed rather than purely problem oriented. Untapped potential becomes a legitimate theme of this preventative/developmental focus which is expanded in Chapter 7. Second, positive counseling might take on a supplementary supportive role as an adjunct to problem-removal programs used in counseling. This involves an effort to unleash untapped potentials, often in a domain of existence not seemingly tied into the presenting problem, i.e., spiritual or physical. Areas which may not contain the heavy blockages associated with the problem can lead to sources of accomplishment much more readily than when confronting the problem head on. This sense of strength then becomes a resource for attacking the primary problem. In contrast to the conservation of energy notion, we believe that adding strengths actually expands the basic energy reservoir which the client can invest in overcoming problem areas. Ironically, this supplemental focus on creating new strength can become so exciting and powerful that the original problem somehow fades into the background. In some cases, there just is not enough energy left over to support the problem anymore.

Beyond the Psychological

In keeping with the increased readiness for multidisciplinary integration within the helping professions, we sense that the current *Zeitgeist* is ripe for expanding the basic Carkhuffian model beyond its psychological (affect, cognitive, behavior) confines toward a more complete view of our clients as they really are—a complex integration of spiritual, physical, and psychological functioning. The foundation for this kind of expansion has already been laid within several publications which deserve mention at this point. Starting from the pioneering efforts of Thorne (1968) and Lazarus (1973, 1976), Hammond and Stanfield (1977) presented a planning model for eclectic intervention [multidimensional assessment and planning form (MAP)]. This system is not bound to any single theory and remains comprehensive and yet quite simple. "This assessment procedure departs from the historical tendency in diverse schools of psychotherapy to emphasize one factor as the prime dimension of problems (e.g. cognitive, environment, emotions) at the expense of other factors and scrutinizes the contributions or involvement of multivariate determinants or factors." In congruence with eclecticism "the multimodel approach achieves unusual comprehensiveness through assessing a broad range of potential determinants, and then intervening across a large number of dimensions." There is no unitary intervention system as the counselor creatively assesses interacting vectors within a holistic orientation. The MAP form serves as a guide for inquiry regarding client problems as well as strengths across seven dimensions—behavior, affect, sensory, physical, imagery, cognitive, interpersonal/environmental context—to emphasize the mutual influence and multicausality inherent in all human situations. A related innovative scheme has been recently developed by Pappas (1979a, 1979b) which stresses the importance of client strengths as well as physiological factors, family, and social context. Whereas both of these systems encourage the expansion of eclecticism into areas outside the strictly psychological, neither adequately deals with the spiritual or physical aspects of intervention. Therefore, Chapter 8 in the present text provides a more specific delineation of these systems and develops guidelines for the consideration of spiritual and physical functioning within the counseling context.

Beyond Eclecticism

Whereas eclectic thought has always placed the counselor above any system, the specifics of maintaining a high-functioning level have not been well developed. The counselors themselves are the most critical ingredients. No system or technique makes for effective helping by itself. It is the counselors who put life into available tools of intervention. Consequently, the issue of counselor renewal becomes vital to our discussion. We, therefore, conclude our book (Chapter 9) by focusing on the counselors themselves and some methods for keeping them at their creative best.

SUMMARY

Chapter 4 presented a historical picture of the emergence of eclecticism and its growing acceptance among professional counselors. The influence of Carkhuff and others in building a conceptual scheme for eclectic counseling was described and an overview of the resulting model presented in some detail. We proposed that this model, along with its core conditions, skill emphasis, and framework for the counseling process, serves as an excellent foundation for creative counseling. It offers a basis upon which we can build our own unique and changing approach to counseling which reflects the individual counselor's personality.

While the Carkhuffian model is a major contribution to effective eclectic counseling, it has its limitations. These limits are clarified and define a starting point for our coverage of creative counseling. The expansion of this eclectic framework outlines the remainder of our book and defines what we have described as the growing direction of the counseling profession. The emerging (creative) paradigm that we present builds on the strengths of the eclectic view but goes beyond the confines of any formal system. Specific skills provide a necessary prerequisite, but creative counseling is more than the application of effective techniques. It is eclecticism at its best as counselors move past their own perceived limits to creatively pull into play their own experiences, personalities, and highly developed intervention repertoires to facilitate desired client change.

REFERENCES

Aspy, D. N. *Toward a technology for humanizing education.* Champaign, Ill. Research Press, 1972.

Carkhuff, R.R. *Helping and human relations* (Vols. 1 and 2). New York: Holt, 1969.

Carkhuff, R.R. *The development of human resources.* New York: Holt, 1971.

Carkhuff, R. R. *The art of helping.* Amherst, Mass.: Human Resource Development Press, 1972.

Carkhuff, R. R. *Teaching as treatment.* Amherst, Mass.: Human Resource Development Press, 1976.

Carkhuff, R. R. and Berenson, B. R. *Beyond counseling and therapy.* New York: Holt, 1967.

Carkhuff, R. R. and Berenson, B. R. *Beyond counseling and therapy* (2nd ed.). New York: Holt, 1976.

Egan, G. *The skilled helper.* Belmont, Calif.: Wadsworth, 1975. (a)

Egan, G. *Exercises in helping skills.* Belmont, Calif.: Wadsworth, 1975. (b)

Farber, L. H. Martin Buber and psychiatry. *Psychiatry,* 1956, *19,* 109–120.

Fiedler, F. A. Comparison of therapeutic relationships in psychoanalytic, nondirective, and Adlerian therapeutic relationships. *Journal of Counseling Psychology,* 1951, *15,* 32–38.

Gordon, T. *Parent effectiveness training.* New York: Wyden, 1970.

Hammond, D. C. and Stanfield, K. *Multidimensional psychotherapy.* Champaign, Ill.: Institute for Personality and Ability Testing, 1977.

Kuhn, T. S. *The structure of scientific revolutions.* Chicago: University of Chicago Press, 1970.

Lazarus, A. A. Treating the "basic id." *Journal of Nervous and Mental Disease,* 1973, *156,* 404–411.

Lazarus, A. A. *Multimodal behavior therapy.* New York: Springer, 1976.

Pappas, J. *Case conceptualization.* Unpublished manuscript, University of Utah, 1979.(a)

Pappas, J. Personal communication, at the University of Utah, Salt Lake City, January 1979.(b)

Rogers, C. R. The necessary and sufficient conditions for therapeutic personality change. *Journal of Consulting Psychology,* 1957, *22,* 95–103.

Szasz, T. *The myth of psychotherapy.* Garden City, N.Y.: Anchor/Doubleday, 1978.

Thorne, F. C. *Psychological case handling* (Vols. 1 and 2), Brandon, Vt.: Clinical Psychology Publishing, 1968.

Truax, C. B. and Carkhuff, R. R. *Toward effective counseling and psychotherapy training and practices.* Chicago: Aldine, 1967.

Wiesen, A. E. *Positive therapy.* Chicago: Nelson-Hall, 1977.

PART TWO

TOWARD CREATIVE COUNSELING

We have come a long way as a profession in moving from schoolism toward an eclectic framework. The growing acceptance of eclecticism hallmarks the leading edge of a maturing profession, but it is imperative that we push beyond these current boundaries if our profession is to continue to develop. As in personal growth, expansion means moving beyond perceived points of security and into relatively uncharted areas. It is in extending the limits of eclecticism that we find creative counseling and generate the content for the remainder of our book. In line here with May's thinking (*The Courage to Create,* 1975), we would add that it is tempting to retreat into safe patterns of thinking, but that seeking new vision requires the courage to create new perceptions of ourselves and related professional roles. As Cole and Sarnoff (1980) suggest, each client demands new roles and skills which stretch the limits of our own creativity. This is what creative counseling is about, and the essence of what makes it an exciting adventure for both client and counselor.

In pushing our eclectic inheritance further, we would like to open several avenues which support creative counseling. Chapter 5 takes us beyond the counseling hour itself into a look at what counselors can do before and after actual sessions to increase the potential for a creative interchange. We explore the context out of which counseling emerges as we set the stage for creative problem solving. Chapters 6 and 7 introduce risk as a major theme in creative counseling. First, we look at risk as a core condition for remedial counseling. Next, we extend the risk theme into the growing concern that helping professionals have with prevention in their work with high-functioning clients. In Chapter 8 we turn our attention toward expanding counselors' roles as we encourage them to become involved with the spiritual and physical concerns of their clients. Chapter 9 concludes with a practical look at keeping the most essential ingredient for creative counseling at its best—the counselors themselves.

REFERENCES

Cole, H. P. and Sarnoff, D. Creativity and counseling. *Personnel and Guidance Journal,* 1980, *59*(3), 140–146.

May, R. *The courage to create.* New York: Bantam, 1975.

CHAPTER **5**

BEYOND THE COUNSELING HOUR

Counseling is a way of life. This phrase captures the essence of the eclectic philosophy and supersedes the skill and technical aspects of this orientation. It implies that counseling occurs within the context of everyday life and cannot be simply switched on when the client enters the counselor's office. In keeping with this theme, we see a need to expand eclecticism toward more consideration of the contextual factors which occur before, after, and in between the actual counseling sessions. The level of creative flow during the sessions is a direct reflection of our utilization of the time surrounding these encounters. Therefore, we would like to extend the eclectic framework that we have presented by developing some guidelines for the contextual phases of counseling. The context immediately preceding and following each session provides the focus of this chapter, whereas the broader issue of counselor lifestyle is dealt with in the final chapter as we deal with the prevention of counselor burnout.

PREATTENDING: GETTING YOURSELF PREPARED

Whereas Egan (1975) refers to a prehelping phase, his emphasis is on prerequisite relationship building during the initial counseling sessions. We would expand this preattending concept to include the time immediately preceding the actual contact with our clients. This time is critical as it sets the stage for the forthcoming session and is influential in determining what will or will not take place. Counseling does not occur in a vacuum. Even the highest-functioning counselors (maybe especially them, in fact) enter these sessions out of the context of their demanding and complex lives. For us, sessions are oftentimes sandwiched in between class preparation, meetings, exercise programs, and other counseling sessions. True, many counseling contacts are relatively spontaneous, i.e., the student who stops you after class to share a concern or an emergency call late at night, but most tend to be built into some kind of schedule. When we know that a session is coming, we can preattend by preparing ourselves and an appropriate strategy.

Effective preattending can only occur when preceded by adequate preparation of technical considerations during the interim between sessions. At times this may involve discussing your client with a colleague while at other times it may require inquiry into a new technique, preparing a handout, locating bibliotherapeutic resources, setting up biofeedback equipment, or a dozen other things. The authors frequently use each other as sounding boards to clarify client concerns and help with strategy building for upcoming sessions. These steps are analogous to client homework assignments designed to carry therapy into everyday life and maintain continuity between sessions. For the clients, much of the success of counseling depends on what they do with insights and action programs between sessions. Likewise, the level of creative involvement for counselors during sessions is a direct reflection of their preplanning efforts. Obviously, some counseling situations will call for more outside preparation and at times demand an addition of new skills to our repertoire of intervention techniques, entailing at times the risk of breaking from what is comfortable in order to meet the clients' needs. This interim period is when we can develop the raw materials to be creatively integrated within the counseling session and evolve a tentative strategy as a practical road map upon which to proceed. We recommend that this process culminate in the development of a brief summary which may or may not (depending on what the client presents) be utilized to bring about initial direction to the session. The summary is designed to provide continuity and demystify the counseling process by clarifying relational, integrational, and behavioral change components of what has taken place and lies ahead to be accomplished. Use of this kind of summary may also convey the powerful message to the clients that you have cared enough to devote outside time to better conceptualize their concerns. In fact, the summary may be introduced by noting, "I've given a lot of thought to what we discussed last time and. . . ." Since the kind of preparation we are discussing may take a few minutes or several hours, it requires a disciplined effort to structure it into your schedule well in advance of the brief preattending period which immediately precedes the session. Athletes entering a marathon run cannot afford to put off their training until the last minute before the event. Likewise, creative interchange will not occur without the hard work, albeit, exciting work, of preparation.

Now for a look at the preattending phase immediately preceding each session. This phase may be initiated by introspection in an effort to clear the deck as we move from the concerns of the day toward the anticipated encounter with our client. In addition to living busy lives, professional helpers are often the collectors of human "garbage" (problems dumped on us by our clients and others), and effective counseling may be preempted when we enter a session while psychologically congested with our own and other people's problems. Without some effort at putting these things aside, we can increase the potential for using the session as a personal dumping ground. Counseling is for the client, and we cannot afford to bring our unfulfilled needs into the session. This kind of thinking is reminiscent of Maslow's (1943) hierarchical conceptualization of needs in which energy related to higher-order needs can be released only when more basic (physiological, safety, love, esteem) needs are at least minimally satisfied. Whereas we would hope that counselors are effectively meeting their own needs on a day-to-day basis, an active suppression of some of their own needs may be necessary at times in order to creatively interact with the clients. Ironically, putting aside personal concerns for the moment and fully engaging clients may at times make those needs seem almost trivial, and we leave a session feeling more in charge of our own situation. We are not recommending the suppression of deep-seated problems, but merely recognizing counselors' own humanness and their capability to choose to enter the session at their highest level of functioning.

Therefore, in addition to a quick review of previously prepared strategies, personal presession focus is highly recommended. This is a conscious effort at breaking ourselves out of the contextual involvements (meetings, other sessions, personal concerns) surrounding the session. It involves a meditative shift and may be facilitated by the kind of relaxation procedures frequently used in helping our clients cope with stress. Too much anxiety (ours or the client's) interferes with creative problem solving and must, therefore, be managed at its optimal level if creative counseling is to take place. Whatever the specific technique we develop, the key is to get in touch with ourselves prior to initiating an intense investment of our energies toward our clients. The authors have each developed their own preattending routine and consider it to be a critical ingredient in the success of counseling contacts.

This transition inward, then, is logically followed by a shifting of focus toward the client in the last few moments before we enter the session. Without this prefocus, our busy lives and mounting caseloads can sometimes leave us cold (or even forgetting the client's name, let alone the critical information and tempo of the previous session) at the wrong time. We suggest that this process might be enhanced through prereflection when we subvocally restate the essence of the client's concerns and summarize them to ourselves as a tune-up exercise to get us in touch with the client again. Our concentration can be further intensified through the use of presession fantasy as we visualize the upcoming session unfolding while identifying potential roadblocks and desired interactions. This is similar to the popular use of pregame visual imagery by many successful athletes as they rehearse the desired maneuvers prior to the actual event. In fact, we compare creative counselors to finely tuned athletes who are able to unleash their skills only to the extent that they are psychologically and physically prepared. We might also insert here that it is often helpful to instruct our clients in the notion of preattending and encourage them to establish a warm-up period preceding each session to prepare themselves. It seems almost ironic, but structured preparation seems to clear the way for the kind of free-flowing, creative involvement which may actually allow the interaction to go beyond preplanned strategies and give way to more productive unplanned directions. Perhaps the real value of this process lies in the commitment of our time and thoughts to the work ahead and the related benefit of tuning into the clients from the moment they enter. Finally, we would suggest that all of these considerations fall into the background as we enter the session and turn our complete attention to the clients' needs.

If the establishment of a minimal level of acceptance (based on the offering of high levels of the facilitative conditions) is a priority goal throughout the stages of counseling, a primary function of preattending is to broaden our level of acceptance for the clients prior to the actual session. At best, our attempts at offering positive regard and empathy are phony imitations when our own concerns and unresolved problems block a genuine feeling of acceptance toward our clients. Our effectiveness in handling outside interaction is directly related to this ac-

FIGURE 5-1
The counselor's window. The window model divides all behaviors into acceptable or unacceptable, depending upon the behavior of the other person and your own decoding system. Therefore, the same behavior may be acceptable within one person's window and not in another's. *(Adapted from Gordon, 1971.)*

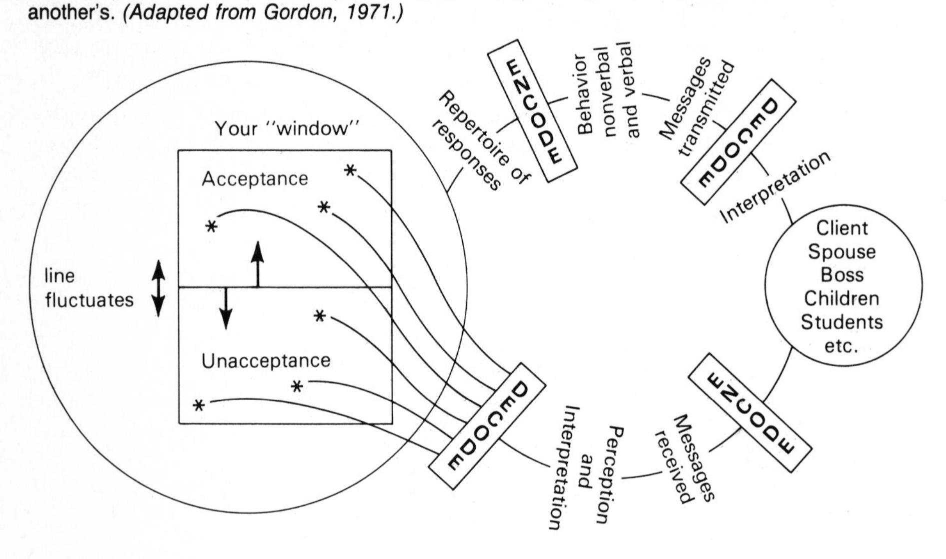

*Acceptance

1 Your boss compliments you on your work
2 A time of positive personal sharing with a spouse or friend
3 A concern presented by a client or his efforts to learn a coping skill or accomplish a personal goal

*Unacceptance

1 A patrolman writes out a traffic ticket on the way to work
2 Your boss hassles you for being late
3 A client fails to show up for a scheduled session

(See case study for personal example — Appendix I, Part C)

ceptance level and concomitant success in dealing with our client. We find it valuable to conceptualize this deck-clearing process through the *window* scheme presented by Gordon (1971, 1975) and developed in Chapter 4 of this book. Within this framework, all the behaviors of other people fit somewhere into your personal system (the *window*) and are decoded as basically acceptable or unacceptable (see Figure 5-1). Note that the messages we send back (encode) will reflect to some degree our interpretation (decoding) of incoming messages from all others in our situation, along with our clients' communication. Here is where unresolved conflicts can be displaced on to our clients. A preattending period helps to sort out these outside messages and increase the chances that client responses will be correctly decoded. The line dividing your unique window into these areas is dynamic and shifts up or down in response to changes in self, others, and the particular situation. Unresolved issues in the unacceptable area tend to push the acceptance line up, and leave less room for us to feel genuinely accepting. Problems tend to compound themselves and can spill over into our counseling contacts. Remember, the clients have windows, too. Perceived nonacceptance by our clients may push their line up also and preclude any real sharing on their part. Sensitivity to the line level (both yours and your clients') becomes an excellent cue for knowing when to push forward or temporarily back off during a session. It also reflects general personality differences. Some people are basically accepting (high-functioning, low-line), while others tend to be relatively narrow and unaccepting (high-line) with little tolerance for the other people in their environment (see Figure 5-2).

FIGURE 5-2
The counselor's "line." Basic accepting and nonaccepting personalities (*behavior of others) as reflected in respective line placement within their windows. Line fluctuates in response to changes in self, others, and situations. It should be noted that low-line individuals are not immune to hassles and feelings of unacceptance (not even Jesus Christ felt unconditioned positive regard for everyone at all times). However, these people tend to make effective counselors and handle their own difficulties so that they generally feel genuinely accepting of others. Part of their effectiveness lies in their ability to preattend encounters as a means for keeping things in perspective. They need to preattend the least but tend to maximize brief preencounter warm-up periods the most. *(Adapted from Gordon, 1971.)*

Mellow, relaxed, open

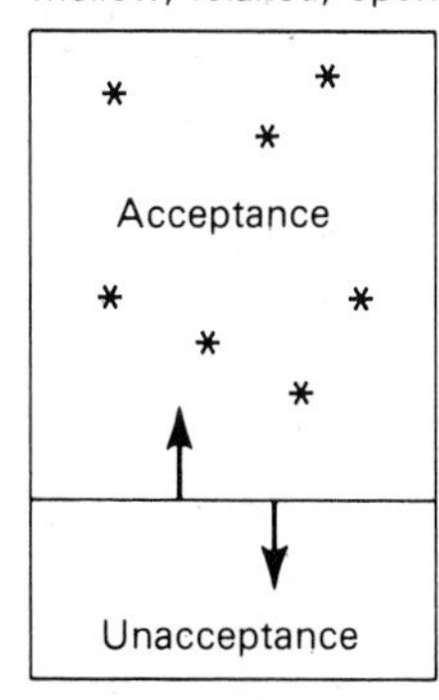

Narrow, tense, closed

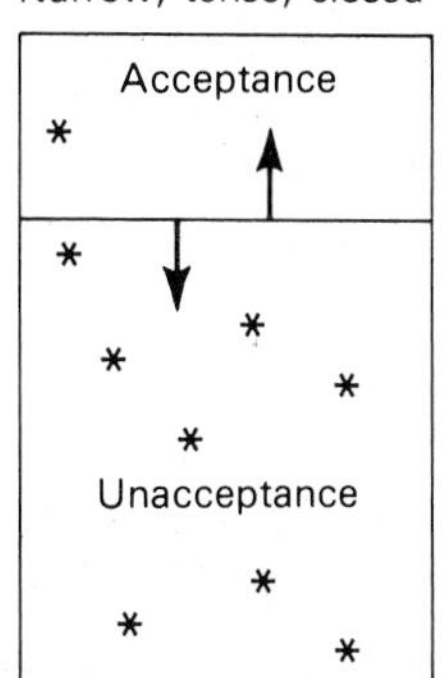

You might picture for a moment, a low-acceptance (high-line) person who you deal with—hardly the kind of resource you would approach for support in a time of conflict or to enhance your own growth. In fact, it tends to be these kinds of individuals who present us with unacceptable behaviors and create problems for us which subsequently elevate our lines (decreasing our tolerance levels) if we fail to cope with them effectively. In contrast, effective people tend to make us feel accepted through their relaxed, caring manner which reflects a low-line (high-acceptance) and their own ability to cope with unacceptable aspects of their lives. Now we can further extend this framework by the division of these two areas into the related dimensions of problem ownership (see Figure 5-3). Obviously, our acceptance of others is limited when our own lines are pushed up by frustration and an inability to resolve problems in our lives which leaves us impotent in our efforts to help others who "own" problems. The authors are both basically low-frustration/high-acceptance people. In other words, our acceptance lines tend to be consistently low, leaving considerable room to offer a sense of acceptance to our clients. If this were not the case, we would have no business offering ourselves as professional counselors. Even so, we are human and subject to periods of frustration and intolerance as our lines move up in responses to unresolved difficulties. When we fail to deal with this rising line phenomenon, the results can be disastrous for those who come to us for help. Perhaps a personal example would best illustrate how this window concept works and why preattending is so important for keeping this acceptance line low. Unfortunately, several instances come to mind. One involved a student who the senior author had known for several years and who had taken an incomplete in a research class 1 year prior to the incident which illustrates the point (See Appendix One, Part C: Mike: When We Fail to Preattend, an illustration of the window concept).

FIGURE 5-3
Boundaries of problem ownership. Problem ownership showing the integral relationship between the counselor's encounters in daily life and helping relationships with clients which flow out of this context. It is essential for creative counseling that counselors are able to separate their problems (personal conflicts, busy schedules, etc.) from those of their clients. Only then can a high level of acceptance and involvement be achieved while still allowing the clients to assume the ultimate responsibility for the solutions to the problems they own. *(Adapted from Gordon, 1971.)*

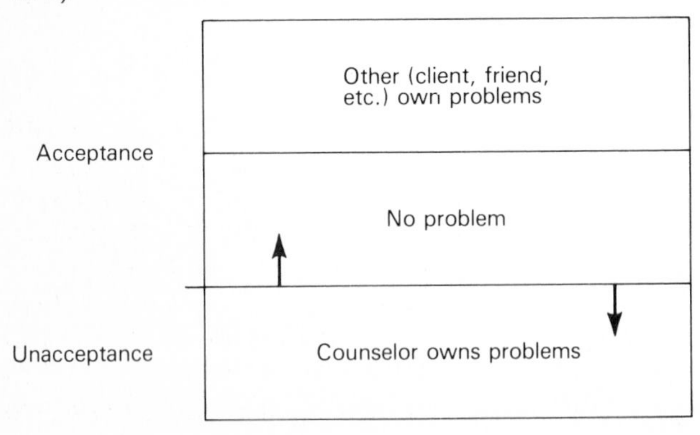

We see this overall framework as an extremely useful conceptual tool for sorting out the interaction with clients and other areas of the counselor's life, and encourage the reader to utilize it as a vehicle for preattending upcoming sessions or any important encounter. The primary goal of this warm-up period, then, becomes the lowering of your line and increasing your presession level of acceptance by moving into the no-problem area before entering into the client's problems. High personal functioning is a prerequisite for creative counseling. While the creative counselor must be basically accepting, a conscious effort at preattending each session increases the probability that a real sense of caring will be both felt by the counselor and communicated to the client.

POSTATTENDING: MAKING AN EFFECTIVE TRANSITION

To further develop the in-session model originated by Carkhuff, we emphasize the importance of a brief postattending period following each session. This can be viewed as a deprogramming time in which we make the transition from intense interaction back into the context of our everyday lives. The function of this unwinding effort is at least twofold: an inward focus geared toward lowering your line (relaxing) and a cognitive focus on identifying the key elements of the session you have just completed. The latter can be translated into a capsule summary to be used in preparing for the next session while serving to identify counselor homework and further clarification of issues presented by the client.

Counseling frequently involves intense periods of interaction which can leave us drained or revitalized depending on our ability to integrate what has occurred and move on to the next item on our agenda. We think that a period (structured until it becomes automatic) of personal deprogramming following each session can be of tremendous value. Just as primed athletes warm-up prior to an event, they also bring mind, body, and spirit back into equilibrium through a brief cooling-off period following the complete investment of their energies. Counselors are called upon to reach this peak level of involvement many times every week and must, likewise, devise ways to maintain the high level of functioning necessary for effective helping. While each individual varies in this capacity to handle stress, the following suggestions might be helpful in establishing personal realignment periods as part of your postcounseling activities.

Clarify Problem Ownership

The clarification of problem ownership might be a logical first step in moving from the intensity of the counseling hour toward the context of your everyday living, i.e., other appointments, meetings, family, etc. In terms of the window, we can conceptualize this transition as a movement from the "client owns the problem area" back into the "no-problem area." However brief your stay in this problem-free state before reinvesting your energy into other activities, a short respite provides a valuable break period and allows you to set the tone (preattend) for the next item on your agenda as we actively move our acceptance line down and refocus our energies. It is the initial step in removing yourself from the frustration and tension which sometimes hit us as a byproduct of our close identification with the client's turmoil. The client truly owns the problem, and this must be kept in perspective in order to keep our lines of acceptance at a productive level.

Focus on the Positive

There are at least two directions for positive focusing immediately following our counseling interactions. First, it is personally revitalizing to recognize the contributions we have just made toward our client's growth and reinforce ourselves for these efforts. Just as in tennis, dwelling on the shot we bungled can negatively affect the way we handle subsequent volleys. It is common, especially for inexperienced counselors, to set unrealistic goals and experience discouragement when they are not realized as rapidly as anticipated. Since counseling is a highly confidential and private process (there is no gallery to cheer us on), we must learn the art of picking out the positive aspects of our efforts. Remember the tremendous boost of encouragement felt when a practicum supervisor praised a particular intervention while listening to one of your taped sessions. We are not overlooking the value of criticism, but feel that evaluation flows more constructively from a basically positive framework. If you have had a good session, enjoy it and allow yourself to appreciate your contributions. The second direction for positive focusing relates to the identification of positive movement on the part of the client. Some clients blossom before our eyes, and it is all right to bask in their excitement. Enjoy every bit of it. At other times, we have to look pretty hard to find anything constructive in the midst of their pain and suffering, but it is worth the effort. It is all too easy to overidentify with the overwhelmed feeling presented by some of our clients, but the last thing they need is a counselor who feels helpless, too. That is not to deny the reality of their difficulties, but to merely warn against the temptation to wallow in it unduly. Identify areas of change and look for what can be done rather than dwelling on the seeming impossibility of their situation.

Using the Model

While the basic Carkhuffian model serves as a valuable guide during the session, it can also function as a cognitive road map for postsession evaluation and strategy planning. It enables us to align messages delivered during the interaction with the four-stage model in order to clarify what has just occurred and delineate appropriate directions for future sessions. Whereas a step-by-step evaluation of audio- or videotapes related to this model is invaluable in counseling training, it is impractical in everyday practice. Nevertheless, the same process can be simulated on a less thorough and time-consuming basis through the use of summary case notes and review of session highlights through our own visual imagery. The use of this format (sorting case material through the model) adds logic to what may have been an intensely creative and free-flowing encounter and defines preparation that needs to take place (the counselor's homework) in order to be ready for the next session. By equating client responses with the messages we have just delivered, we have a check on our pace and can define our location within the stages and the skills needed to promote movement next time. It enables us to monitor whether we are moving too fast or slow as well as indicating the timing for moving from one stage to another. This process parallels the counseling model itself and should foster increased understanding, goal specification, and a plan of action which we can prepare to implement.

Interpersonal Process Recall

Whereas the four-stage model is a helpful organizational scheme, the interpersonal process recall (IPR) system developed by Kagan and his associates (1967) is a viable complement to the model as a means for adding details to our session-related evaluation and planning. The technique involves a self-assessment of taped interactions but can be simulated without the actual recorded session through fantasy playback. The process involves a clarification of what was happening at each juncture of the interaction through recalling the underlying affective/cognitive ingredients of the transactions. It is a self-monitoring system based on the assumption that we are our own best critics. It can be particularly revealing when done overtly in the presence of the client, but this certainly is not appropriate in all cases. The real contribution of this self-learning approach lies in the reexperiencing and clarification of central themes and nonverbalized aspects of the session. It is also a meaningful vehicle for transferring critical information from short-term to long-term memory storage to make details more available during future sessions.

Reverse Application of Carkhuff's Steps of Responding

Originally designed as a teaching tool for skill training, a five-step sequence of counselor responding (Carkhuff 1972, 1975) summarizes the actual communication taking place in the general four-stage model. We have found that a verbalization of this sequence from the counselor's perspective can be helpful in tuning in to our own feelings and recycling the counseling interaction in a self-correcting manner. The sequence evolves in the following fashion: (1) Repeat verbatim a statement you made during the preceding session; (2) ask yourself how that makes you feel; (3) fill in the following format to personalize the feeling, "I feel___________"; (4) to personalize blockage of change, "I feel___________ because___________"; and (5) personalize the goal, "I feel ___________ because___________and I cannot___________but I want to ___________." Once a goal has been established, it can be operationalized into its component parts and concrete steps for implementation developed. For example, if the basic goal is to improve client self-esteem through assertion training, this process helps me identify my reaction to offering this kind of training and may lead to a sequence of preparation steps—confrontation of client, homework assignment to delineate feared situations and underlying beliefs, having reading material ready for client

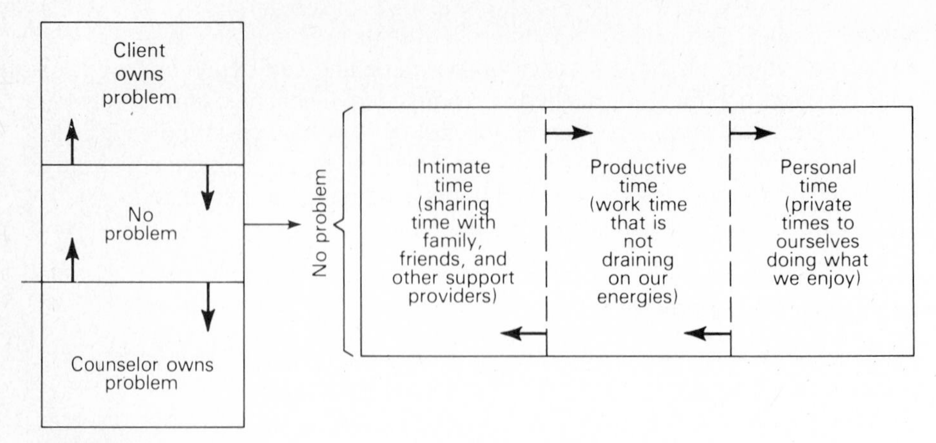

FIGURE 5-4
The no-problem area. No-problem area of your window dividing allotment of energy expenditure into intimate, diffuse, and personal time. *(Adapted from Gordon, 1971.)*

to take home, preparing a script for in-session behavioral rehearsal, copy handouts which clarify steps in assertion, and so on. This becomes a guide for the counselor's homework between sessions to be worked into his busy schedule sometime prior to the next meeting with the client.

This postattending period then flows logically into the in between structuring of our time and can be seen as an extension of the two major considerations just outlined—self-renewal and preparation. The self-renewal theme will be developed more thoroughly in our final chapter on preventing counselor burnout, and basically entails the management of the counselor's personal life space. In terms of the window (see Figure 5-3) it involves the optimal handling of our own and shared problems, along with continual expansion and effective use of the no-problem area. Our preventive work with healthy clients also fits into this area and can be professionally and personally revitalizing (Productive Time in Figure 5-4). Whereas the problem-free area is critical for healthy functioning, it can readily be sandwiched between the problem areas to the point at which it is almost nonexistent. That is where many of our clients find themselves—helplessly engulfed by problems. The last thing they need is an equally overwhelmed counselor. It is these problem-free times in our lives that offer maximal regeneration potential and therefore must be safeguarded. We must have time for privacy as well as for intimate contact with friends, family, and those individuals who give us support. In addition to dealing more effectively with the problem aspects of our own living context, it is of vital importance to effectively manage the time we spend in our no-problem areas. Whereas these time allotments involve a unique equation for every counselor, each of us must have revitalizing periods built into our daily activities.

SUMMARY

This chapter focused on counseling as a way of life. The importance of the counselor using a period of time before and after counseling sessions to influence positive client change was discussed. Methods which can help counselors prepare for client contact were presented as a part of effective preattending. Basic issues involved in preattending include personal/professional technique development, a review of appropriate skills which are applicable to specific clients, and development of a personal facilitative mind-set immediately prior to meeting with a client. Thomas Gordon's (1971) window concept was proposed as a visualization useful in delineating problem ownership in effective counseling.

Steps which enhance postattending were also presented as methods to assist counselors to make the transition from the intense interaction of a counseling session back into the context of their everyday lives. Steps presented by the authors include:

1. Clarify problem ownership.
2. Focus on the positive.
3. Recall the interaction (capturing key points to store for future use).
4. Utilize Carkhuff responding in reverse to tune in to your own feelings as the counselor and recycle the process so that self-correcting of the counseling session can occur.
5. Identify preparation steps and a plan for accomplishing prior to the next session.
6. Transition: Put last session aside as you move on to other things.

Counselor planning before and after sessions influences self-renewal and professional growth. The procedures discussed in the chapter aid counselors as they accomplish these two goals.

REFERENCES

Carkhuff, R. R. *The art of helping*. Amherst, Mass.: Human Resource Development Press, 1972.

Carkhuff, R. R. *Living constructively in a destructive world*. Paper presented at the meeting of the Colorado Personnel and Guidance Association, Denver, Colo., October 1975.

Egan, G. *The skilled helper*. Belmont, Calif.: Wadsworth, 1975.

Gordon, T. *Parent effectiveness training*. New York: Wyden, 1971.

Gordon, T. *Teacher effectiveness training*. New York: David McKay, 1975.

Kagan, N., Krathwohl, D., Goldberg, A., Campbell, R. J., Shankle, P. G., Greenberg, D. S., Danish, S. J., Resnickoff, A., Bowes, J., and Bandy, S. B. *Studies in human interaction: Interpersonal process recall simulated by videotape*. East Lansing: Michigan State University Educational Publication Sources, College of Education, 1967.

Maslow, A. H. Dynamic theory of human motivation. *Psychological Review*, 1943, *30*, 370–396.

CHAPTER 6

RISK IN REMEDIATION

Risk is a pivotal dimension in determining the quality of life for each of us. Whether we are forming a new relationship or trying out an untested approach to solving everyday problems, risk taking appears to underlie all aspects of growth and development. Helen Keller confirmed this point in her graphic portrayal of life. She stated (Viscott, 1977):

> Security is mostly a superstition. It does not exist in nature, nor do the children of men as a whole experience it. Avoiding danger is no safer in the long run than outright exposure. Life is either a daring adventure or nothing. (p.9)

Viscott (1977) defines risk as the loosening of our grasp on the known so that we can reach for something better and suggests that it is "central to everything worthwhile in life."

Risk is sometimes the only antidote for indecision. The approach/avoidance conflict depicted by Lewin (1935) symbolizes the dilemma in which we find many of our clients. Unable to decide between the potential gains from new directions and the apparent safety of withdrawal, the individual may vacillate in a painfully ambivalent state of confusion. Perceived helplessness stemming from a lack of control over life outcomes lies at the root of most human misery (Seligman, 1975). Nevertheless, the risks inherent in change can yield immobilizing fear in anyone, particularly at times of personal vulnerability. It is during these periods of crisis when energy can become consumed by irrelevant uncertainties while our fears build up perceived barriers to change. Coleman, Butcher, and Carson (1980) identify three key principles of self-defeating lifestyle that can block personal growth: feelings of anxiety, avoidance of threatening situations, and self-defeating behavior. The latter has been further identified as the neurotic paradox in which ineffective behavior yields dissatisfaction but is nevertheless perpetuated because it somehow buys monetary relief from the perceived threat. Whereas the short-term defensive tactics yield immediate relief, they may ultimately prevent the individual from learning appropriate coping skills. Consequently, the feared object becomes an even greater source of threat. The person remains in the grip of a destructive cycle as limited defensive strategies are repeated and increase the potential for becoming ingrained in addictive patterns of chronic dysfunction. Wiesen (1977) further elucidates this picture with his notion of self-perpetuating "trap circuits" which are fed by negative emotions, defeatist sentences, and self-defeating behaviors that trap and consume psychological energy. The production of negative projections of future events, i.e., "I can't do it" or "It will never work out," signal trouble, activate bioemotional systems, and may put a self-fulfilling prophecy into play. These imaginary disastrous outcomes then immobilize the individual and preclude self-assertion. Beck (1976) also indicates that the feedback cues from anxiety can themselves produce additional anxiety-producing ideation. Repetitive thoughts about feared events not only reduce problem-solving capacities but tend to feed upon themselves until any life change is perceived as a threat.

The push toward breaking out of the apparent security of routine is contrasted by drive forces which keep us striving for balance and consistency in our lives. The need for homeostasis pervades every aspect of living from biological responses to stress and temperature change to our need for keeping incoming stimuli within comfortable limits. Glasser (1976) believes that the basic struggle of life is reflected in seeking balance between affiliative and self-esteem needs. This notion is reminiscent of the classic portrayal of motivation presented by Maslow (1962) in which the satisfaction of high-order needs (and the risks involved in satisfying them) is not pursued until more basic needs are at least minimally satisfied. Success at one level serves as an impetus for reaching the next level. A cumulative spiraling effect may consequently evolve in either the growth (risk) or deteriorative (withdrawal) direction. This continual push toward possible fulfillment and pull away from potential loss is seen by Sheehy (1976) as an inevitable sequence of predictable crises or "passages" which unfold throughout life. She sees periods of disruption as prerequisites for change which can lead to growth. The process is depicted in the following analysis:

> We are not unlike a particularly hardy crustacean. The lobster grows by developing and shedding a series of hard, protective shells. Each time it expands from within, the confining shell must be sloughed off. It is left exposed and vulnerable until, in turn, a new covering grows to replace the old. With each passage of growth to the next we, too, must shed a protective structure. We are left exposed and vulnerable but also yeasty and embryonic again, capable of stretching in ways we hadn't known before. The shedding may take several years or more. Coming out of each passage, though, we enter a longer and more stable period in which we can expect relative tranquility and a sense of equilibrium regained (p. 20).

Growth occurs when we can let go of illusionary safety and the tactics which have failed to allow for change and personal expansion. There appears to be growing support for the promotion of risk as a vehicle for personal development.

Whereas safety and balance may be represented by our biological and psychological needs for homeostasis, many high-functioning individuals seem to thrive on risks which allow boundaries to be expanded. Jencks (1977) suggests that "taking risks within the limits of common sense is useful for meeting the challenges and stresses of life." In contrast to popular misconception, Ogilvie (1974) found that competitors in high-risk sports—sky-diving, race driving, technical rock climbers, and so forth—tended to be emotionally stable with positive personality organization. While high-risk takers have been previously viewed as driven by unconscious death wishes and underlying feelings of inadequacy, this research (based on studies of 250 national- and world-class athletes) yields a markedly contrasted profile. These individuals were characterized as ranking extremely high on independence, leadership potential, abstract thinking, and creativity while maintaining a strong sense of reality. At the same time, this same group scored "extremely low on measures of anxiety." However, risking certainly does not have to mean endangering our lives. Everyday life is full of opportunities to move beyond our known limits. The critical issue, then, is in terms of overcoming the fear that holds us back (Kopechy, 1980). In this sense, we believe that risk lies at the core of creative counseling—risk for counselors as they leave the security of prescribed programs of intervention to become fully involved with clients' concerns and risk for the client who is challenged to replace nonproductive patterns with alternate ways of handling life's issues.

RISK AS A CORE CONDITION

Risk is an essential element in counseling. The entire process pivots around the issues of helping our clients break out of unhealthy (yet comfortable) patterns of attitude and behavior. More effective patterns cannot be developed without taking the risks inherent in moving toward untapped areas of life adjustment. Much of the counselor's efforts focus on setting the stage for and facilitating the implementation of successful risking at each stage of the counseling process. Likewise, creative counseling is impossible without the counselor's ability to risk the kind of involvement necessary to promote client change. Whereas this theme has been largely overlooked in the literature, we see it as an extension of the basic core conditions (Carkhuff and Berenson, 1977). In fact, risk is so integral to the counseling process that it both supersedes and ties together the other core dimensions (empathy, concreteness, confrontation, etc.).

Viscott (1977) outlines five steps (included within three phases) of risking which bear a striking resemblance to the model of counseling we presented in Chapter 4. We will briefly present this parallel process and then attempt to expand on the risk-taking aspects of counseling as they unfold within each stage of the process by focusing specifically on overcoming process impediments experienced by both counselor and client. First, we will examine the steps presented by Viscott. Phase one is seen as a preparation component and is subdivided into two interrelated steps: recognizing the need for risk and deciding to move toward it. In this phase, the individual attempts to make a realistic appraisal of needs and prepares to initiate the risk (hopefully acquiring the skills necessary to make the risk pay off). Deciding that something must be done to improve the life situation may become the logical extension of appraisal, but indecision and the tendency to postpone unresolved areas of needed change can get in the way. Fortunately, the choice of taking charge tends to greatly alleviate fears and can replace the anguish of indecision with a renewed purpose and directionality. Phase two of commitment is subdivided into risk initiation and moving past the point of no return. Fear may reappear, but it is too late: the commitment toward risks locks you into an unfolding progression. In building to the point of no return, momentum is collected by reasserting the basic convictions underlying the risk. It is that point at which you cannot turn back and is generally accompanied by a sense of closure and resolution. Finally, phase three involves risk completion. Exhilarated and perhaps a bit shaken, care must now be taken in adapting to the new position and preparation before the next risk commences.

How does all of this relate to counseling? We would like to make the connection more explicit by focusing on the potential risks contained in each of the three major phases of counseling—relationship, integration, and action. We will also explore our assertion that the real business of change through counseling extends the boundaries of the counseling hour. As counselors, we can help the client explore, evaluate, and program for change, but the critical work is done between sessions and in transferring new learning into everyday life long after formal counseling has been terminated.

The degree to which the counselor can creatively engage the client in this risking process ultimately reflects the counselor's level of personal functioning and capacity to let go of set patterns. As Carkhuff and Berenson (1967) put it:

> Traditional psychotherapy, in its emphasis upon the implementation of stereotyped role models and the dispensing techniques, falls short of effective practices, for at the crisis point the therapist reaches into his own resources or extends the boundaries of his resources. The therapist handles the crisis or not as he is a whole therapist or not; the therapist handles the crisis or not as he is a whole human or not. There are no rules for functioning in unknown areas, and crises are crises because they are unknown areas for the therapist as well as the client (p. 169).

Ironically, it is the element of creative risking that enables the counselor to facilitate client change, and at the same time expand on the limits of the core dimensional structure and eclectic framework we have previously outlined. The guidelines can serve counselors well, to the extent that they free them to become totally involved with the flow of the process itself. Rigid adherence to lock-step methods is precisely what creative counseling is not. The essence of our orientation lies in the awareness of the tremendous complexity and individual uniqueness that both counselor and client bring into their interaction. It is the interaction itself, then, that is most critical, with the element of risk lying at the core of every step. Whereas our present focus is on relating risk to the three basic phases of counseling, we might remind ourselves that adequate preparation and follow-through by both the counselor and client are essential for setting the stage for the actual counseling contact.

In developing the theme of risk within counseling, we would like to focus on the counselor/client interaction throughout the process. Counseling is in many ways analogous to creative problem solving and does not occur effectively without the risks necessary to overcome the barriers associated with each phase. First, success in the relational phase is dependent upon clients' willingness to take the risk of sharing meaningful information, whereas counselors risk the personal energy required in setting the stage for client self-exploration. The relationship actually forms as a byproduct of this kind of interaction. The primary barriers here seem to center around the clients' perceptions of acceptance by the counselors and their ability to verbalize significant problem-related material. Second, the integration phase evolves around the risks inherent in the clients' internalization of new insights and problem reconceptualization. Overcoming related barriers is a prerequisite to placing the pieces of the client puzzle in order and promoting increased self-understanding. Third, the fear of failure (or fear of success in some cases) looms as an obstacle in phase three and can prevent the client from translating goals into constructive action. The counselor here may be in a position to promote movement from perceived helplessness toward active behavioral change. Finally, we assert again that the ultimate purpose of counseling is found in the movement from the security of the counseling relationship into the fears of establishing more effective supports and lifestyle patterns. In this light, we will conclude the present chapter by focusing on the barriers and risks involved in moving beyond the counseling involvement to extensions in everyday life.

RISK IN THE RELATIONAL/EXPLORATION PHASE

Whereas the core dimensional attitudes (empathy and positive regard) are critical to the relationship phase, rigid adherence to their related skills (reflective interpretation and active listening) can defeat creative interaction. Counselors' preoccupation with their responses can detract from sensitivity toward the clients' personal framework and related decoding system. It is, therefore, not simply what counselors say but the interpretation of these responses by the clients that become critical. As indicated in our outline of the counseling model presented in Chapter 4, the counselor's job here is to create an atmosphere of acceptance and to facilitate client self-exploration. According to Cole and Sarnoff (1980), a key ingredient in the creative process is deferred judgment, which allows clients to engage their rational cognitive powers and more clearly express their concerns. Whereas the underlying relationship that forms as a byproduct of this interaction is essential to the entire process, it becomes apparent that the actual communication cannot be set by exact rules of responding. This phase itself can become the primary focus of counseling with some clients (absorbing much of the time and energy we invest in our clients), whereas others we work with move smoothly into a solid relationship and meaningful self-exploration. In the latter cases, the relationship remains important but is easily established, and its formation absorbs only a fraction of our efforts. We are free early on in the process to move quickly into integration and action-related concerns. Consequently, we cannot be locked into specific modes of responding. In fact, the overall process itself may have to operate in reverse order with some clients by initiating the process with directive actions and then moving back to build a relational base. It is simplistic, also, to think of the counseling process as unidirectional (relational——integrative——action) with each phase being accomplished prior to the next. While the flow tends to move in this manner, it is more realistically characterized by its complexity and constant interaction of phases throughout the process. It would be nice if we could simply follow a road map made up of clearly marked paths (process model) and road signs (core dimensions and related responding skills), but it is just not that easy. There are many exceptions to the rules, and the creative counselor moves flexibly along with these differences.

I am reminded of a former student who approached me (the senior author) recently with some problems. I had worked with her several years ago and had seen real progress in gaining self-control and a more assertive approach to life issues. Unfortunately, she had become very dependent upon another psychotherapist during the preceding year and had slipped back into indecision and a whiny self-pity. Her therapist had moved, and she felt helpless. I listened for awhile. Perhaps the rule book would call for gentle responses geared at renewing our relationship. It did not fit. I did not know why at the time, but I unleashed a very firm series of confrontations telling her to stop this self-pity and take charge of her life. I even surprised myself with the harshness of my approach. She became angry and stomped out of my office. Somehow I felt right about our interaction and left it at that. I believed that she could hear the care coming through my apparent attack. I was convinced that she was basically strong and that pampering was the last thing she needed. Creative counseling or bad judgment? Time would tell. She came back 2 months later to thank me for my help. She had used the confrontation to take a hard look at herself, and had set down specific new directions on her own. These goals had been largely attained, the self-pity had diminished, renewed confidence gained, and she felt fantastic about her accomplishments. She did not need a lot of support or even someone to map out a course of action. She needed to tap her own resources which had been buried in self-pity. She needed someone to challenge her to risk coming out of the security of her depression. She needed an honest confrontation from someone who really cared, and that is what she got.

In maintaining our focus on the goals of the relational phase (clients' perceptions of acceptance and their exploration of meaningful life issues), we can move beyond the mechanics of effective responding skills and invest our energy into facilitating the clients' efforts at self-expression. Sensitivity to our clients' decoding systems can enable us to respond in ways which penetrate defenses and allow our clients to feel accepted. These mechanics must be in the counselor's repertoire, but their release becomes dependent on a free-flowing sensitivity to client receptiveness rather than a preset game plan. Responding skills become readily accessible when our intuitive hunches suggest their release. Ultimately, it is this sensitivity to incoming client messages that serves as a basis for initiating our responses. This is the essence of empathy and rests on the risks of entering the client's frame of reference, while leaving our decoding systems open to hear what the client really has to say. This in turn (not a rigid responding format) serves as the framework for our corresponding behavioral responses (the actual things we say and do) that we emit to the client. Both functions—decoding client messages and encoding our responses back to them—rest on the risk inherent in letting go of formal systems and relying on ourselves to find the most accurate interpretation and effective response. These risks, in turn, are not reasonable without the underlying skills and sense of confidence we must have built into ourselves. As Viscott (1977) puts it, these risks cannot be taken without first being open to yourself.

Now for an appraisal of the specific barriers found in the relational phase of counseling. The first barrier clients face involves their motivational and emotional systems. Our clients risk losing an element of control—while ultimately increasing the chances of gaining a better sense of control—when they begin sharing their concerns. They further risk the possibility of rejection as they define areas of imperfection and disclose parts of themselves that need to be changed.

Too much anxiety, or too little motivation, can stop the process. Either extreme becomes a barrier to meaningful self-exploration. It is the client's subjective assessment of the initial counselor responses that is critical and determines the depth and quantity of client sharing. Consequently, our sensitivity to client perception of responses may be more important than the actual responses we emit.

How can the counselor, then, facilitate the client risks of involvement and self-exploration? There is no fixed answer. Effective problem solving relies on participant flexibility and brings out the best of the creative counselor. To begin with, the previous discussion suggests that the initial flow of client self-exploration depends on client anxiety levels which must be decreased in most cases but occasionally increased. For the skillful counselor, the primary risk in initiating the problem-solving process is to move from reliance on techniques toward full involvement with the client's frame of reference. This reflects the historical development of client-centered therapy (Corey, 1977) which has shifted its emphasis from reflection toward counselor genuineness and now offers many good insights into the facilitation of the relational development in counseling. This kind of involvement, then, frees the counselor to creatively offer the most effective helpful responses, even if they appear on the surface to contradict preprogrammed response patterns. This is not to disown the core conditions and related responding skills (reflection and active listening), but to allow the counselor to risk reliance on intuitively produced responses stemming from genuine involvement with the client's situation. With a broad response repertoire at the counselor's command, the focus can shift toward intense empathetic communication with the client.

As indicated by Carkhuff and Berenson (1967), crisis is the essence of constructive client change. Counseling is often initiated at a crossroads and then progresses toward "a series of interrelated crises." Here is where low-functioning counselors tend to cling to the security of lock-step methods or drop out completely; either way, the client in crisis stands to lose and move further away from the risks needed to start any process of constructive change. Carkhuff and Berenson

(1967) seem to have captured the essence of this point in their description of the "hourly intensification of life" in counseling:

> The only real psychotherapy takes place at the crisis point, most often with the focus initially upon external crisis for the client but eventually crisis involving both client and therapist, in and out of therapy. At the crisis point, both client and therapist are stripped of all facade, which is indicated by what they do or do not do. This communication is the most intimate person-to-person communication that there can be. There are no rules for responding the crisis, no techniques, no rituals. The therapist simply has to "be" to experience the moment and stand the tests. The effective therapist responds most honestly from the deepest wells within him. His responses reflect his recognition of the life and death urgency of the situation. He responds the way he lives his life and he chooses life in his response. In his "being" and acting he discloses the meaning and efficacy of his approach to life (p. 147).

High-functioning counselors flow with clients' self-presentations, and utilize crises to stimulate their own creativity.

Brammer (1973) suggests that threat associated with initial counseling contacts stems from the client's fear of exposure, perceived sense of problem uniqueness, and a personal threat to esteem. But creative counselors know that self-exploration sets the stage for assimilation of more productive patterns of attitude and behavior. Consequently, they must help clients to risk personal vulnerability. Whereas listening skills conveying empathy and regard may stimulate client expression, the counselor/client interaction remains as the primary ingredient itself. Egan (1975) has made a meaningful distinction between "primary-level" and "advanced accurate-level" empathy. We emphasize that the application of these dimensions may not always flow in logical sequence. Generally, we would initiate the counseling process with a focus on explicit client expression of feelings and experience (level-3 empathy in Carkhuff's terms), while reserving more implicit interpretive influences until a more accurate perspective of the client's frame of reference is developed. Certainly, premature movement into the client's personal life space can increase the level of threat and corresponding defensiveness, but rigid adherence to an interchangeable reflective mode can be equally damaging. There is no substitute for accurate perception of client readiness. There are no absolutes here as the counselor risks movement beyond the safe confines of models and schedules of responding. The tone is set, and hopefully modeled for the client, for the risks of self-exploration. In the process, the counselor may become an increasingly potent reinforcer (Carkhuff and Berenson, 1967) who can help the client break the vicious cycle of stress, confusion, and perceived helplessness.

Egan's (1975) discussion of counselor genuineness seems particularly appropriate in the present context. He identifies five characteristics of genuineness which clearly reflect our representation of creative counselors. First, genuineness implies the risks of moving beyond counselor roles. They can be themselves in a wide range of interactions without relying on credentials, degrees, or social stamps of approval. Second, these individuals move from facade to spontaneity. They are not continually gating their responses by caricaturing the "right" thing to say. They are thoroughly based in the basic principles and skills of helping but do not rely on anything but themselves within the actual flow of counseling. Third, the element of risk is reflected in nondefensiveness as they move beyond client resistance and negativism toward understanding what is really being communicated. Fourth, genuine individuals are consistent—not within any contrived system of counseling, but within themselves. Feedback to the client springs from intuitive perceptions guided by past experience and broad knowledge of counseling. Finally, they are self-sharing and capable of choosing what bits of personal self-disclosure can be used constructively by the client. Rogers and Truax (1967) express it as a "direct personal encounter with the client" in which the counselor moves beyond facades toward experiencing the interaction as it unfolds.

We would like to emphasize here that an active cultivation of client strengths needs to begin in this relational phase. Our sensitivity to client resources and outside supports interacts with our assessment of chronicity and problem severity to set the stage for appropriate responses. In general, creative counselors do not take over for clients unless absolutely necessary, but realistically assess the clients' abilities to overcome blocks to self-exploration. Consequently, clients' expressions of psychological pain may be seen for their motivational value (client strength) rather than as something to be relieved through supportive efforts. Whereas counselors may take the risk of temporarily taking over for some clients, they may need to risk letting clients fall back on their own strengths in other cases. The clients are ultimately responsible for themselves.

A final obstacle to self-exploration may come in the clients' inability to express themselves, and again demand the counselors' flexible and resourceful approach. Since self-exploration provides the data for problem solving, it must be concrete and specific to become useful. This involves moving the client toward explicitness which is generally facilitated by the counselor's own increasing level of specificity. Egan (1975) suggests that since "concreteness can be painful, it is evident why some clients take refuge in generalities." He goes on to indicate that vagueness can be decreased by keeping the client from rambling and by direct probing of specific key issues. He concludes that "concreteness means that the client must risk more in the counseling interaction, but little happens without risks and without facing the crises precipitated by reasonable risk-taking."

Whereas some clients (generally higher-functioning ones) seem to explore critical issues spontaneously without direct counselor coaxing, others may need to be taught what kinds of materials are to be disclosed and how to share them. In either case, the creative counselor keeps in mind that exploration is functional to the extent that it leads to more effective client self-conceptualization and responds accordingly. This may mean a relatively passive approach which enables the client to charge into critical issues, or it may mean actively structuring client expression. In the latter case, it may be necessary to confront or lead the client through effective exploration by the use of relevant homework assignments. Cole and Sarnoff (1980) believe that the key here is in helping the client suspend judgment which can stop idea generation. Behind all of these efforts lies not only the counselor's willingness to risk venturing into the unknown, but an ability to cut off seemingly deep exploration which may not be ultimately productive for the client. This sensitivity is, then, paired with openness to underlying risks inherent in moving from exploration (which can become seductively safe) to the business of integration and action.

Once again, counselor barriers in phase one revolve around low personal functioning and rigid adherence to a set format of responding. In summarizing his comments regarding self-exploration, Egan (1975) suggests that the effective counselor draws from a wide range of skills and "does whatever is most useful for the client at any given moment in the helping process, whether it is called for by any stage of the model or not." Handling problems in a strictly sequential fashion begs the risks involved in creative counseling. He concludes:

> It is true in some cases that the counseling process proceeds more or less according to the model. In other cases it does not. The final criterion for the steps taken during counseling, however, must be what is helpful for the client. The model is for the helping process and not its master, and helping is for the client (p. 126).

RISK IN THE INTEGRATIONAL/UNDERSTANDING PHASE

The action phase can only become effective to the extent that clients are able to translate a more accurate perception of their problems into specific goals and related change. We see the integrational (self-understanding) phase as pivotal, mediating action on one side and enhancing the relational quality as a byproduct on the other side. The clients' development of a clearer and more realistic picture of themselves becomes the goal of this phase. The raw data for building this self-portrait come from self-exploration, whereas the major obstacles involve inaccurate perception of the life situation, rigid clinging to ineffective conceptual schemes, and the fears associated with breaking out of nonproductive patterns of thinking. Helping the clients take the risks inherent in overcoming these barriers becomes the counselors' challenge. The counselors' task is to help the clients integrate meaningful disclosure within a usable conceptual framework without themselves clinging rigidly to preconceived notions of human functioning. Whereas counselors naturally build their insights around some fundamental principles (as outlined in Chapter 3), noncreative application of any rule of human behavior can block this phase of the problem-solving process. Whereas responding models can be valuable tools, we would again place our emphasis on the uniqueness of every counseling interaction and the counselors' ultimate reliance upon intuitive resources and sensitivity to client presentation. Keeping the goal of this phase in the forefront (self-understanding as a basis for increasing client self-control and movement toward constructive change) is a key for counselors' effectiveness here. Once again, however, creative counselors must be well grounded in the basics of responding skills and human understanding in order to be free to help clients do whatever is necessary to put their self-pictures in order. After making many excellent observations about the mechanics of phase-two interaction, Egan (1975) concludes:

> The helper should not be too literal with respect to the timing of Stage II interactions. The model exists for the helper and the helpee, not visa [sic] versa. If, on occasion, Stage II interactions seem called for earlier than is indicated by the model as presented

> here, they should be used. Ultimately, the high-level helper depends on himself and his judgment rather than on a paper model. He does whatever is necessary at the moment to help the client, even if it involves some rearranging of the stages of the model (p. 180).

What, then, can we gain from the Carkhuffian model (embellished by Egan and others) that can serve as a basis for responding in the integrational phases? In helping the client move toward more objective self-understanding, Egan (1975) has identified a composite of responding skills: advanced accurate empathy, self-disclosure, confrontation, and immediacy. He warns that these are potent skills and should be used appropriately in response to client needs for putting the issues in perspective and probing for missing pieces needed for improved understanding. He further suggests that these dimensions reflect "a shift in perspective" as we move from trying the facilitation of client sharing toward helping them develop a more accurate self-perception. We would focus on the role of advanced accurate empathy and confrontation as becoming particularly relevant to facilitating client risk related to the goals of this phase.

In looking at the dimension of accurate empathy, we point to the real value of developing personal guidelines for its applications. We would prefer general guidelines which become operational within the context of the actual counseling interaction rather than a scriptlike approach which can be seductively simplistic. Consequently, we appreciate the basic principles generated by Egan (1975) in this regard as tools to provide a firm foundation for the creative counselor who can use them directly, mix them up, or go beyond the guidelines, depending on the contextual flow of the particular session. First, advanced accurate empathy may mean expressing what is implicit in client messages. This may involve interpretive reflections or probing questions which fill in gaps that may have been recognized through seemingly unrelated pieces of client-presented data. The timing again is critical which rests on the element of counselor risk. Sometimes our timing reflects subtle cues picked up in the communication, while seemingly spontaneous comments come to the forefront at other times. Second, the summarization of relevant material can be used to pull together facts, feelings, and even seemingly disconnected pieces of the overall puzzle. This is a heavily cognitive function at times and goes on (subvocally) throughout the exploration process as hypotheses are stored and checked against client input. In fact, summaries can be useful in building continuity between phases as well as for pulling together core materials within the integrative function. While the sorting of pieces is an intellectual function on the counselor's part, the actual formulation and release of summary responses rests on timing and risk. Third, missing links can be joined by helping the client connect pieces of experience revealed in self-exploration (Ivey, 1971). In addition, we see accurate empathy reflected in every effort made toward helping the client develop unifying themes. Once the picture forms something of a Gestalt, we can then (either in a passive, collaborative, or directive manner) move with the client toward translating these themes into goals and related schemes for change.

Whereas elements of confrontation flow throughout the counseling process, this dimension tends to come into primary focus in promoting client insight. Again, general principles tied together via the risk dimension seem to be helpful. The principles provide a foundational framework whereas risk mobilizes their expression. Egan (1975) sheds light on the potential targets of confrontation—discrepancies, distortion, games, tricks, smoke screens, evasions, and incongruities—and then provides some useful guidelines for the actual confrontive response. These suggest that confrontation should be a reflection of our understanding of the client and be conveyed tentatively with the expression of care. The relationship itself provides the cues for the level of confrontation while the counselor focuses on client strength and related motivation indices. Once again, we would emphasize the creative blend of general principles as being superior to the rigid application of rules. Above all, confrontation must be for the benefit of the client and, therefore, must come out of a counselor choice rather than impulse. Preattending a confrontation can be valuable, especially when the risks of confrontation have been weighed and the counselor is subsequently free (during the actual utilization) to confront or not.

Similar guidelines for confrontation in counseling have been developed by Eisenberg and Delaney (1977) and can be quite valuable in generating client self-motivation. The first guideline suggests that confrontation should lead to increased counselor involvement. Confrontations are sometimes painful and a shift to supportive responses may be in order. At other times, increased involvement might be appropriately conveyed by pushing the new insight directly toward action and behavioral change. Second, confront only when you sense a feeling of caring. We concur and believe that confrontation out of displaced counselor frustration is rarely helpful to the client. Third, relational considerations are important, and confrontation should not go beyond a level that the relationship cannot support. Finally, a sensitivity toward client defenses may lead to an avoidance of confrontive material or to an effort to prepare the client for necessary confrontation by working on defense reduction. A corollary that we add here suggests that constructive confrontation must ultimately be client self-confrontation since only material which penetrates the internal perceptual system can lead to insight or serve as a stimulant for change in perspective and behavior. We also add an insight from the authors of the new eclecticism (Carkhuff and Berenson, 1967) to conclude our discussion of confrontation:

> Confrontation precipitates crisis; but crises are viewed as the fabric of growth in that they challenge us to mobilize our resources and invoke new responses. Growth is a series of endless self-confrontations. The therapist who serves as an authentic model of confrontation offers the client a meaningful example of effective living (p. 179).

In addition to creatively blending responses during the integrational phase, the creative counselor may borrow from a wide range of theoretical views to enhance client insights. Several of the more prominent contributions deserve mention here as potential resources upon which the creative counselor can draw. We would in no way promote any of these systems in their entirety, but would encourage critical analysis of each and the creative application of any related concepts and techniques which promote improved client self-conceptualization.

Albert Ellis has produced several publications which identify irrational belief systems (similar to earlier Freudian conceptualization of the superego and the scripting notion fundamental to transactional analysis) as the root of human misery (Ellis and Harper, 1973). He has identified a list of irrational beliefs which block appropriate risk taking and suggests that "catastrophizing" external events and dwelling on possible negative outcomes leads to self-destructive behaviors. He suggests that internalized "self-statements" can tie individuals to past perceived failures and lock them into negative self-fulfilling prophecies. Whereas this conceptualization has definite merit as applied to some client problems, it is far from explaining the complexity presented by most. Likewise, the heavily directive/confrontive interaction modes associated with this system can be invaluable at times, but certainly do not meet all client integrative needs. Its challenging tone may stimulate appropriate restructuring risks with some clients, but fail to penetrate the defensive systems of others. The creative counselor might at times conceptualize some of the client concerns in rational emotive therapy (RET) terms and confront accordingly, while implementing a more collaborative low-keyed remolding of thought patterns at other times.

Two other contemporary systems have extended the cognitive emphasis of RET into more expanded usages and have a great deal to offer the creative counselor. *Cognitive Therapy and the Emotional Disorders* (Beck, 1976) views both psychological disorders and related treatment as being concerned with thinking processes. He suggests that "the challenge to psychotherapy is to offer the patient effective techniques for overcoming his blindspots, his blurred perceptions, and his self-deceptions." The focus is on alleviating distress through "correcting faulty conceptions and self-signals" and helping the client make a realistic self-appraisal. After outlining the basic principles of this approach (with which we largely concur), he presents a detailed picture of specific techniques which are aimed at unleashing the client's judgment systems and problem-solving abilities. These are outstanding contributions, and we strongly recommend a thorough reading of this excellent book. We also caution that it is a seductive scheme, and that buying this or any specialized system is simplistic and potentially counterproductive. Take what is relevant to your expanding personal framework and apply those concepts and techniques which can facilitate more effective self-understanding with your clients.

Wiesen (1977) has also developed a cognitively based scheme with considerable merit. While critiquing RET and most other therapeutic schools as negative and destructive, Wiesen emphasizes the critical importance of our cognitive perceptual systems. Increasing positive self-beliefs is seen as the key to producing positive feelings and strengthening constructive action. The task of *positive therapy* is to program the client for success by creating "images of future success" and directing energies toward success attainment. By risking the recognition of client strength (a taboo among many approaches), the client may, in turn, risk an assessment of personal conceptual blockages and the risks involved in attempting different problem-solving strategies. A wide range of techniques is utilized in moving the client toward increased control over feelings, thoughts, and actions. Thoughts are seen as primary with the replaying of past failures as setting in motion the programming of future failures. We concur wholeheartedly with the major thesis of this approach which is to help people move toward important positive goals. We also agree that destructive mental forces—anxiety, depression, hostility, ambivalence—tend to diminish in power when the client can make a commitment to positive goals. Once again, the basic premise and related techniques have profound merit, especially for those who can integrate them within a broad eclectic framework.

The integrative phase, then, confronts client discrepancies between illusion and objective reality and provides a basis for constructive behavioral change. However, whereas the emphasis among most therapists tends to be on promoting a reality orientation among their clientele, creative counselors can also choose to move away from these narrow conceptualizations. At times they may risk the encouragement of denial by some clients. There is growing evidence (Lazarus, 1979) that illusion and denial may provide a more constructive perspective in some cases than stark reality. In contrast to the cherished assumption that self-deception and unexamined beliefs are pathological, he suggests "a temporary disavowal of reality helps the person get through the devastating early period of loss and threat." Denial can buy time for individuals to assimilate the impact of their dilemma and gradually gain coping strength to do something about it. Illusion can gradually be replaced by pieces of reality brought into the perceptual field in a sensitive and creative manner through the interaction of counselor and client. Some clients must be encouraged to risk facing an illusion in order to find themselves, whereas others may, in fact, need help in building a more livable fantasy screen from parts of their reality (Seligman, 1981). In either case, the challenge of the creative counselor is to bring principles, skills, and techniques into the interaction as a means of setting the stage for evaluating alternatives. As Carkhuff and Berenson (1967) put it:

> The therapist, in a very real sense, clears away the "crud" for the client at the choice point. The therapist takes the responsibility (and risk) for precipitating the crisis—but the client takes the responsibility (and risk) for this choice (p. 175).

The integration/understanding phase might be depicted as a cognitive effort at piecing together the client puzzle—making sense out of confusion and distortion. The entire range of mental, physical, and spiritual concerns may become integral to accomplishing the self-understanding goals of this phase. In developing a holistic framework for dealing with life's stresses, Pelletier (1977) suggests that biofeedback training (usually viewed as action-oriented techniques) can be used by the individual exploring the relationship of physiological and psychological events and lead to a more sophisticated understanding of their interaction. Brown (1975) describes this approach as a means of improving the "interaction with the interior self" through which the individual can learn about the relationship between feelings, thoughts, and bodily functions. Likewise, clients may also need to deal with value-laden issues during the integrative phase or even move directly into the structure of their spiritual life. Both the physical and spiritual areas of counseling are pursued in more depth in Chapter 8. The point here is that the creative counselor is able to move into all areas of client experience that generate meaningful insights. This risk is in breaking away from the traditional boundaries of counseling set in theory and responding formats when those structures do not serve the client's best interests.

RISK IN THE ACTION/BEHAVIOR CHANGE PHASE

Whereas exploration and improved insight are important foundational steps, the ultimate purpose of counseling is to translate understanding into action. This may involve the development of new attitudes or a systematic attack on self-defeating behaviors. It may entail skill development on the client's part to increase the probability of successfully accomplishing goals, but it necessarily entails heightened levels of risk. Whereas the cognitive roots for change are set in the integration phase, the client now risks facing threats that may have been previously avoided and moves into unknown areas of previously untapped strengths. A sense of helplessness may need to be overcome in order to put specific goals into action. The clients are at the crossroads again, and counselors risk putting their credibility on the line. Risks in this phase need to be carefully and creatively balanced against potential losses.

We introduce the phrase *rational risking* to reflect the critical issues of the action phase. The Chinese word for "crisis" illustrates the key elements of this concept. Two Chinese characters make up the word "crisis"—the first means "danger" and the second "opportunity." Successful action becomes a real opportunity for clients to achieve life goals. The counselors' task is to lead clients to a point at which goal implementation can be handled successfully. Counselors may need to risk letting the clients take the steps on their own at this point, or risk further dependency with some clients in order to eventually support directional movement. Counselors may choose to help clients sort out probable outcomes, and then move clients toward the steps of behavior change. This can be hard work for both participants and may demand that creativity be based on high personal energy levels and commitment to integrating the pieces of change. Many gray areas remain; as Egan (1975) puts it:

> The client should learn how to risk himself. He must learn that, paradoxically, it is "safe" to risk himself. This means that he must first take small risks and be reinforced for success and help to weather failure. Again, the helping process itself, from Stage I on, should be teaching the client how to take reasonable risks (p. 40).

Whereas there are many excellent guidelines for promoting successful plans of action (Bootzen, 1975; Goldfried and Davison, 1976; Krumboltz and Thoreson, 1976; Osipow, Walsh, and Tosi, 1980; Redd, Porterfield, and Anderson, 1979, to name only a few) many gray areas remain in facilitating client movement past perceived danger toward opportunity. We see the underlying process as evolving around three basic components of the action phase: (1) developing an optimal motivational level while promoting the client perception of behavior change as opportunity; (2) teaching the skills necessary to make risks rational; and (3) timing the client's action steps so as to increase the potential of success. Obviously, relational and integrational elements continue to play a vital role throughout this phase. In fact, the creative counselor shifts emphasis from phase to phase (goal setting to support to action to integration, etc.), while the overall process may be recycled again and again. The following diagram is not presented as a lock-step sequence, but reflects the interaction between the various components of the counseling process (see Figure 6-1). The arrows could actually be bidirectional as we certainly do not mean to represent a smooth progression and emphasize the potential for jumps and recycling at any juncture.

FIGURE 6-1
Points of risk. Arrows represent potential risks to client and counselor.

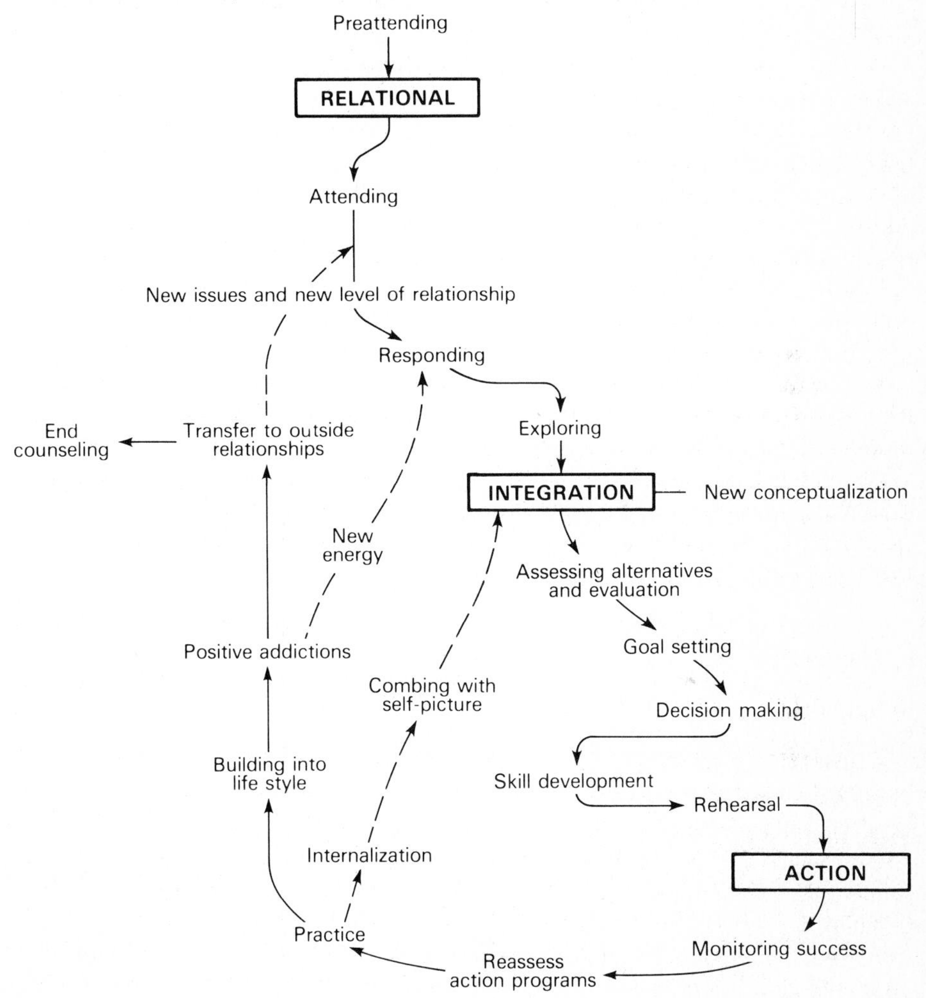

Before we attempt to identify some of the available theoretical resources, we caution that movement into action is not always an automatic extension of the previous phases. The integration phase hopefully brings about a choice point as the client must evaluate the potential gains and losses of the risks ahead. It is possible that change may not be worth the risk in some instances. The counselor is in a position here to help with this assessment and move the client through a rational system of decision making. When the alternatives and possible consequences are defined, the client faces the decision (to act or not to act) squarely and is better able to assimilate responsibility for the chosen direction. Weisberg, Sofair-Fisch, and Fisher-McCanne, 1978 have designed a procedure for identifying client strength and related assessment of the risks of possible action direction. They point out that whereas "the choice of translating new insights into change is best in some cases, the acceptance of the unchangeable is the appropriate choice at other times." The appropriate choice in either direction can bring about a renewed sense of control.

As we have indicated, there are many theoretical and practical guidelines which can be creatively integrated into the counselor's personal eclectic framework to facilitate client change in the desired direction. Whereas a survey of these methods is beyond the scope here, we would like to identify some of the underlying principles which provide a foundation for this phase. Mastery and creative application of the dozens of specific techniques stemming from these principles becomes a lifelong challenge for the creative counselor.

Whereas some clients may gain most of their counseling benefits through the catharsis and insights of the initial phases, most clients will choose to put new insights into action as part of the behavioral change phase. In good eclectic fashion, we will outline some of the principles related to this phase as we pull together ideas from Egan (1975), Eisenberg and Delaney (1977), and a recent discussion of contingency management (Walker, Hedberg, Clement, and Wright, 1981). In the process we will briefly delineate five steps of problem-solving methodology. After reviewing the following steps, we would invite the reader to apply the principles through example from the authors' caseload (see Appendix One: Part D, Sherry: Putting Insights into Action).

Goal Identification

This step is a logical extension of the integration phase and bridges the gap between understanding and action. The problem is translated into solution terms and may be defined in workable units. Problem ownership sets the stage for the client's acceptance of responsibility in the implementation step to follow. The establishment of solution priorities which enhance the probability of moving the client toward success is a primary focus. Who actually does the work of goal setting relates to another priority issue. In general, it is preferred to support the client goal identification efforts, but there are cases where the counselor may choose a highly directive role. Most cases involve an integral effort between counselor and client in order to define the specific goals to be accomplished.

While the goals may then need to be stated concretely (actually writing them out in contract form when appropriate) with most clients, the creative counselor may sense an advantage to relatively broad goal statements with other clients. This is another pivot point and the risks center around breaking from a cognitive (which can be quite safe for some) into a change focus. The whole range of counselor responses from supportive to confrontive may be brought into play and applied accordingly.

Assessment of Client Resources

Identifying the client's unique assets and liabilities serves to mediate the transition between goal identification and selection of a specific plan of action. This may redefine approach/avoidance conditions as we clarify forces within the clients and their environments, which may inhibit as well as enhance goal attainment. Whereas much of the literature has focused on the assessment of psychological resources—intellectual functioning, self-concept, interpersonal skills, support systems, expectations—and related environmental factors, an assessment of physical strengths may also be important. Counselor risks involved in breaking into the boundaries of the client's physical domain (nutritional, exercise, etc.) are developed in Chapter 8. The creative counselor is also sensitive to the possibility of a medical referral where actual physical barriers impede the client potential for successful implementation of goals.

Action Program Selection

Client goals and resources now serve as a basis for developing a strategy for client change. Strategy selection itself can be a creative process as a personalized blend of intervention techniques may be developed. Once again, the arbitrary plugging in of programs is antithetical to our philosophy as the program must be adapted to the client's needs and not vice versa. The actual strategies are extremely varied but rely on several basic principles. Eisenberg and Delaney's (1977) coverage of intervention principles is particularly relevant, and we invite the reader to utilize this resource for a more detailed presentation of these guidelines. First, they suggest that verbal instructions can be effective once the counselor has been established as a viable provider of advice. This principle is related to instructional approaches such as assertion training, systematic desensitization, bibliotherapy, and others. It may also involve active instruction in effective decision-making methods. Second, the principles of modeling can be applied toward developing more constructive beliefs, attitudes, and behaviors through specific application of role-playing strategies. They see modeling as an integral part of the counseling relationship itself. The client hopefully learns many of the responding skills (and core conditions) presented by the counselor and transfers those into improving other interpersonal relationships. The modeling effect may be enhanced in some instances by identifying (to the client) specific parts of the counseling interaction that merit client adoption. Third, client gains may at times be made by changing the environmental influences which have supported destructive behaviors or modifying reinforcement contingencies in support of new, more constructive attitudes and behaviors. The creative counselor is thoroughly knowledgeable of behavior modification principles and can call on them (operant conditioning, shaping, extinction, etc.) when appropriate. Finally, the strategy may be to continue efforts aimed at facilitating additional client insights about themselves and their environment. A continuing interaction between integrative and action functions may move some clients to successive increments in insights and behavior change. Behavior change may need to be integrated into the emerging self-picture to set the stage for the next level of risk. It may also be important to clarify criteria for assessing the success of action programs. As Egan (1975) points out, concrete success measures can be a key to sustaining client motivation as identified successes encourage the next risk in the change process.

Implementation

The time eventually comes (in small pieces or large units) to put the strategy into practice. Insight again may be important in reformulating tactics for change, and counselor support continues to serve as a basis for further risks. This process may become cyclical as insight leads to change and change is integrated into the emerging self-picture as a stimulus for further insight and change. Relational skills may again emerge as the nature of the relationship tends to intensify during the steps of implementation. In fact, more meaningful levels of self-exploration may emerge as the client continues to build confidence on the building blocks of successful changes.

Evaluation

Since this appears to be a logical extension of the preceding steps, it is all too easy to overlook its importance. Weighing attempts against previously established success criteria not only serves a valuable feedback function, but may provide the data and impetus for readjusting the game plan. Rigid adherence to initial plans may be necessary at times, but can be disastrous at other times. Similarly, the creative counselor can not afford to become so goal-oriented that it replaces sensitivity to client needs ("jumping for joy" over client successes not only reinforces the client but can reaffirm our own capacity for genuinely appreciating another's accomplishments). Watching a problem-solving process translated into improved self-esteem and personal effectiveness can be exhilarating, and our expression of this excitement can be mutually enhancing.

The extensive contributions from behaviorally oriented theorists have yielded a renewed sense of confidence among effective counselors as we face the challenges of programming action packages. The old debate between relational versus cognitive versus behavioral approach supremacy seems to be giving way to an integrated eclecticism. While we continue to build our counseling repertoires with the innovations that are being developed, we might again remember the advice of Egan (1975): "The ultimate test is not whether these strategies fit into a theoretical system but whether they meet the needs of clients."

RISK IN TRANSITION

This phase (largely ignored in the literature) is an extension of the continuity generated between sessions as the client applies in-session insights toward experiences between sessions. We would again affirm our belief that as valuable as counseling is in its supportive and directive functions, its primary function remains that of setting the stage for what happens between sessions. And even as important as the work is between sessions, the eventual goal must be to transfer insights and coping skills into future lifestyle directions. In the process, the theme of risk will hopefully become woven into the fabric of the client's continuing lifelong pursuits. Creative counselors are able to empathize with client risks to the extent that they incorporate challenge into their own lives, and also model the related attitudes throughout the counseling process. This modeling may eventually provide a foundation for the integration of risk into the everyday life of the client.

In each phase there appear to be major barriers to progress and risks related to overcoming them—the transition phase is no exception. Whereas there are many potential barriers, the primary risks at this point generally evolve around giving up, or changing, the relationship which has provided the support and impetus for moving the client toward independence from the onset. The transition (weaning away) comes in progressive steps and may be enhanced by increased counselor disclosure and a conscious effort to redefine the relationship itself. Carkhuff and Berenson (1977) call this the immediacy dimension (an action condition) in which the relationship itself may be explored explicitly as clients learn from the process they have been through. Where do I fit in your life now? This becomes a critical issue at times and should not be ignored. In fact, the continuing redefinition of the purpose of counseling and the relationship should be a part of virtually every session. Clients must know where they stand. Understanding the underlying ingredients of this healthy relationship (what has made it successful) can then serve as a basis for transferring relevant components into everyday life. Some clients move through this transition quickly and immediately into other healthy relationships in the natural environment which can continue to support personal growth. With other clients, the transition phase offers genuine barriers which must be dealt with in considerable detail. The relationship has served as a safe testing ground for developing interpersonal skills and the confidence to take rational risks. Now, these attitudes and behaviors must be translated into everyday life (on a more permanent basis) as the client builds a healthier outside support system. Old relationships may have been given up in the process of "stacking the deck" with a more constructive structure of significant others. In fact, evidence for the permanence of counseling-related change can be found in an assessment of the level of functioning among the clients' close associates. It is unlikely that they will continue with growth-related risks if surrounded by negatively oriented individuals. Consequently, a major function during this phase is the transfer of counseling learning to outside relationships.

The remedial risks of the first three phases set the stage for prevention-directed risks in the transition phase and beyond. Whereas danger may have predominated over potential opportunities during the crisis throughout counseling, the success of risks taken helps to build the foundation for a clearer perception of self and environment. Hopefully, opportunities outweigh perceived dangers. The upward spiral continues to the degree that the client is able to take the risks inherent in overcoming future barriers to growth. At a higher level, future development hinges on the client's ability to tap previously dormant areas of strength by actually seeking out new challenges. We continue this theme in the next chapter as we consider the preventative role that risk plays with high-functioning individuals.

SUMMARY

Chapter 6 introduces risk as a pivotal ingredient in creatively dealing with client problems. Risk is so central to creative counseling that we have identified it as a basic core condition that must be present if the real and perceived barriers to change are to be overcome. Risk is examined as it relates to the major phases of the counseling process. The relational/exploration phase demands a great deal of sensitivity and flexibility as the client risks sharing personal materials, and the counselor risks moving beyond the safety of models and techniques. The integrational/understanding phase also incorporates risks for both client and counselor as they build a workable picture of the problems to be resolved. The action/behavior change phase rests on small steps (rational risks) that move the client toward desired changes and further break the counselor out of any lock-step systems for change promotion. Finally, risk is seen as critical in the transition process as both client and counselor move toward transferring gains beyond the temporary security of the counseling context.

REFERENCES

Beck, A. *Cognitive therapy and the emotional disorders.* New York: New American Library, 1976.

Birch, G. G. The role of motivational factors in insightful problem-solving. *Journal of Comparative Psychology,* 1945, *38,* 295–317.

Bootzen, R. R. *Behavior modification and therapy.* Cambridge, Mass.: Winthrop, 1975.

Brammer, L. *The helping relationship: Process and skills.* Englewood Cliffs, N.J.: Prentice-Hall, 1973.

Brown, B. *New mind, new body.* New York: Harper & Row, 1975.

Carkhuff, R., and Berenson, B. *Beyond counseling and psychotherapy.* New York: Holt, 1967.

Carkhuff, R., and Berenson, B. *Beyond counseling and psychotherapy* (2nd ed.). New York: Holt, 1977.

Cole, H. P., and Sarnoff, D. Creativity and counseling. *Personnel and Guidance Journal,* 1980, *59*(3), 140–146.
Coleman, J. E., Butcher, J. N., and Carson, R. C. *Abnormal psychology in modern life* (6th ed.). Glenview, Ill.: Scott, Foresman, 1980.
Corey, G. *Theory and practice of counseling and psychotherapy.* Monterey, Calif.: Brooks/Cole, 1977.
Egan, R. *The skilled helper.* Monterey, Calif.: Brooks/Cole, 1975.
Eisenberg, S., and Delaney, D. J. *The counseling process* (2nd ed.). Chicago, Ill.: Rand McNally, 1977.
Ellis, A. *Reason and emotion in psychotherapy.* New York: Lyle Stuart, 1972.
Ellis, A., and Harper, R. *A guide to rational living* (7th ed.). Hollywood: Wilshire, 1973.
Glasser, W. *Positive addiction.* New York: Harper & Row, 1976.
Goldfried, M. R., and Davison, G. C. *Clinical behavior therapy.* New York: Holt, 1976.
Ivey, A. *Microcounseling: Innovations in interviewing training.* Springfield, Ill.: Charles C Thomas, 1971.
Jencks, B. *Your body, biofeedback at its best.* Chicago: Nelson-Hall, 1977.
Kopechy, G. Take a chance: You have nothing to fear but fear itself. *Family Week,* 1980,
Krumboltz, J. D., and Thoreson, C. E. *Counseling methods.* New York: Holt, 1976.
Lazarus, R. Positive denial: The case for not facing reality. *Psychology Today,* November 1979, 44–60.
Lewin, K. *Dynamic theory of personality.* New York: McGraw-Hill, 1935.
Maslow, A. H. *Towards a psychology of being.* New York: Van Nostrand, 1962.
Ogilvie, B. Stimulus addiction: The sweet psychic jolt of danger. *Psychology Today,* October1974, 88–94.
Osipow, S. H., Walsh, W. B., and Tosi, D. J. *A survey of counseling methods.* Homewood, Ill.: Dorsey, 1980.
Pelletier, K. R. *Mind as healer, mind as slayer.* New York: Delta, 1977.
Redd, W. H., Porterfield, A. L., and Anderson, B. L. *Behavior modification.* New York: Random House, 1979.
Rogers, C. R., and Truax, C. B. The therapeutic conditions antecedent to change. In C. P. Rogers (ed.), *The therapeutic relationship and its impact.* Madison: University of Wisconsin Press, 1967, pp. 97–108.
Schachter, S., and Singer, J. Cognitive, social and physiological determinants of emotional state. *Psychological Review,* 1962, *69,* 379–399.
Seligman, M. E. P. *Helplessness.* San Francisco: Freeman, 1975.
Seligman, M. E. P. Personal communication, Alamosa, Colorado, June 1981.
Selye, H. *The stress of life* (2nd ed.). New York: McGraw-Hill, 1978.
Sheehy, G. *Passages.* New York: Dutton, 1976.
Viscott, D. *Risking.* New York: Pocket Books, 1977.
Walker, C. E., Hedberg, A., Clement, P. W., and Wright, L. *Clinical procedures for behavior therapy.* Englewood Cliffs, N.J.: Prentice-Hall, 1981.
Weisberg, M., Sofair-Fisch, T., and Fisher-McCanne, L. A relationship skills training program for college students. *Personnel and Guidance Journal,* 1978, *57*(4), 220–221.
Wiesen, A. E. *Positive therapy.* Chicago: Nelson-Hall, 1977.
Yerkes, R. M., and Dodson, J. D. The relation of strength of stimulus to rigidity of habit formation. *Journal of Comparative Neurology and Psychology,* 1908, *18,* 459–482.

CHAPTER 7

RISKS IN PREVENTION: ALTERNATIVE ENVIRONMENTS IN MOVING UPSTREAM

As indicated in Chapter 1, the preceding decade marked a period of rapid change in the counseling profession reflecting a growing dissatisfaction with the narrow remedial focus of the past. The trend favored a new direction toward moving upstream (Carkhuff and Berenson, 1976) in an effort to reach people before they become bogged down in self-defeating life patterns. Even beyond this, we began to turn our professional energies toward promoting continued growth in basically high-functioning individuals. Along with an emerging rationale for prevention, outreach-based and multifaceted models were developed to provide a structure for expanding the role of counseling. As preventative forces became an integral part of our profession, their revitalizing potential became apparent. This was supported by a growing number of self-help programs and the translation of remedial models into preventative terms. We should not only be pleased with these positive changes but anticipate further expansion of preventative themes and related intervention approaches.

In looking ahead to the future of our profession, a growing impact of preventative themes is anticipated. In a recent issue of the *Counseling Psychologist* designed to cast future projections, several prominent figures in our profession were asked to visualize the future. The unifying theme revolved around the expectancy of a deeper commitment toward prevention in order to make an expanded contribution to society. Wrenn (1980) expressed his vision of the future in which "prevention is stressed rather than treatment, health rather than illness, integration of self rather than the development of parts." Wrenn's dream of the future presents a welcome challenge and is supported by other major contributors to innovation who have shaped the direction of our profession in past decades (Bordin, 1980; Krumboltz and Menefee, 1980; Tyler, 1980). Each of these contributor's description of future, prevention-based directions can be characterized by contagious enthusiasm which is evidenced by a review of any segment of the current professional literature.

A review of the *Psychological Abstracts* since 1979 reveals that special interest areas within the profession have turned their focus toward prevention. The following specialty areas are only a sample of those generating preventative approaches in the current literature: alcohol education, child abuse, minority attitudes, behavior modification, vandalism, sexually transmittible disease, child training, dropouts, early learning, stress-related disorders, midlife crisis, and cultural issues. We are impressed by the diversity of attempts to deal with remedial issues in a preventative manner. This parallels a secondary movement directed at translating theories and techniques of remedial origin into the preventative context. Ironically, the professional mind-set is still imbedded in remediation. We still tend to see a problem after it has been manifested and then work backwards toward heading off similar future problems. Nevertheless, the growing list of preventative techniques gives the eclectic counselor a wide range of methods from which to select and creatively integrate into the needs of a particular situation.

Two major professional contributions paved the way for the current preventative emphasis (Drum and Figler, 1973; Morrell, Oetting, and Hurst, 1974). These efforts stimulated initial enthusiasm for prevention and provided a model for its conceptualization and implementation as well. A perceptual scheme was generated (cube model presented in Chapter 1) to enhance visualization of the activities which would broaden our professional boundaries. A more recent extension of this thinking (Chaney and Hurst, 1980) provides guidelines for direct intervention into areas of client growth and moving into outreach efforts by extending the traditional office-based boundaries. A strong case is made for making resources accessible in areas of need rather than waiting for the client to come to us. A further contribution has involved a movement away from a purely individual focus toward changing the institutional structure in which the client operates. The "school climate" banner is illustrative of this emphasis, and we see the role of counselor as consultant to institutional change as becoming increasingly legitimatized. We sense that an increasing proportion of the consulting functions performed by counselors have become preventively oriented in recent years. Goodyear (1976) identifies efforts made toward meeting personal needs for growth through institutional change. He defines the impact of this direction in an article which identifies institutional systems and healthy individuals as targets of prevention. The counselor becomes a change agent with a focus on environmental forces. The task of the professional from this reference point is to develop systems and environmental atmospheres that promote individual growth (Jones and Stewart, 1980). Sprinthall (1980) also supports this view. He makes an impressive plea for counselors to work with teachers in developing positive learning environments.

Lifestyle change through preventative programs offers another example of current extension of the prevention theme. Stachnik (1980) supports the development of lifestyles "congruent with good long-range health" as a priority concern for our profession. Ardell (1977) also recognizes the discrepancies found as we compare these goals with many of the counterproductive themes in our society. In evaluating the potential for major lifestyle change, Pelletier (1977) concludes that radical shifts are not feasible without a pervasive holistic approach. This kind of change may be large in magnitude and involve reevaluation of friends, philosophy, job, and other major environmental forces.

Interest in stress and its consequences has almost become a national pastime (at least among counselors) in recent years, and offers another example of an area which has moved beyond traditional remedial boundaries. The "Peace, Harmony, and Awareness" series (Lupin, 1977) is only one example of the application of remedially developed techniques (relaxation training and visual imagery) within a preventative context. This program is geared toward teaching young children skills which can be used to face future stressors while building a sense of confidence and control. Girdano and Everly (1979) have further popularized stress prevention programs, as they apply a wide range of techniques to assess stress level. They also go beyond the building of a personal stress profile, and suggest the development of a personalized strategy for heading off the potentially destructive force of stress. Individuals in every walk of life (and at all levels of functioning) are attending workshops throughout the country designed toward self-assessment of stress levels and related methods for controlling life activities.

Transpersonal psychology provides a further example of preventative efforts in recent years. This framework for visualizing client potential offers a major contribution to the preventative movement. Recognition of client strengths and relative-supported motivational forces is central to the preventative orientation (Otto, 1979). This perspective also emphasizes the impact of total systems on individual lives and the potential for positively impacting both of these forces (Carlson, 1979; Dinkmeyer and Dinkmeyer, 1979). These themes are further extended through Wiesen's (1977) emphasis on the recognition of our client's positive attributes. Ivey (1980) supports this view in the following terms:

> Counseling psychology has a long history of emphasis on positive mental health with accompanying stress on assisting individuals, groups, and organizations to develop their full potential. Rather than search for pathology, counseling psychology seeks to build on assets. (p.14)

Ivey assumes that all counseling interventions should be based on the premise of a growth potential for the client. Ardell (1977) also emphasizes a positive focus and the importance of an integrated lifestyle. The positive health movement calls for building upon personal assets and utilizing a wide range of approaches to support a consistent upward movement in lifestyle. Obviously, these themes are congruent with the emerging preventative direction within our profession.

The preventative movement comes at a time of increased appreciation for diversity. The schoolism upon which the remedial component of counseling was founded does not necessarily have to transfer into its preventative counterpart. In fact, prevention and remediation can be seen synergistically as supporting each other within a single continuum. Whereas some remedial concepts can be translated directly into the preventative context, creative counselors are selective in the blending of models and are always governed by the needs of their clientele. The major block to the growth of prevention is the inflexible adherence to any rigidly formulated system of thought. Landsberg (1977) identifies this potential block in the following manner: "One reason for the ineffectiveness of preventative measures in mental health may be that definitions of prevention generally follow the public health model, or medical model, which is disease oriented." In general, preventative plans have originated from the problems we have observed in society rather than from our ability to see individual and institutional potential.

We believe that our profession in the future will be increasingly characterized by a preventative focus based on the perception of client strengths. This potential was set in motion during the preceding decade as prevention became a legitimate theme of an expanding structural framework for counseling. The counselor's role was extended and intervention repertoire enhanced through the development of a wide range of techniques which were taken out of their remedial origins and translated for use in the preventative context. Even though the prevention of human misery has become an increasingly accepted part of the counselor's function, the developmental end of the helping continuum (development——prevention——remediation) deserves more attention. The creative counselor is capable of working at all points of this continuum, but we sense that working with healthy people in a developmental/preventative effort (keeping the upward spiral in motion) will become a higher priority in the future. In keeping with the "conservation of energy" theme presented earlier (Wiesen, 1977), counselors, too, have only so much energy to invest. An overinvestment in strictly remedial cases can be potentially destructive for both client and counselor. In contrast, the growth emphasis of the developmental/preventative end of the continuum offers benefits in two directions. First, the investment/payoff ratio tends to be extremely high with healthy individuals and upstream activities geared toward heading off problems. Confronting chronically ingrained problems is exhausting work and may reap relatively small changes in all too many cases. In addition to the direct benefits of helping our clients build strengths, developmental/preventative work tends to be revitalizing for the counselor. The energy gained in these efforts can then be reinvested with clients who present remedial needs. Obviously, a uniquely personal equation is necessary in managing the flow of our personal/professional resource energies into the needs of our clientele. A choice on our part has been to channel an increasingly higher percentage of energy into the developmental/preventative end of the continuum. In turn, we would encourage a shift in our profession from a preventative/remedial to a developmental/preventative emphasis which highlights the strengths of our clients and the expansion of untapped areas of potential.

We have already documented the fringes of this upstream movement in the preceding paragraphs. Hopefully, the impact of expanded preventative resources may eventually serve to change the profession's "illness" mind-set. In the meantime, the process for remedial counseling (Carkhuffian model) seems to have merit as a guiding force for prevention. However, this model may need to be modified in order to support efforts directed at stimulating growth in relatively high-functioning clientele. In this light, we sense that the developmental/preventative counseling experience may actually flow in the reverse direction of remedial counseling. In remediation the initial focus tends to be on relationship building in order to set the stage for integration and eventual action. The major risks, at least initially, are generally relational in nature. The relational risks are less ominous when working with relatively high-functioning individuals who have good ego strength and a previously established personal support system. Strengths may be readily apparent. Consequently, initial risk can focus on action activities which, in turn, set the tone for later integrational and relational issues. Our experience with developmental/preventative counseling has generally been reflected in the following sequence: (1) initiation of action (high risks and crisis precipitation in many cases); followed by (2) an integration of the action experience within existing understanding while extending insights back into everyday life; and then (3) the development of additional mutually enhancing relationships as a byproduct. While crisis is an integral part of remedial and preventative counseling, the former deals with breaking down barriers to self-exploration and change as the dangers inherent in opportunity are reduced. In contrast, the reverse may characterize developmental/preventative counseling. In other words, opportunity predominates over dangers. The barriers of action (danger) may be placed in front of the client to offer new challenges (opportunities). This, of course, is not offered as a lock-step sequence but as a general backdrop for supporting the counselor's developmental/preventative interventions. As with remedial counseling, the actual flow emerges only within the context of counselor/client interaction. Nevertheless, a model can become an invaluable resource for structuring creative counseling, and we identify the risks and potential benefits of each of these phases in the remainder of this chapter. An overview of this model is presented in Figure 7-1.

FIGURE 7-1
Prevention/developmental counseling with high-functioning clients.

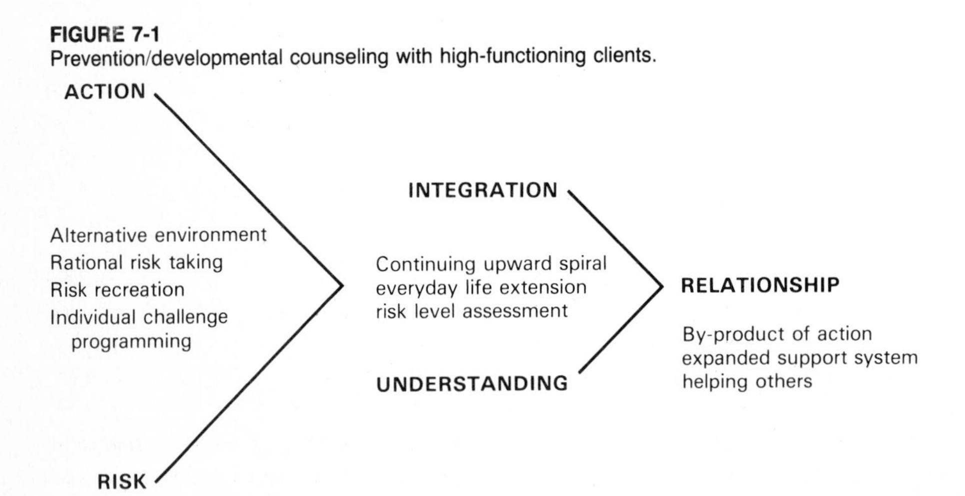

ACTION: THE ALTERNATIVE ENVIRONMENT AND RISK PROMOTION

Whereas behaviorists have supported the notion of early movement into action in remedial counseling, we see considerable merit in the promotion of action to initiate the process of developmental/preventative counseling with relatively high-functioning clients. The initial focus is placed on the identification of client strength and related ways to challenge the use of potential resources. The risks shift toward the initiation of action in an effort to stimulate continued growth in upwardly spiraling clients who can be challenged to draw from previously untapped reservoirs of potential strength.

During the action phase of developmental/preventative counseling, the client may be presented with personally unfamiliar territory in an effort to test and expand personally perceived limits. Exposure to alternative environments (any unfamiliar setting which offers intense challenge) can provide a context for self-testing and an opportunity of exceeding (or becoming more attuned to) previous limitations. Along with a clear contact with strengths, healthy clients may move toward an expanded perception of their own potentiality. Whereas small gains are sometimes painfully slow in remedial counseling, high-risk activities with healthy people can promote dramatic insights and related lifestyle changes. Within a framework of previously established self-confidence and interpersonal support, the high-functioning client may eagerly seek the opportunity to move from safety into risk situations. The challenge for the creative counselor comes in designing personally relevant alternative experiences for the client which provide maximum challenge but do not push the client beyond reasonably safe limits. Rational risking governs movement into alternative environments as the counselor builds for client success and facilitates the client's efforts to cope with failures. While the emphasis in the action phase is on the risk itself, adequate preparation remains the counselor's responsibility. Taft (1979) builds on this issue in discussing the importance of preparation for high-risk activities: "The principle is not to avoid activities involving danger, but to prepare participants both by technical training and physical fitness to deal with the risk competently. The aim is to teach that the more adventurous an undertaking, the more care and prudence are needed to succeed." Meier (1978) goes on to suggest that intelligent assessment of risks involves defining goals and evaluating the odds of success against the potential benefits and hazards related to the activity.

Just as risk involves a highly unique personal perception, the alternative environment concept also involves an individual equation. What is risk for one person is mundane for another. What is an exciting challenge offered by an alternative environment to someone, may be comfortable, safe, and routine for someone else. There are no universals in defining an alternative environment, and the creative counselor is consequently faced with an unlimited range of possibilities in creatively matching growth-seeking clientele with personally challenging experiences. We explore the dimensions of these potential alternative environments later in this chapter, but would like to focus initially on "risk recreation" as a potential direction for providing our clients with growth experiences.

A special issue of the *Journal of Physical Education and Recreation* (April 1978) was devoted to the assessment of high-adventure activities performed in alternative environments, and it offers some excellent insights into this increasingly popular movement. We feel that eclectic counselors can borrow from an exposure to the growing variety of recreational activities which contain elements of risk, challenge, excitement, and adventure to expand their awareness and intervention repertoire.

According to Peterson (1978), risk recreation can be divided into three major components. First, high risk involves cooperation with the elements of the alternative environment—natural elements may not be conquered but offer the experience of moving into the unpredictable and unknown as individuals challenge their limits. Second, the challenges are highly individual as reflected in the subjective nature of risk itself—"participants are testing themselves against a task, a challenge that can be defined and met on an individual basis." The third element is the risk itself, "which stimulates an exciting emotional response and a sense of self-confidence and accomplishment." Exposure to the alternative environment maximizes the potential for healthy individuals to reach what Maslow (1971) described as a "peak experience." Individuals may move beyond perceived limits and develop a firmer sense of being at their own creative center. Placed in an unpredictable environment where forces are beyond their control may be humbling and allow individuals to gain a new perspective on their place in the scheme of life. As Miles (1978) puts it:

> In the end, the ultimate value of high adventure risk recreation may be that one person confronts existentially the decision as to whether or not to venture forth into the unknown. Choice is exercised, the mind and body committed, and the consequences accepted. No one is drafted into the activity, but chooses to face the test. There are limited opportunities to exercise personal freedom so dramatically in the world today (p.4).

What is an alternative environment? In a world of modern technology, life may be highly structured and predictable. For some people, then, the natural outdoor environment offers optimal exposure to realize their potential and engage the uncontrollability of nature. White (1978) identifies three activity clusters of natural challenge activities which the counselor can help participants select in light of individual skills and strengths: "mountain activities (rock climbing, ice and snow climbing, ski mountaineering, caving); white-water activities (kayaking, canoeing, rafting); ocean activities (surfing, kayak surfing, wind surfing, ocean kayak touring)." The authors emphasize the importance of leader-facilitated calibration of risk level for each participant. According to Miles (1978), individual freedom can be maximized by encountering the natural environment alone and on its own terms. He suggests that one can counteract the unnaturalness of the contemporary city environment by "periodically renewing oneself in the wilderness." On the surface it may appear ironic that we can benefit from a high-risk contact with our natural environment, when urban living today is so frequently overstimulating itself. However, nature offers a significant contrast to challenges met in the man-made environment and offers unique potential for personal expansion (Schreyer, White, and McCool, 1978). There may be geographical limitations with some target groups, but creative counselors can challenge their own imaginations in setting up natural, alternate environmental experiences for their clients as they move out of their counseling offices to explore natural settings for growth counseling (Miller, 1980).

In reality, alternative environments reflect the client's past experience and represent perception more than a specific geographical location. A return to the wilderness is not the only alternative and in fact may be impractical from a financial and resource standpoint for most counselors. Creative counselors can develop challenging environmental contingencies regardless of their proximity to natural environmental settings. Webster (1978) points out that the Project Adventure program developed for educational settings has been creative in moving the client into dynamic challenge experiences. In allowing students to explore areas of uncertainty, this program utilizes "fields, trees, empty lots, buildings, and whatever exists in and around school." Dickey (1978) suggests that the basic elements of risk recreation programs can be generated within urban environments. He sees the city as a learning environment which can offer the same risk ingredients to participants as natural outdoor settings at a low cost, close to home. We are limited only by our imagination (and safety precautions) as we structure risk activities for high-functioning clients. Mountaineering simulation can be executed through rope courses built within the urban environment whereas others may enter the challenges of alternate environments by involvement with geriatric homes, psychiatric patients, or institutionalized children.

The experience of an alternate environment means moving into previously unexplored areas of our existence. Counselors who place themselves in risk situations as part of their own growth process potentiate their ability to remain empathic for the risks their clients take. While our offices may be safe and familiar to us, they may represent the risk of entering an alternative environment for many of our clients. Eder (1976) clarifies our point: "As the thought of climbing a wall of stone terrifies some, so does the schoolroom loom fearsome and oppressive to others." Dealing with the terrible feeling of failure in a technical rock-climbing experience, a teacher in one of his outdoor risk programs said, "The paralyzing fear I'd just felt gave me a basis for understanding the fears these children (unsuccessful students) have and their emotional turmoil, both ignored so easily by parents and teachers." In an expanded sense, alternative environments may reach beyond the physical setting, and into the psychological and even spiritual domains of our existence. For emotionally reactive individuals, processing their experience from a rational cognitive framework may enter them into an alternate environment and open new potentials for growth. It is a basic premise for us that creative counseling actively seeks to move the client beyond comfortable areas of experience into the potential opportunities inherent in previously untapped areas. Creative counselors must also be open to the risks of alternative frameworks as they continually expand their open eclectic model by developing the skills and techniques required to respond to client needs.

Whereas our remedial clients may seek desperately to maintain equilibrium (even if self-defeating) in their lives, our high-functioning clientele may actively seek opportunities for moving beyond their ordinary level of control. With these clients, our challenge is to enter into their need for personal expansion and actively promote and integrate relevant alternate experiences. Our job involves helping our clients successfully tap previously unexplored areas of themselves. In depicting the core of the high-risk experience, Miles (1978) states:

> Routine living and too many amenities may dull one's emotions. Tied up with multiple demands and bombarded by multiple stimuli, a person withdraws and struggles to maintain an equilibrium, always striving to control the swing of emotions. Away from routine and in a risk situation, emotions surge up and are given a release. Watch any group rafting a river, they approach the big drop pensively, with knitted brow and nervous giggle, but once into the roaring white water they yell, laugh, and even cry (p. 29).

This whole issue of sensation seeking (breaking out of ordinary limits) may be central to understanding the alternative environment growth experience of high-functioning individuals. People whose lives are destructively governed by high stress may be least likely to seek and benefit from high-risk activities and in fact may tend to recoil into the safety of their own environment. For others, stress is sought periodically in an effort to expand the limits of established sensation levels. High-functioning individuals who are secure in their support systems and own self-images can unleash energy to invest in seeking new experiences. According to Schreyer, White, and McCool (1978), "The greater the arousal created, the greater the high resulting from the experience." Tension builds as the risk is anticipated which is released upon completion of the activities and translated into exhilaration and an emotional peak experience.

We are reminded here of Selye's (1976) eustress principle, and suggest that high-functioning people may use stress to their advantage while maintaining relative immunity to the destructive impact of distress. By periodically pushing the limits of perceived boundaries, the individual builds a broader band of stimulus tolerance which may serve a functional role in meeting the high demands of everyday life. Furthermore, expanding these limits may enhance our creative capacities as we allow ourselves to view our world from a different perspective. Glasser (1976) points to the potentially addictive properties of exposing ourselves to varied stimulation levels and describes a positive addiction state to which new neural pathways may be developed along with highly creative patterns of thought.

In a series of publications, sensation seeking has been identified as a personality trait manifest in a need for change in variety and intensity of stimulation level (Brown, Ruder, Ruder, and Young, 1974; Zuckerman, Bone, Neary, Mangelsdorff, and Brustman, 1972; Zuckerman, 1978; Zuckerman, Buchsbaum, and Murphy, 1980). These people have been characterized as being sensitive to internal cues, independent, spontaneous, assertive, and enjoying complexity and challenge. Zuckerman (1978) states that the sensation seeker approaches high-risk activities "with more pleasure than anxiety, while low sensation-seekers experience nothing but anxiety." He implicates biologically based differences in causing high needs for sensation seeking among some people. We would add the possibility that sensation-seeking experiences may in turn impact our neurophysiological systems and increase our needs to risk. A controlled and systematic approach to this bootstrap cyclical process would appear to have considerable implications to personal expansion. Whereas these studies have also pointed out the negative side of sensation seeking, we see high-functioning individuals as those who do seek out challenges and are eager to test their limits.

The reasons for participation in risk activities are complex and involve psychological, physical, and environmental factors. Meier (1978) suggests that the motivational forces beyond the pursuit of risk activities range from self-testing and exploration needs to needs for camaraderie and aesthetic contact with nature. Ogilvie (1974) has found that athletes who participate in high-risk sports consistently reflect a healthy and positive personality profile. He sees them as "stimulus addicts" who have a periodic need for extending themselves to the absolute physical, emotional, and intellectual limits. He suggests that these people tend to incorporate and adjust to high sensation readily, and therefore may need to continually escalate the level of risk in the activities they pursue. Obviously, there is a point beyond which risk is unrealistically dangerous, and it may be up to the activity leader to put limits on overzealous participants. Counselors cannot afford to get so caught up in the excitement of the activity as to forget reasonable boundaries. They are also there to encourage an individual assessment of activity risk level and encourage some clients not to take risks beyond their limits only because of peer group pressures. The counselor who utilizes risk activities will emphasize the importance of the choice not to participate, placing equal value on any *rational* decision made by individuals relative to their personal participation. We should also emphasize that the counselor should call on the expertise of recreational specialists to help structure risk activities and provide appropriate safety precautions. Our experience with such specialists has been invaluable and has led to several lifelong friendships.

Challenging limits through heightened stimulation level may be presented to participants through the altering of several dimensions of more ordinary experiences. These dimensions offer nearly unlimited potential for creating an alternative environment experience uniquely relevant to the group or individual. We will look briefly at four possible dimensions and then let your imagination carry you into other possibilities. Part of the fun of developing alternative environment experiences for high-functioning groups is the brainstorming that goes into the creation of new activities. (1) The *time* of day is one dimension in providing an alternative environment. What is simple and nonthreatening during daytime hours may be just the opposite after dark. A raft trip down a gentle river stretch becomes an entirely different experience for some when the sun goes down. Learning to deal with this change in environment, i.e., climbing down a mountain at night, can offer unique challenges to those who typically avoid such experiences. Night walks in the high country have become a climax experience for some of our risk classes. (2) The location can further precipitate a change in the activity's stimulus value. An isolated rural environment can offer new opportunities for learning to the city dwellers. Likewise, the reverse can promote challenge for those accustomed to a rural setting. Both authors can relate to the risk taken by inner-city kids in spending a night in the mountains where even the new sounds (particularly coyotes) challenge the individual's coping resources. (3) Being *alone* can turn a formerly innocuous activity into a new and different challenge. Stimulus deprivation itself offers an alternative to the stimulus-laden fast pace of many of our clients (and ourselves). Whereas some of us actively seek out personal time alone, others virtually never experience it. According to Ogilvie (1974) high-risk takers tend to be very independent and autonomous, choosing often to do things alone. They also tend (as many counselors) to be comfortable with having others depend on them. Consequently, to move to the other extreme of this dimension may create an alternate environment for some where they are part of a group and dependent on others for successfully accomplishing tasks. The whole issue of dependence/independence emerges when we move an individual to an unfamiliar end of this alone/together continuum. Learning to receive assistance from others may be as difficult for some as giving support is for others. (4) The *physical dimensions* of our environment may offer the clearest ways to manipulate sensation level. What is comfortable on the ground may take on an entirely different perspective when the same activity is performed at a height. Again, the experience is subjective and varies from person to person. Fear may be evoked at 6 inches above the ground for some whereas extreme heights do not elicit much reaction at all for others. Likewise, the person who sees little risk associated with height may encounter considerable challenge when performing an activity under water or underground. The creative counselor is challenged here to develop personally relevant risk experiences for healthy clientele by expanding these and other dimensions of altered stimulation levels.

We emphasize here that the initiation of risk counseling with the action phase tends to be effective with people who are already high-functioning. Even then, we may not want to rush into high-risk activities without "testing the water" with regard to the atmosphere of support within the group. Indeed, with lower-functioning people the process may be more likely to parallel the process of remedial counseling where relational considerations are paramount to moving clients into the risks of action activities in alternative environments. In fact, the relational context for some of the individuals may actually provide an alternative context where the threat and risks are in terms of developing a closeness with another human being. Webster (1978) describes the Project Adventure program as involving three phases which offer both interesting parallels and contrasts to our sequence. This program, however, is geared toward direct infusion into the academic curriculum in an effort to add potency to the academic experience for a majority (high- and low-functioning) of students in secondary education. Phase I in this project emphasizes preparation and anticipation. Students ready themselves for physical risk activities by rhythmic exercises and cardiovascular conditioning. Phase II is geared toward developing mutual support and personal confidence. Efforts in this phase are built upon group problem-solving activities which maximize cooperation and the utilization of the individual member resources. Common goals are emphasized so that group success (rather than individual failure) is the key ingredient. Finally, phase III uses the natural environment (buildings, telephone poles, trees) to form a "ropes course." This kind of course involves "a series of ropes, cables, trees, and logs designed and constructed to present elements which require a combination of balance, agility, coordination, and commitment to navigate. Some parts of the course are upwards to 60 feet off the ground and may appear imposing. At any rate, the action phase follows relational considerations, and we are certainly open to this sequence even with high-functioning groups. Once again, there are no hard and fast rules for the creative counselor, only general guidelines and an endless array of techniques to be pulled together to help the participants meet their needs. Hammit (1980) also proposes the multiphase model for outdoor experience which incorporates five phases: anticipation, travel to, on-site, travel back, and recollection. We see this as a supplementary method of conceptualizing the risk experience and emphasize the importance of moving beyond the on-site experience where we tend to locate the phases we have presented to include the entire context of the experience. Whereas we emphasize action which occurs on-site in risk recreation and involves the actual risk activities within alternate environments, the surrounding context provides a framework for integrational and relational work. Some integrational efforts can be made during the activity itself, but a structured time before or after each challenge activity generally optimizes the opportunity for personal insight.

Because of the potential dangers of high-risk recreation, the counselor may want to approach these activities through cofacilitation with someone who has highly developed skills in overseeing risk activities and providing maximum assurance of their safe execution. There are also a variety of training programs, i.e., National Outdoor Leadership School and Outward Bound, which can help the counselor gain leadership skills and the confidence to venture into outdoor risk activities with clients. This is simply an extension of the eclectic concept which moves the counselor into a previously uptapped area of expertise. At the same time, McAvoy (1978) suggests that many qualified outdoor leaders do not have the skills necessary to promote optimal group interaction, problem-solving, and integrational themes. This area appears to offer an excellent opportunity for extending professional boundaries and having some fun in the process.

INTEGRATION: CONTINUING THE UPWARD SPIRAL

As Wiesen (1977) has pointed out, negatively oriented remedial therapy can actually perpetuate client problems by reinforcing cathartic wallowing in areas of misery which are difficult to change. In contrast, the integration phase in the preventative context is generally a springboard for insight toward new action, and the extension of clearer personal conceptualizations into everyday life. This second phase should support the client's upward spiral toward higher functioning and involves a personal integration of the experience contacted in the alternative environment. Rather than draining client energy through continual rehashing of negative life experiences, our emphasis is on generating new energy as a revitalization source and for enabling the client to better cope with areas of difficulty. We focus on strengths as we move into action, and this theme generally extends into our integrational efforts preceding and following the risk activities. Often the exhilaration that comes with the risk activity spills over and sets the tone for personal insight in the individual or small group integrative sessions. Intensity level may be as high as in working with chronic areas of human misery, but the tone is generally positive and enthusiastic. The immediacy of the risk experience places the integrational focus on the current life situation so that immediate concerns tend to emerge (instead of unworkable historical baggage) and can be dealt with more readily. Facing difficult challenges head on seems to predispose toward a willingness to deal with areas of needed change. Instead of gradually (often painfully) working upward through a hierarchy of fears, the risk context may enable clients to see their life perspective from the top as they come off of or approach peak experiences. New insights generated from this perspective may be translated into goals and strategies for change. We have had these clients move quickly into constructive changes since we have already established a strong relational base.

The motivation in remedial counseling may typically be nurtured through relational means, but the motivational base in risk counseling stems from the action activity itself. Maslow (1962) saw motivational forces as organized hierarchically. Lower-level (fundamental) physiological and safety needs were seen as preemptive of intermediate psychological needs (love and esteem). Likewise, the minimal satisfaction of psychological needs was seen as a prerequisite for the release of energies directed at higher-level needs. Only then can the individual be freed to deal with metaneeds or self-actualization concerns surrounding creativity and the fulfillment of individual potential. Risk activity brings these need systems into clear focus and optimizes the opportunity for transcending a sequential hierarchy (Maslow, 1971). Rather than plodding upward through a need sequence as typifies remedial counseling, the risk experience may allow the individual to see all motivational sources from the top downward. Energy gains related to risk activities may serve as an impetus to increase motivation directed at esteem and interpersonal needs and certainly provide a unique perspective on the individuals' requirements for safety. The lowest-level needs (physiological) may actually support high-level creativity as mind and body work in unison to accomplish the task. Glasser (1976), in fact, emphasizes this intense interaction as it emerges out of total involvement with intense physical activities. Consequently, we would capitalize on the expanded motivational base in our integrative work and develop client insight through an expanded version of Maslow's scheme. We visualize their motivational interaction by extending the familiar triangle of needs into a more complex and synergistic picture which is characterized by expanding each level of the motivational picture (see Figure 7-2). This can serve as a theoretical guide for the counselor's integrational work in developing client insight related to the risk experience.

We are not so naive as to think that all participants in alternative environment

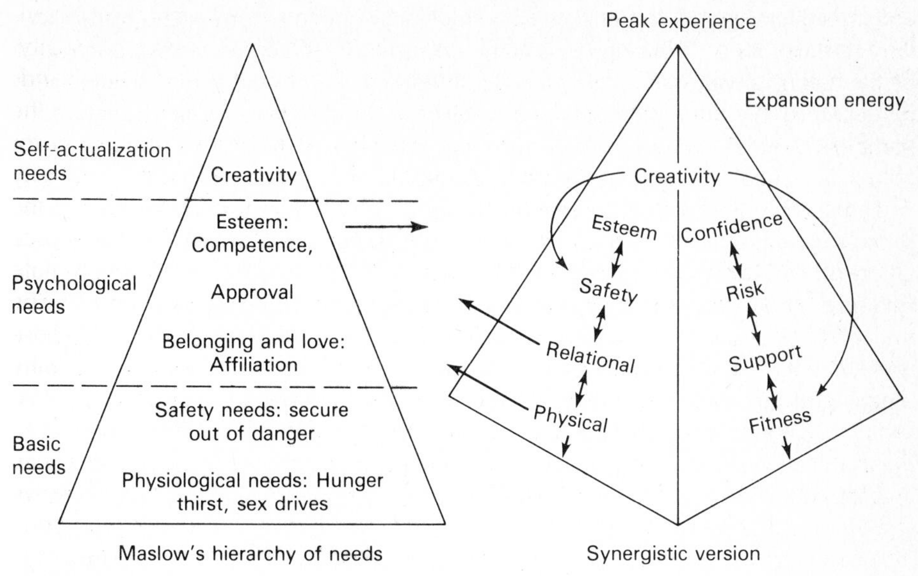

FIGURE 7-2
Maslow's hierarchy revised. *(Adapted from Maslow, 1962.)*

risk experiences (no matter what selection procedures are used) will be high-functioning. Physical prerequisites for risk activities are relatively easy to establish (cardiovascular fitness, agility, etc.), but the more subtle psychological levels of preparedness may be difficult to identify. Consequently, all group compositions will reflect a certain level of heterogeneity in terms of overall health. Thus, risk activities offer opportunity for highlighting strengths and identifying areas of needed change. The counselor in this context is on the site where the risks take place and becomes a model as well as a coauthor for the client's efforts. The counselor is actively involved (in vivo) rather than providing homework assignments to be carried out in between therapeutic sessions. The counselor is also in a key position to offer remedial resources for problem concerns that emerge during the integration work. The referral (to self or another counselor) can be handled smoothly as an extension of the risk program. Counselors themselves have become natural resources through building trust and presenting themselves as models for healthy living. The counselors' visibility and vulnerability set the stage for client accessibility to them as therapeutic resources. Stress situations may serve to break down defensive facades presented by some participants. As a chronic weakness is uncovered, the counselor is in an excellent position to develop a remedial program as an extension of the risk experience and integrational work. As strengths emerge among higher-functioning clients, the counselor's job is to help the client formulate new areas of challenge and to facilitate the transfer of insight into lifestyle considerations. The counselor may rely on the same integrational skills outlined in the preceding chapter, but healthy clients often generate their own insights and are generally able to translate new understanding into construction programs for action. In these kinds of groups, the counselor's efforts are further enhanced by the high motivational level and natural helping skills of other high-functioning participants. We have witnessed many cases in which relatively low-functioning participants have become linked with high-functioning members and have been able to translate this involvement into a mutually beneficial friendship.

The question highlighted in the integrational phase becomes how to apply self-knowledge gained during the experience into daily life (Rice, 1979). The translation process flows automatically for some and yet may require considerable skill on the counselor's part with others. Perhaps the translation process itself (and the ability to apply it to future situations) becomes the most important thing that some clients may take with them. Ultimately, the goal is to promote a more meaningful integration of physical, spiritual, and psychological aspects of personality. Enhanced self-esteem may become the structure upon which these elements develop. Miles (1978) suggests, "having confronted self and met a physical and spiritual challenge, a person may become more secure in their identity, more confident in themselves."

As Rice (1979) points out in his discussion of Outward Bound programs, the opportunity for limit testing offers personal renewal potential for *all* participants. Active participation on the part of counselors sets the stage for revitalization in their own lives. The energy generated by seeing potential come to life and the activities themselves offer an alternative to the energy drain so frequently experienced in our remedial efforts. As the professional perspective begins to slant toward seeing potential rather than weakness in others, a renewed sense of personal potential may also emerge. A different perspective on professional skills may also be generated as remedial methods are placed in an alternative context. Surrounded by basically high-functioning clients, the counselors themselves may gain new energy and insight which can be transferred back into their personal and professional lives.

RELATIONAL BYPRODUCTS: ESTABLISHING A BROADER SUPPORT BASE

Whereas the initial focus (and considerable ensuing energy) in remedial counseling is concerned with building a relational support system and counselor credibility, the relational aspects of developmental/preventative counseling may emerge as a byproduct of the activities themselves. In preventative programs emphasizing risk, the initial investment of energy is focused on the challenge activities themselves. While some group/relational activities may be consciously built into the program (particularly with lower-functioning groups), the relational component primarily forms as a natural complement to intense involvement in the activities. Stress situations are confronted in a peer context and interdependence encourages individual risk and even survival in extreme cases. Whereas the individual in his or her challenge effort is often highlighted, a sense of group cohesiveness and mutual respect may merge parallel to individual accomplishments (Brown and Simpson, 1977). Individual confidence is enhanced through helping others as high-functioning participants have an opportunity to invest their skills and positive attitudes into peer success.

Whereas the emphasis in these activities is on individual esteem, Yalom (1970) points to the close interrelatedness of self-esteem and group cohesiveness. Whereas the relationship holds true in the present context, we envision dramatic differences in the group dynamics of preventative risk groups as compared with the classic picture of remedial group therapy. Participation in risk-group activities with healthy people puts negative self-elements into a state of dissonance and serves as a motivational force to improve the self-picture. In this case, the group experience (when properly facilitated) brings out the best in its participants and emerges as a positive force in itself. This tends to be in stark contrast with remedial group therapy in which destruction may feed off of destruction and the only initially healthy individuals succumb to the negative group process. (Unfortunately, group therapists are not immune to these effects.) In depicting the development of high-functioning groups involved in risk activities, Lee and Bednar (1977) identify the following sequence: "(a) initial ambiguity, (b) increased structure, (c) increased risk taking, (d) development of group cohesion from shared group experiences, and finally (e) increased personal responsibility." While the counselor looks for opportunities to build on group support, it tends to develop as a natural byproduct of the challenges being faced. Cooperation rather than competition is encouraged. As Webster (1978) concludes, cooperation emerges as the group recognizes individual strengths which can contribute to the accomplishment of group goals.

Once again, we would actively seek out high-functioning clients as participants for developmental/preventative risk activities. This is a key to their success and the success of not-so-high functioning members who may inadvertently become involved. Success breeds success, and the experience of success (or even acceptance of failure) within a group context promotes mutual support. This kind of support not only promotes successful engagement in the challenges themselves, but also becomes the material for extending individual support systems beyond the adventure activities. These people tend to have a sound support base to begin with, but even the highest-functioning individuals can expand their relational supports. In fact, they tend to be continually open to new relational facets of their personal development. One of the most gratifying aspects of our involvement with these kinds of programs has been the lifelong friendships we have established as byproducts of intense risk-related experiences. Our own bond of friendship has also intensified in the process. While issues of dependency and the relational transfer to out-of-therapy supports involves some of the most difficult work of remedial counseling, solid relational supports often emerge naturally in the context of risk programs with healthy clients.

APPLICATIONS AND IMPLICATIONS: OUR EXPERIENCE

Our involvement with outdoor risk programs evolved as an extension of our experience with remedial counseling. While integrally involved in helping clients prepare for change, the action phase generally remains an extension of the work done during counseling sessions into everyday life. Much of the excitement and reward of remedial counseling comes as we process successful homework assignments and gear toward transferring counseling gains into future life directions as we near termination. Still, we tend not to be there when change occurs. Perhaps this need for increased participation in the actual change process gradually moves us more and more out of our own offices and out to where the action occurs. Of course, the authors' lifelong interest in outdoor recreation and geographic location helped set the stage, too. Our first efforts were also motivated by a need to increase group cohesiveness within our graduate counseling program. Consequently, we sponsored a series of social events for our graduate students staged in the outdoor environment (rafting, picnics, hiking). These experiences were so successful (and fun) that we expanded our applications to some of our smaller undergraduate psychology classes. The next application was an effort at staff development within our division of psychology and counselor education and eventually to other divisions on campus in the form of wilderness retreats. We were greatly encouraged by the enthusiasm and improved communication generated through these adventures. We saw relationships change in positive directions at the personal, professional, and group levels. One of our staff members experienced a professional rebirth through the insights and renewed support generated in one of our programs. Some of our activities have since become the core of our summer orientation programs for new students and have been met with refreshing enthusiasm.

Gradually we moved from a social development emphasis in the outdoor environment toward a direct effort at promoting risk activities which was stimulated by three risk recreation professionals (Gregg Simmons, Bill Howell, and Ben Cossman) from our outdoor program and a grant-funded premountaineering training course that we helped develop. This ropes course was located on our campus and modeled after those designed through Project Adventure (Rhonke, 1977). We began using this course as a pivotal ingredient in our outdoor adventure program for the purpose defined by its designer: (1) increase participant's sense of personal confidence; (2) increase mutual support within a group context; (3) develop agility and physical coordination; (4) develop a sense of physical self-appreciation among participants; and (5) increase familiarity and identity with the natural environment. Some of our early work with this course was remedial as we worked with youth delinquent groups, but also focused on basically healthy groups of adolescents and adults from our local community and college.

More recently we have felt a need to expand our efforts into a more formal structure. As a consequence, we offered a 3-semester-hour, 5-day class (Psychology of Risk: An Outdoor Adventure) last spring. We used a wide variety of outdoor risk activities to structure personal challenge for our class members (see Appendix Three for an outline), and the results were gratifying. Whereas we became involved in remedial therapy with a couple of the participants after our program, most of our integrational efforts were positively directed as healthy people applied new insights into their life situations. While several months have passed since this class, members (although varying widely in age and cultural background) are still maintaining close contact and are asking for a repeat class.

Several lifelong friendships have been formed and new lifestyle formulations implemented. We presented a slide show of our experiences on campus and had 130 students and community people in attendance. We are currently planning some exciting challenging activities for our sequel class. We plan to develop this class along with one of our recreational specialist friends, but are also engaged in risk leadership training ourselves.

Since our initial application of outdoor risk activities within our counselor education program a number of years ago, we have seen several new directions emerge. A brief "get acquainted" exposure to the outdoors has evolved into an expanded and integral part of our graduate students' practicum experience (Golsan, 1978). Our initial focus in counselor education is logically personal awareness and development—outdoor experiences have provided an excellent stimulus for accomplishing these goals. While we have structured activities early in the first semester, our graduate groups have intended to develop their own outdoor activities. At the time of this writing, most of our present group of students are involved in a student-led retreat in our nearby mountains. One of our students formalized these activities into a winter camp retreat (Tozer, 1979) as part of his research requirement. This particular program was carried out under his direction in the middle of a bitterly cold winter. Snow-shoeing, skiing, snow-caving, and winter survival camping were used as mechanisms for challenge. As a result, new areas of strength emerge and several near crises serve to test participant endurance. The experience served as a stimulus for intense discussion in numerous in-class practicum sessions that followed. This has spilled over into outdoor risk programs, developed and facilitated by graduate counseling students, which have been offered to undergraduate and community people (Baldwin, 1981; Hitchcock, 1981). The initiative on the part of our students to share their experience reflects the enthusiasm for this part of our graduate program and allows us to experience an alternate supervisory role while our students develop skills in preventative counseling. We have been further encouraged by the response we have received from presentations given on these themes to groups of counselors and counselor educators (Golsan, Nicholson, and Simmons, 1979; Nicholson, 1980). The response has been enthusiastic to say the least, and has stimulated plans to develop risk workshops for various professional groups ranging from physicians to teachers. A lot of possibilities exist and meaningful formats can range from 1-hour slide show awareness overviews to intensified semester-long programs. Webster (1978) suggests that these themes can even be successfully integrated into overall curriculum structures as is evidenced by Project Adventure. Learning in the classroom has a vital role to play, but personally relevant education should not be limited to the confines of four walls. Experience in the alternative environment can reinforce and add potency to the material of the academic setting. Concepts become more immediate and reinforce the student's motivational investment in the subject matter.

Before we allow our enthusiasm to get out of hand, a couple of words of caution may be in order. Growing participation in high-risk activities has led to some hesitancy on the part of sponsoring agencies related to a fear of possible accidents and resulting litigation. Meier (1978) points to the increasing number of deaths resulting from adventure activities, and cautions that actual risk must be carefully weighed against potential benefits. We emphasize rational risk programming with careful preparation and adequately trained leadership. From a legal perspective, Frakt (1978) suggests that adventure activities are not particularly vulnerable to liability when properly supervised. Participants must be of an age level that allows a reasonable assessment of actual risks and a level of physical conditioning and skill that allows them to reasonably encounter the challenges presented. He points out that liability is much less in wilderness and unimproved land activities than where man has created unnatural hazards. Also emphasized is the importance of explaining and demonstrating potential hazards so that prospective participants become responsible for their choice in engaging in the activities. As he suggests, "Although there seems no reason to fear undue or excessive liability, the carelessly or foolishly run program still runs a high risk." He encourages leaders to adhere to basic safety standards and to make provision for personal injury insurance. Rankin (1978) adds to the legal picture by stating that most courts hold that individuals are responsible for their own actions when they have been made fully aware of possible dangers and have voluntarily selected to engage in the activity. Understanding the risk is a critical ingredient and points to the responsibility of the risk leader to carefully explain the activity.

A second area of concern involves the selection of activity participants. Whereas remedial applications have their place, we have emphasized the use of risk programming for high-functioning individuals. We also recognize the values and inevitability of a certain level of heterogeneity in any group composition. Since an understanding of activity risks is critical from a legal point of view, Rankin (1978) cautions toward carefully screening for those who might have "diminished mental capacity" because of age, maturity, or retardation. Safeguards in the selection of those with physical problems is also warranted. Whereas the psychological testing industry has invested tremendous energy in identifying human weakness, its effectiveness in strength assessment is dubious. We know of no instrument designed specifically for the screening of high-functioning individuals. Consequently, we see the self-selection process as the logical alternative. We would recommend that leaders present a thorough overview of program rationale to facilitate client decision making and to specifically model and clarify the risk involved with each specific activity. Nothing can replace the sensitivity of leaders to participant needs and risk expectancies as they interact with participants at each juncture of the program.

While participation in risk programming offers revitalization potential for counselors, program preparation provides a stimulus for their personal/professional creativity. Planning the next "trip" has been a source of excitement and expectancy for both authors since we were kids. Visual imagery is recharged by the anticipation of the next risk experience, and we are challenged to create a unique exposure to alternate environments which may also demand "off-season" skill building and commitment to physical fitness programs. Both authors have greatly reduced their weight control problems (losing over 30 pounds each) since their involvement in risk activities and fitness programs began about 7 years ago. Unlike remedial counseling, modeling is most prominent in the action phase, and this puts demands on the leader to stay in shape and continually assess potential personal challenges. With the basic physical and attitudinal building blocks in order, the creative counselor is freed to develop an unlimited array of alternative environment experiences for clientele and have fun doing it.

SUMMARY

We have presented a modification (reverse order: action, integration, relational) of the Carkhuffian remedial model of counseling for preventative/developmental work with high-functioning clients. The actual risk-related experience becomes the focus and serves as a stimulus to generate personal insight which can be translated back to everyday life. Group cohesiveness and close relationships tend to form as a byproduct of the intense involvement inherent in high-risk activities. Each of these phases was developed in some detail along with suggestions for creating risk-based programs and some precautions regarding high-risk activities. The concept of alternative environments was presented as involving any unfamiliar setting offering intense challenge and was seen as a context which can be created by the counselor in an effort to develop client strengths. Implications for the use of risk activities in counselor education and other applications were also discussed.

REFERENCES

Ardell, D. *High level wellness.* New York: Bantam, 1977.

Baldwin, P. *Risk recreation: Its effects upon the group cohesiveness of college students.* Unpublished research project, Adams State College, Alamosa, Colo., May 1981.

Bordin, S. Counseling psychology in the year 2000: Prophecy or wish fulfillment. *The Counseling Psychologist,* 1980, *8*(4), 24–26.

Brown, L. T., Ruder, V. G., Ruder, J. H., and Young, S. D. Stimulus seeking and the change seeker index. *Journal of Consulting and Clinical Psychology,* 1974, *42*(3), 311.

Brown, W. K., and Simpson, B. F. Group and individual growth through the out-of-doors. *American Journal of Correction,* November-December 1977, 8–38.

Carkhuff, R. R., and Berenson, B. G. *Teaching as treatment.* Amherst, Mass.: Human Resource Development Press, 1976.

Carlson, J. Health, wellness, and transpersonal approaches to helping. *Elementary School Guidance and Counseling,* 1979, *14*(2), 85–90.

Chaney, A. C., and Hurst, J. C. The applicability and benefits of a community mental health outreach model for campus ombudsman programs. *Journal of College Student Personnel,* 1980, *21*(3), 215–222.

Dickey, H. L. Outdoor adventure training. *Journal of Physical Education and Recreation,* 1978, *49*(4), 34–35.

Dinkmeyer, D., and Dinkmeyer, D., Jr. Holistic approaches to health. *Elementary School Guidance and Counseling,* 1979, *14*(2), 108–112.

Drum, D. J., and Figler, H. E. *Outreach in counseling.* New York: Intext Educational Publishers, 1973.

Eder, S., Learning on the rocks. *American Education Magazine,* 1976, *12*(3), 16–21.

Frakt, A. N. Adventure programming and legal liability. *Journal of Physical Education and Recreation,* 1978, *21*(3), 49–50.

Girdano, D., and Everly, G. *Controlling stress and tension: A holistic approach.* Englewood Cliffs, N.J.: Prentice-Hall, 1979.

Glasser, W. *Positive addiction.* New York: Harper & Row, 1976.

Golsan, G. Trust at twelve feet. *Colorado School Counseling Newsletter,* Fall 1978, 1–5.

Golsan, G., Nicholson, J., and Simmons, G. *Daring to try—using the natural environment in counselor education.* Presentation at the American Personnel and Guidance Association meeting, Las Vegas, Nev. April 1979.

Goodyear, R. K. Counselor or community psychologist. *Personnel and Guidance Journal,* 1976, *54,* 512.

Hammit, W. E. Outdoor recreation: Is it a multi-phase experience? *Journal of Leisure Research,* 1980, *12*(2), 107–110.

Hitchcock, R. *The effects of a wilderness experience on group cohesiveness.* Unpublished research paper, Adams State College, Alamosa, Colo., May 1981.

Ivey, A. E. Counseling psychology—the most broadly based applied psychology specialty. *The Counseling Psychologist,* 1980, *8*(4), 12–16.

Jones, M. D., and Stewart, N. R. Helping the environment help the client: A sequenced change process. *Personnel and Guidance Journal,* 1980, *58*(8), 501–506.

Krumboltz, J. D., and Menefee, M. Counseling psychology of the future. *The Counseling Psychologist,* 1980, *8*(4), 46–48.

Landsberg, G. The state of prevention in mental health. Perspectives *in Psychiatric Care,* 1977, *15*(1), 15–17.

Lee, F., and Bednar, R. L. Effects of group structure and risk-taking disposition on group behavior, attitudes, and atmosphere. *Journal of Counseling Psychology,* 1977, *24*(3), 191–199.

Lupin, M. *Peace, harmony, and awareness.* Austin, Tex.: Learning Concepts, 1977.

McAvoy, L. Outdoor leadership training. *Journal of Physical Education and Recreation,* 1978, *49*(4), 42–43.

Maslow, A. H. *Toward a psychology of being.* New York: Van Nostrand, 1962.

Maslow, A. H. *The farther reaches of human nature.* New York: Viking, 1971.

Meier, J. R. Is the risk worth taking? *Journal of Physical Education and Recreation,* 1978, *21*(3), 7–9.

Morrell, W. H., Oetting, E. R., and Hurst, J. C. Dimensions of counseling functioning. *Personnel and Guidance Journal,* 1974, *52*(6), 355–359.

Miles, J. C. The value of high adventure activities. *Journal of Physical Education and Recreation,* 1978, *21*(3), 27–29.

Miller, T. M. Outdoor counseling. *Journal of College Student Personnel,* 1980, *21*(1).

Nicholson, J. *Risks in moving upstream.* Presentation at Colorado Personnel and Guidance Association meeting, Colorado Springs, Colo., October 1980.

Ogilvie, B. Stimulus addiction: The sweet psychic jolt of danger. *Psychology Today,* October 1974, 88–94.

Otto, H. A. The potential of people. *Elementary School Guidance and Counseling,* 1979, *14*(2), 92–96.

Pelletier, K. R. *Mind as healer, mind as slayer: A holistic approach to preventing stress disorders.* New York: Dell, 1977.

Peterson, C. A. The right to risk. *Journal of Physical Education and Recreation,* 1978, *21*(3), 47–48.

Rankin, J. S. The legal system as a proponent of adventure programming. *Journal of Physical Education and Recreation,* 1978, *21*(3), 51–52.

Rhonke, K. *Cowtail and cobras.* Hamilton, Mass.: Project Adventure, 1977.

Rice, B. Going to the mountain. *Psychology Today,* December 1979, 65–81.

Schreyer, R. M., White, R., and McCool, S. F. Common attributes uncommonly exercised. *Journal of Physical Education and Recreation,* 1978, *21*(3), 36–38.

Selye, H. *The stress of life.* New York: McGraw-Hill, 1976.

Sprinthall, N. A. Guidance and new education for schools. *Personnel and Guidance Journal,* 1980, *58*(7), 485–489.

Stachnik, T. J. Priorities for psychology in medical education and health care delivery. *American Psychologist,* 1980, *35*(1), 8–15.

Taft, H. W. *Risk and safety in outward bound.* Greenwich, Conn: Outward Bound, 1979.

Tozer, R. J. *Developing self-concept in guidance and counseling students.* Unpublished masters thesis, Adams State College, Alamosa, Colo., Summer 1979.

Tyler, L. The next forty years. *The Counseling Psychologist,* 1980, *8*(4), 19–21.

Webster, S. E. Project adventure: A trip to the unknown. *Journal of Physical Education and Recreation,* 1978, *21*(3), 39–41.

White, B. Natural challenge activities. *Journal of Physical Education and Recreation,* 1978, *21*(3), 20–22.

Wiesen, A. *Positive therapy.* Chicago: Nelson-Hall, 1977.

Wrenn, C. G. Observations on what counseling psychologists will be doing during the next 20 years. *The Counseling Psychologist,* 1980, *8*(4), 32–35.

Yalom, I. *The theory and practice of group psychotherapy.* New York: Basic Books, 1970.

Zuckerman, M. Sensation seeking: The biological need for high stimulation. *Psychology Today,* February 1978, 39–99.

Zuckerman, M., Bone, R. N., Neary, R., Mangelsdorff, D., and Brustman, B. What is the sensation seeker? Personality trait and experience correlates of the sensation seeking scale. *Journal of Consulting and Clinical Psychology,* 1972, *39*(2), 308–321.

Zuckerman, M., Buchsbaum, M. W., and Murphy, D. L. Sensation seeking and its biological correlates. *Psychological Bulletin,* 1980, *88*(1), 187–214.

CHAPTER **8**

A MULTIMODAL MODEL: ENTERING THE SPIRITUAL AND PHYSICAL DOMAINS OF COUNSELING

Paralleling the strides made toward prevention, a movement toward an expanded scope of counselor intervention has gained considerable momentum during the last decade. Whereas prevention can be seen as an emerging component of eclecticism, the expansion of the boundaries of eclecticism itself reflects the current *Zeitgeist*. Previous boundaries for counselor intervention not only stopped at remediation, but tended also to focus narrowly within the confines of the client's psychological functioning (affective, cognitive, behavioral). Unfortunately, this was often to the exclusion of the spiritual and physical domains which are a part of everyone of us. As indicated in Chapter 2, there appears to be a growing openness to humanity's true complexity. This awareness needs to be translated into an expansion of counselor roles which will hopefully lead to an increased interdependence among helping professional subgroups. We believe that the expansion of these boundaries will serve as an impetus for a more creative perspective on counseling as we move through the present decade.

As we indicated previously, the antagonistic schoolism that marked the earlier stages of development of our profession must give way to a more comprehensive eclecticism that is flexible and sensitive to client uniqueness and complexity. Ever since the defections of the neo-Freudians, our profession has been characterized by a proliferation of competing theories of psychotherapy. Whereas these theories have typically focused on limited aspects of human functioning, they have generally been presented in global panacean terms. These dogmas have tended to overgeneralize the relevance of specific causes and treatments of human problems and have perpetuated dichotomous thinking. These unidimensional theories have been mutually exclusive in their view of the human condition as basically predominated by one domain of existence. In recent years we have become increasingly aware of the absurdity of elevating any monolithic theory to a status of universal applicability. It appears unlikely that even the simplest forms of human interaction are anything less than multicausal and complex. The creative counselor orients all existing theory to the unique needs of the client by permitting the best of all schools to exist simultaneously (Diamond and Havens, 1975). Consequently, we need a broad-based conceptual framework—one that recognizes client complexity by allowing the counselor to enter (when appropriate) the client's spiritual and physical world.

Considerable interest has been generated recently regarding the movement toward concepts of holistic health. Wrenn (1980) points to the mind/body/spirit interaction as a primary theme for counselors in the next 20 years. Gross (1980) also challenges counselors to consider the implications of the holistic movement and defines it in terms of three criteria—integration of mind, body, spirit; preventive emphasis on fitness; and deliberate elicitation of client self-responsibility. Whereas the roots of this trend toward more holistic schemes can be traced to Thorne (1967), the professional climate of his era was apparently not prepared to accept his ideas. Carkhuff and Berenson (1967) added to Thorne's initial efforts, but their framework remained largely within the confines of psychological functioning. Pappas (1970) described a system of "multiple counseling" that provided a broader basis for assessment and technique application but his efforts fell largely on a deaf professional ear. Kaplan (1974) also emphasized "the principles of multideterminism and multilevel causality in the eclectic treatment of a wide range of human disorders," but her system of determinants (environmental, relational, intrapsychic, biological, and learned factors) made a relatively small impact on the therapeutic community.

It was not until the middle of the last decade that our profession showed signs of accepting this broader perspective. The efforts by Lazarus (1973,1976) finally provided momentum to the notion that counselors might become involved beyond the confines of the psychological aspects of client functioning. His multimodal approach has stimulated the production of related model construction and serves as an excellent guide for us to build upon. His scheme organizes problem definition and intervention along seven modalities: behavior, affect, sensation, imagery, cognitive, interpersonal relations, and drugs/diet. This system (BASIC-ID in acronym form) integrates diagnosis and treatment and extends counseling past its traditional boundaries. It cuts across the gamut of areas involved in the remediation of human problems. Judah and Keat (1977) suggest that the BASIC-ID model "is limited only by the imagination of whoever applies it" and have adapted it to a wide range of counseling settings. They have developed a 29-item, 5-point rating scale for assessment of client functioning on the seven relevant areas. In addition, it appears to have considerable potential for use in the definition and delivery of developmental and preventative counseling services. Keat (1979) has also translated the Lazarus model into his own format, using the acronym HELPING to represent a system for "creating your own personal orchestration." It is a practical eclectic approach "for imposing a personal multimodal growth profile." An example of this model has been abstracted from his article and is presented

TABLE 8-1
MULTIMODAL GROWTH: HELPING CHILDREN

Health	Diet Sleep	Nutrition information Turning-off training
Emotions-feelings	Expression of feelings Joy attainment Anxiety	Relationship enhancement Fun training Relaxation training
Learning-school	Auditory appreciation Motor coordination Study skills Sensory awareness	Music, e.g., multiplication rock Movement dance How to study; tutors Yoga
Personal relationships	Getting along with others	Friendship training
Imagery-interests	Developing self-worth Awareness of imagery Meditation	IALAC story Imagery training Transcendental meditation (TM)
Need to know	Decision making Identifying irrational ideas	Problem solving practice Rational therapy
Guidance of A,B,Cs	Attention paying Assertiveness	Game playing Behavior rehearsal

Source: Adapted from Keat, 1979.

in Table 8-1 for the reader's use. This example focuses on HELPING children, but the model has been adapted for parent education, peer counseling, and other target groups. He suggests that the content in each mode should be rank-ordered to establish a starting point. Subsequently, work in each mode can be added as the client builds and transfers successes. We would add that the selection of modes and related intervention techniques (in response to evolving client needs) is the essence of creative counseling. The personal eclecticism of creative counselors is multimodal, and they are free to simultaneously integrate interventions across interacting modalities.

The most thorough multimodal guide for counselors involves a further refinement of the earlier work done by Lazarus (1973) and Lazarus and Fay (1975) and is presented by Hammond and Stanfield (1977) as a means for "conceptualizing multidimensional determinants of problems and for treatment planning." It offers flexibility, simplicity, comprehensiveness, and is not bound to any simple theory. The Multidimensional Assessment and Planning Form (MAP Form), as it is known, offers an excellent theoretical extension of the basic Carkhuffian model. These two models then can be used simultaneously with the MAP Form extending the boundaries of its predecessors.

From an assessment perspective, the Hammond and Stanfield (1977) model moves beyond the confines of traditional systems and away from the labeling of individuals. The problems of other systems (diffuse goals, self-fulfilling prophecies, confusing jargon, dehumanization, unreliability, etc.) are dealt with through an emphasis on multicausality and specific patterns of response. As the authors put it, "The goal of this model is not to assign people to diagnostic categories, but rather to serve as a basis for making intervention decisions for broad-based, eclectic treatment." It encourages the assessment of a wide range of factors in defining the clients' problems and related counseling goals. They conclude:

> The MAP Form was designed to be a tool, guide, and summary sheet for assessment and treatment planning to facilitate multidimensional therapy in the spirit and tradition of Lazarus, Kaplan, and Thorne. Its use fosters thoroughness in assessing problems and assets across six dimensions, promotes systematic analysis of the adaptive function and situational determinants of symptomatic behavior, encourages systematic treatment planning, and reminds one to consider when and where to intervene rather than approaching therapy with specific direction (p. 16–17).

This model can then serve as a valuable resource for the creative counselor who applies it with flexibility as it is modified by the ongoing needs of the client. In keeping with our historical perspective in Chapter 2, we would like to adapt these earlier works to reflect the five basic domains of human existence. While the Carkhuffian model is an excellent guideline for eclecticism, its emphasis is on the psychological domains (affective, cognitive, behavioral) as reflected in the movement from relational to integrative to action phases of therapy. This focus has largely been to the exclusion of the spiritual and physical domains of functioning, and we believe that the creative counselor cannot afford to ignore these two important areas. All five major areas inevitably interact, thus our real concern becomes how and when to deal with them. They represent an indivisible unity in which the interactive whole is more than a sum of its parts. Their relationship is reciprocal so that any domain can only be understood within the context of its interaction with the remaining domains. Whereas we establish no universal hierarchy, the creative counselor may certainly prioritize domains and their relative importance within the context developed with each individual client. Consequently, this model not only highlights the theme of expanded eclectic intervention but also reminds us of the issues surrounding the timing of our interventions. Priorities not only emerge within each domain, but also between the various major areas of client functioning. Hammond and Stanfield (1977) provide some good reminders in establishing these priorities: flexibility as a guiding force; intervention in areas of relative strength initially to maximize the success potential; use of less complex approaches initially.

The current *Zeitgeist* appears to support the expansion of the counselor's involvement to incorporate, or at least be open to, consideration of the spiritual and physical domains along with the areas of psychological functioning. As with the expansion toward developmental/preventative counseling, movement into the spiritual and physical functioning of our clients places additional demands on counselors for expanding their conceptual and interventional perspectives. Before developing these two forgotten areas, let us explore the major areas of concern within the psychological domains. This coverage focuses logically on affect first since this area tends to be most heavily weighted early in counseling as reflected in the relational phase presented previously. In keeping with Hammond and Stanfield's (1977) analysis of affectual considerations, emotions are the products of physiological, cognitive, and behavioral determinants. First, emotions may be conditioned physiological responses to social/environmental events which are reduced or intensified as they interact with cognitive and behavioral cues. The second set of determinants involve internal stimuli of a cognitive nature in which imagery and self-talk provide the labels for internal states of arousal. Third, our behavior serves to act out our emotions and may intensify or reduce the related affect. Finally, emotions themselves may serve adaptive functions as they are used to manipulate the client's interpersonal environment. Given this perspective, it becomes clear that the emotional domain of the client is an integral consideration as we move from the relational to integrational and action phases of the counseling process. The communication framework presented in Chapter 3 offers a useful way to conceptualize this interaction. Furthermore, the basic Carkhuffian model provides us with an excellent response resource for creatively dealing with the client's emotional areas of concern. Our responses can set the stage for acceptance and also serve as a vehicle through which the client can gain control over affective states. Attention to the external and internal antecedents of emotion and their related cognitive and behavior counterparts can serve as a structure for helpful counselor intervention. The client can move toward controlling negative emotional states and the creation of more constructive ones.

Within the cognitive domain, we move into the client's evaluative perspective. The integrative phase of counseling focuses on restructuring the client's perception of self and his or her interpersonal world while leading to goals for related behavior change. This cognitive domain includes our perceptual, logical, and interpretive processes and serves (via visual imagery) as a pivot upon which emotions and behavior are built. Packaging their self-exploration into a workable picture of their current condition is of critical importance in paving the way for behavior change and the emergence of a healthier self-concept and lifestyle. Numerous resources have evolved to help creative counselors in their efforts at cognitive restructuring (Beck, 1976; Mahoney, 1974; Raimey, 1975; Lazarus and Fay, 1975, for example). Whereas Hammond and Stanfield (1977) include convictions and beliefs within the cognitive domain, they suggest that spiritual considerations evolving around value and moral issues may deserve special attention. They conclude that a "truly comprehensive system for analyzing human behavior" might include spirituality as a separate dimension. However, they point out that this area is controversial and give it only passing recognition. We would propose that the spiritual domain is of critical relevance to the human condition and is inevitably interwoven into virtually all client problems. It cannot simply be ignored because it may be controversial and difficult to assess. Indeed, we will develop this area as related to the expanding involvement of the creative counselor as a major thrust of this chapter. Perhaps a formal sanction (with related guidelines) for counselor involvement in the client's spiritual arena will open the door for more realistic and comprehensive involvement.

The behavioral domain has been largely equated with the action phase of the Carkhuffian model where relationship and insight are translated into more constructive lifestyle patterns. Whereas the consideration of client behavior obviously runs throughout the counseling process, it frequently becomes the major focus as counseling progresses beyond initial insights. The behavioral domain includes specific lifestyle problems related to situationally or chronically self-defeating patterns. Consideration of client behavior may move us into every aspect of lifestyle from interpersonal to vocational to issues of responsibility and client self-control. We may focus on the elimination of destructive patterns or the creation of constructive behaviors through the help of a wide variety of techniques offered from behavior therapists. (We have identified some of these resources in Chapter 6 and new publications are continually being added.) Hammond and Stanfield (1977) have developed the physical dimension as a separate category in their multidimensional system, and point out that human behavior is ultimately mediated at a biological level through neurochemical change. They point to a growing body of research directed at the influence of genetic and biochemical factors in psychopathology. Any comprehensive system of counseling cannot afford to ignore these factors. While the medical model has frequently been dismissed as narrow and dogmatic, human psychological and spiritual functioning cannot be arbitrarily separated from physical considerations. The necessary interaction between medical and other helping practitioners has been highlighted by the increasing concern over the causes and treatment of stress-related (psychophysiological) disorders. Certainly, the creative counselor is aware of the potential physical contributions to client problems and is willing to make a referral to medical practitioners when appropriate. Beyond the remediation of physical problems which may demand medical attention, we would like to extend our consideration of the physical domain into areas in which the counselor can effectively intervene and incorporate physical concerns into a counseling framework. Once again, creative involvement in any domain cannot occur without the fundamental background of attitudes and skills. Consequently, we would like to expand our coverage of the physical domain in the latter part of this chapter.

INSIGHT INTO THE SPIRITUAL DOMAIN

According to Pelletier (1977), the waning influence of organized religion in recent decades has given way to a "devaluation of spiritual concerns in contemporary society." Many people today seem to lack a central unifying life theme upon which to form their approach to life stressors. Uncertainties surrounding a basic life direction become a major source of stress itself. As Pelletier puts it, "When belief is absent, there is a feeling of incompleteness and a spiritual vacuum which can be extremely disconcerting." He notes a marked absence of philosophy with which we must approach a continually changing scientific and social community. Spiritual issues are fundamental to all human efforts at living. We cannot afford to ignore this fact simply because these issues are difficult and the quest for a viable set of life principles may itself be confusing. As Collins (1976) states:

> Man is a unity who rarely has a strictly spiritual need, a solely psychological abnormality, an exclusively social conflict, or a purely physical illness. When something goes wrong with one aspect of the unified person, the individual's whole being is affected. A healer

> may specialize in medicine, psychotherapy, or spiritual counseling, but each must remember that there is no sharp line between spiritual, emotional, volitional, or physical in man. One symptom may cry for healing, but at such time the entire body is off-balance. We must not deal with the spiritual and forget the person's psychological or physical needs (p. 56).

Likewise, ignoring spiritual needs may be counterproductive to our interventions at the psychological or physical level. The question for the creative counselor is really not which area is most important, but where to place our initial emphasis and how to intervene effectively in each area as they interact. As with any area of counselor intervention, however, the first issue is with the counselors themselves. It is clear that counselors can deal effectively within the clients' spiritual arena only to the extent that they are dealing constructively with the spiritual concerns in their own lives. Our spiritual existence cannot, and should not, be completely separated from our professional involvement with client problems any more than we can draw a fine dividing line between our personal and professional lives. Certainly there is a need to monitor value-laden interventions and to remember that counseling is for the client. But counseling must also be a way of life for us in order to be effective. Only when our own lives are in basic order (and growing) can we hope to creatively enter into the wide range of issues facing our clients.

In order to help our clients wade through the spiritual dimensions of their existence, we must be in a process of facing the personal and professional ramifications of our own spiritual lives. This can be tough, and healthy models, both personal and professional, may be difficult to find. Maybe it helps to accept a degree of uncertainty as part of the search. Wrenn (1973) points out that there is a degree of certainty in accepting ambiguity and that some confusion can serve as a stimulus for growth and change. It is important not to be self-critical in a destructive sense as we engage in the search for our own meaning and model this attitude in facilitating client integrative efforts. Tentativeness can be a freeing agent that can reduce our fear of exploring and open up new potentials for assurance and commitment. Mosher, Carle, and Kehas (1965) define a need to examine dogmas that produce a false sense of security. They also recognize a remarkable ability that human beings have, or can develop, "to blend a tentative outlook with firm commitment to chosen values." They note that William James recognized the ultimate uncertainty of value foundations while acknowledging the constructive force of a mature religious conviction. The seeming irony of tentativeness and commitment can actually be the basis for developing a healthier life perspective within ourselves and our clients.

Wrenn (1973) suggests that religion is an evolving dimension of life. Religion is not changeless. As our method of serving others changes with maturity, so does our religious experience change with increased wisdom. God does not change. Basic universal truths remain stable, but our perception of these things evolves. If it does not, then a destructive gap between faith and philosophy (intellectual understanding) may emerge and erode our very foundations. Disillusionment with organized religion can easily ensue along with a related rejection of basic commitment. Unfortunately, our need to relate to the infinite may be irrevocably damaged by our critical evaluation of its vessel (the organized church). We see the resulting crises reflected in our client's agonizing battle between childhood assumptions and adult intellectual conceptualization. Guilt over examination or change may be paired with unfulfilling acceptance or ironic rejection. Risk emerges again as a key element for spiritual self-examination and our client's pursuit of increased personal understanding.

Some theologians have moved beyond a focus on individual guilt and inadequacy to emphasize the spiritual basis for human potential. For example, at age eighty-three E. Stanley Jones (a fundamental theologian) believes that everything from the lowest cell to the highest man has within it an urge after a fuller, higher life (Jones, 1968). Emerging dimensions in spiritual growth emphasize the importance of achieving meaning in life by finding commitment outside one's self. The authors have discovered that client spiritual growth is often accompanied by increased involvement in constructive church-related programs, community service projects, and peer group activities in which human relationships are supportive and the individuals feel that they are providing for other people's needs. Meshing the belief in the unlimited potential of human beings and the need for personal commitment necessitates a creative process. We believe that focusing on these two ideas while working within the spiritual dimension of our client's life has greater potential (in most cases) for successful client movement than a process which limits its attention to guilt and human frailty.

The theme of helping the maturing individual struggle with spiritual development is increasingly reflected in our profession's growing tolerance for diversity. We have been impressed with a new willingness among our colleagues to deal openly with the spiritual aspects of counseling. As with most maturing processes, however, this openness has emerged out of a long history of rigidity. Collins (1976) points out that the major responsibility for counseling once resided with theologians. Only in the last century has this shifted into medicine and later into psychiatry, psychology, and social work. As it became removed from the church, counseling was seen by some as beyond the limits of the untrained clergy. Freud developed his esoteric system which seemingly placed counseling on an academic pedestal beyond the reach of the clergy. In the process, the spiritual dimension became largely ignored or even viewed with disdain. Whereas the neo-Freudians largely rejected Freud's overemphasis on libidinal forces, Victor Frankl reacted to his negativism and dehumanization. Frankl (1963) brought the spiritual dimension back into counseling through logotherapy. He saw the individual as a unity between physical, psychological, and spiritual. The spiritual domain was seen as central and the basis for self-understanding. Freedom was defined as a key for moving beyond the biological and determining the quality of our existence. The choices inherent in freedom are further based in responsibility to oneself and God. The basic aim of this approach is to confront the clients with their responsibility for their symptoms. The counselor is a critical ingredient in forming a relational basis for self-confrontation. The counselor's own philosophy becomes integral to the entire process but is not directly forced upon the client who is ultimately responsible for a personal system of beliefs.

Revised interest in the spiritual aspects of counseling in the last two decades has fostered a growing body of pastoral counseling literature. Even most conservative seminaries now have courses in pastoral counseling. The clergy remain in a critical position to intervene in the lives of individuals, and some of the literature generated from this perspective has relevance to counselors in general. Unfortunately, some orientations have been dogmatically pushed on secular counselors while suggesting that Christian counseling should have no similarity to secular approaches. Once again, the creative counselor may want to thoughtfully work through some of this dogmatism in search of pieces which can be blended constructively into a personal eclectic framework.

Several recent contributions offer considerable potential for organizing our involvement in the spiritual aspects of our client's struggles. Carlson (1979) sees spiritual development as providing meaning and direction to life and offers some excellent guidelines for integrating these times into counseling. Tyler (1980) offers a focus on choice within value development and some helpful hints on confusion reduction. Shostrom (1976) has included a spiritual growth synergy component as a major theme of "actualizing therapy" and offers a conceptual expansion of earlier humanistic models of counseling. Collins (1976) also presents a system of counseling consistent with the basic Carkhuffian model and biblical principles. He builds his approach on the core conditions and offers a scriptural basis for each. These principles are then translated into techniques for intervention in the psychological and spiritual areas.

We find that spiritual considerations are an essential component of any comprehensive efforts at integrative understanding. Increased spiritual integration is also pivotal in the sense that it may increase the client's support seeking (from God as well as the counselor) while intensifying the motivational basis for behavior change. Helping the client clarify spiritual beliefs may foster a sense of acceptance and generate new hope as a motivational resource. Integration of spiritual beliefs may also serve as an impetus for assessment and constructive change in the physical dimension.

Regardless of their level of skill in dealing with spiritual issues, creative counselors remain aware of their own limitations. Referral to competent pastoral counselors may be the preferred route at times. Their intervention may be critical and pave the way for your efforts in other areas. A couple of examples may clarify this point.

One of the authors received a severely depressed patient as a referral from a local physician. A woman in her forties, this client had withdrawn from virtually every healthy life involvement (work, family, sexual activity, etc.) during the preceding 6 months. The depression appeared initially to have been precipitated by changes in family composition (two of her children had moved away from home) and physical problems which had led to a hysterectomy. However, once a good relational level of trust was established, a much more basic ingredient was reluctantly revealed. During a series of personal crises, she had begun to attribute her bad fortune to the controlling forces of a distant relative. This person was perceived as having "cast an evil spell" on the client as a means of revenge regarding a long-term family feud. Every ensuing piece of misfortune reinforced this belief. The impact was devastating. She rarely left her home and refused to answer the telephone. Unfortunately, her devout religious upbringing served to further support her irrational beliefs. It was apparent that drastic behavior changes were in order, but her belief system blocked the chances for change. Direct confrontation of her belief system would have only met with defensiveness and a loss of counselor credibility. A referral was in order. In this case, a contact with a "curandera" (folk medicine practitioner) was made and an appointment arranged. Maybe we could work from within her belief system. After several sessions with this healer, the client became convinced that no evil spell existed. The door was open now for behavior change. She was also open to hear her physician's confrontation regarding the actual effects of the hysterectomy which were previously misunderstood. It also opened the door to counseling interventions that could be accepted and translated into constructive directions. Change occurred rapidly, and a positive cycle was initiated. Her depression dissipated dramatically as she became reinvolved with her work and all aspects of family life.

More recently, a student from one of our classes came in for help. A chronic history of destructive heterosexual relationships had culminated in a recent unwanted pregnancy. A two-stage approach was set in motion. Stage one was to focus on the alternatives to the immediate pregnancy-related crisis. Stage two would be concerned with the chronic self-destructive patterns related to men and her corresponding low self-esteem. Building counselor credibility in handling stage-one concerns was seen as a prerequisite for moving on to the long-term issues. We began to look at alternatives for handling her pregnancy. Alternative one: get married and keep the child herself (a series of meetings were set up with the young man involved). Alternative two: carry the child full-term and then turn it over for adoption. An appointment was arranged with a local adoption agency. Alternative three: arrange for an abortion. She was asked to consult with a local nurse practitioner regarding the actual process of abortion. Through a series of sessions, considerable information was gathered and it became clear that abortion was to be her chosen alternative. Now some real value-related problems emerged. She was a strict Catholic, and a lay person had in essence told her that she would lose contact with God should she have an abortion. Once again, a referral was in order. Not to just any priest, but a very special one who combines a firm belief system with compassion. The alternatives were reassessed, the crisis faced squarely, and we are now working on the more basic issues surrounding self-destructive attitudes and behaviors.

A final note on remedial referrals for spiritual concerns is in order. One of the devastating aspects of client problems is the sense of hopelessness and alienation. Positive steps can rarely be taken in counseling without the establishment of a support system. And yet, counselors themselves are too frequently the only immediate usable support for the clients. Once the upward spiral is initiated, and motivation toward change increased, the potential for expanding the clients' support systems may emerge. Here is where an assessment of a possible local religious affiliation can become part of the integration process. As with any referral, caution is warranted. However, there are healthy groups of spiritually oriented individuals in every community and an appropriate referral can help to maintain the positive strides made in counseling. This may also appear as a termination consideration as we transfer changes in attitude and behavior into an ongoing supportive environment.

Beyond the remedial concerns, the spiritual dimension plays a potentially important role in preventive/developmental counseling. Once again, we can often make more impact by moving our interventions "upstream." This may be particularly true in the areas of values and moral development. Unfortunately, churches often resemble battlefields of gossip and conflict rather than a prototype of a therapeutic community. Collins (1976) offers some guidelines for preventive counselor involvement in the local church, but our intervention may be much broader. The values clarification approach (Simon, 1974; Simon, Howe, and Kirschenbaum, 1972) has considerable practical and conceptual value for moving the counselor into a wide range of proactive involvements. This is a formal system built on specific strategies geared toward helping clients understand their own values and those of others. It is readily applicable in small or large group settings and offers considerable support to the counselor's efforts at helping their clientele sort out life purposes. Rokeach and Regan (1980) have also extended this approach into a systematic model for allowing the counselor to assist clients in formulating plans for life change and growth. The approach helps clients take a personal look at current values and possible alternatives while encouraging them to translate new understanding into a more effective lifestyle. Once again, the integrative work (including the spiritual domain) sets the stage for constructive change in the behavioral and physical domains.

BEYOND BEHAVIOR CHANGE: ENTERING THE PHYSICAL DOMAIN

While the cognitive schools of psychotherapy have emphasized insight and perceptual restructuring, they have largely ignored the inextricable connection between thinking and physiological changes which support our emotional responses to life events. Likewise, action-oriented therapies have tended to focus on behavior change to the exclusion of the inevitable interplay between physical and behavioral functioning. All client problems and strengths are ultimately mediated (inhibited or enhanced) by biological variables. To overlook this important aspect of client functioning is to dismiss potentially crucial points of understanding and limit our efforts at improving their quality of living. We believe that counselors have overlooked (out of ignorance or fears) their clients' physical well-being for too long. The time has come to constructively approach this area of potential client involvement. We feel that the time is ripe for extending counselor awareness and expertise into the physical dimensions of client functioning. Hopefully, the structure and resources presented in this section provide an impetus for this emerging direction. However, our discussion is only a starting point with any real expertise coming only from extensive study and experience.

Current professional trends support a more realistic appreciation of human complexity and a related diversity of approaches designed to enhance human effectiveness. Physical development has been included within the framework of eclectic counseling (Carkhuff and Berenson, 1976), but has been only partially delineated. They suggest that physical fitness interacts with emotional and intellectual determinants of human behavior but approaches the physical area from a primarily diagnostic viewpoint. Physical functioning is presented on a five-point continuum ranging from sickness to stamina and equated with the level of client strength, endurance, and cardiorespiratory functioning. Within the medical arena, a holistic orientation toward health care has also emerged (Pelletier, 1979) which emphasizes "The recognition that each state of health and disease requires a consideration of all contributing factors: psychological, psychosocial, environmental, and spiritual." Traditional mind/body (psychological/medical) dualism is seen as increasingly giving way to a new medical model which places more of the responsibility for physical health on the patient and encourages an expansion toward a lifestyle orientation among practicing helping professionals. This also entails a shift from a strictly disease-based model toward a prevention and optimal-health viewpoint. The importance of crisis medicine is not negated but seen as extremely limited and even counterproductive at times.

BEYOND BEHAVIOR CHANGE: THE COUNSELOR'S ROLE IN PHYSICAL REMEDIATION

For centuries the medical profession has rested on the assumption that human functioning as a whole could be analyzed through its biological foundations. This classic view served as a basis for scientific inquiry focused on "minute aspects of biological processes" which have tended to exclude psychosocial considerations (Pelletier, 1979). The physicians' purpose became analogous to the repairperson who fixes machines. The ultimate source of illness has been seen as biochemical entities which attack the body from the outside, while the physician's task is to target surgical and chemotherapeutic cures at the afflicted area. Consideration of the person as a whole became secondary to a growing body of medical technology. The view of the passive victimized patient and authoritative healer was transferred into the medical model of psychiatry formulated a century ago. This mental illness concept still pervades much contemporary thinking. Whereas we agree that this orientation is extremely limited, it may still have a viable place in the overall treatment picture. There is always a biological component to our clients' problems, and we must keep medical factors in mind as we deal with our clients. There are times when a referral to a competent medical practitioner is appropriate and when their specific expertise may need to complement or supersede our interactions. We suggest that creative counselors are sensitive to organic contributing factors among their clientele and have developed a good working-referral relationship with local physicians.

There may be a tendency among counseling professionals to dismiss physical problems as being "in the client's head." This narrow-minded thinking can be potentially disastrous for the client. We can recall numerous cases over the years which mandated appropriate referral to medically trained healers. A couple of examples may illustrate our point. As a counselor in a university counseling center, the senior author received a variety of referrals from the student health services. Some of these were made out of frustration that physicians felt with complaining students who were perceived as needing psychological help (which was frequently the case). One young man had made repeated visits to virtually all the staff physicians complaining of a buzzing noise in one ear. They had exhausted their diagnostic resources and patience, so he was sent my way as a last resort. My impression was that of a basically high-functioning individual under increasing stress due to unsuccessful attempts to treat his presenting problem and the not so hidden message that he was "crazy." I felt a definite need for further physical examination and made a referral to a neurologist at the university medical center. To my surprise, this intensive examination revealed a treatable disease-based problem which was completely cured in a few days through chemotherapy. My would-be client was elated and so was I. More recently, a middle-aged woman entered my office and began a long dissertation concerning her numerous physical ailments. Before writing her off as a hopeless hypochondriac, I queried her regarding her use of medication. She proceeded to provide a live demonstration by pouring over 20 medicine bottles onto my desk (maybe the weight of her purse was part of the problem). Once again a medical referral was in order so I called an extremely competent colleague and presented the picture to him. Following a diagnostic interview, her drug intake was limited to two prescriptions, and the physician assured her that the interactive effects of her other medications played a major role in her lethargy and generally poor health. Positive physical changes were evidenced dramatically within a few weeks, and we were able to take a close look at building a more constructive approach to handling relationships and alternatives to self-destructive behavioral patterns. The creative counselor must be sensitive to the physical factors which contribute to client problems and call upon the expertise of the medical community when in doubt.

Beyond the need for occasional medical referrals, the emerging treatment of psychophysiological disorders (hypertension, asthma, migraine headaches, and so on) has expanded the counselor's boundaries for direct intervention. We are becoming increasingly aware that stress interacts with biochemical factors to change the onset, severity, and duration of a wide range of organic disorders (Pelletier, 1979). Whereas the physician remains the sole administrator of surgery and medication, other health care providers can deal with expanding the range of exercise, dietary, and lifestyle modifications to alleviate stress-related disorders. Counselors can also educate their clients regarding their responsibility in determining the course and intensity of their physical problems. Pelletier (1977) reminds us, however, that it is our legal and ethical obligation to have appropriate medical support in dealing with physically related disorders.

A growing body of research provides strong support to the notion that physical and psychological fitness go hand in hand. Exercise programs have been successful in relieving depression (Kostrubala, 1977), whereas fitness training has been helpful in reducing anxiety (Folkins, 1976) and problems with headaches (Atkinson, 1977) and asthma (Marley, 1977). Others have applied an intense physical fitness program to counselor education, and found that it can help improve self-concept while reducing depression, somatic complaints, fear, and fatigue among student participants (Hilyer, Jenkins, Denton, Dillon, Meadows, and Wilson, 1980). Harper (1978) builds a case for the spiritual, physiological, and psychological benefits of "jogotherapy" and provides some excellent guidelines for developing a jogging program with our clients. Miller (1980) goes on to clarify the close relationship between nutrition and behavior and outline the key points of dietary invention. He concludes that the importance of a healthy diet can no longer be ignored by counselors. We agree and encourage the reader to develop a wide range of awareness and related strategies for interventions within the physical domain.

Behavioral medicine deals with genuine organic problems but emphasizes the role of the person's behavior in the development and alleviation of medical illness (Shapiro and Surwit, 1976). Biofeedback training is a prime example of behavioral medicine. This approach encourages self-control developed through practice as a means for symptom alleviation in a variety of disorders. As with chemotherapy, these techniques are really effective only to the extent that the client breaks the stress cycle at a physiological level long enough to develop better lifelong stress management patterns. A major difference lies in the fact that alleviation is through self-control rather than through the ingestion of external agents which may not adequately consider unique individual differences. Biofeedback involves an operant procedure through which voluntary control can be gained over autonomic nervous system responses. Physiological processes are monitored electronically and information sent back to the individual (usually auditory or visual) which can be used to shape these functions. This process can then be used to train the client toward a more effective use of the damaged system. Biofeedback training has clearly become a legitimate component of the counselor's repertoire and may be used after supervised instruction or brought into play on a referral basis. It may serve as a primary care technique or be integrated into other intervention approaches. Either way, the creative counselor cannot afford to ignore the potential value of this approach in dealing with stress-related physical disorders. Several excellent resources are available which provide specific guidelines for therapeutic application (Gatchel and Price, 1979; Green and Green, 1977; Wickramasekera, 1976). Olton and Noonberg, 1980 provide perhaps the most thorough and practical guide for clinical practice and delineate a basic model for biofeedback training as well as specific steps to follow for different disorders.

There appears today to be a growing acceptance of biofeedback training. Wickramasekera (1976) suggests that the biofeedback movement is reminiscent of the popular reception of behavior therapy in the 1960s. He attributes its popularity to its scientific base, electronic packaging, and a growing paranoia regarding traditional medical practice. He goes on to indicate that "biofeedback has brought the body back into clinical psychology" by providing the practitioners with the hardware to help their clientele monitor internal processes. He adds that "The range of biological knowledge required to do biofeedback research or to intelligently and more specifically treat functional syndromes (e.g. headache, ulcer, cardiovascular dysfunctions, et cetera) will cause increasing convergence between medical and psychological education." We have come a long way from the old mind-body dualism. Once again, biofeedback training provides a good example of how divergent fields (psychology, medicine, electronics) have been brought together to improve our ability to help our clients live healthier lives (see Figure 8-1).

Both authors have had considerable success in applying biofeedback techniques with stress-related disorders, and continue to receive a steady flow of clients referred from local physicians (stemming in part from workshops we have conducted for medical professionals). Perhaps an example will illustrate the use

FIGURE 8-1
The biofeedback movement.

Mind psychology	Advances in electronic monitoring systems	Psychosomatic medicine
Respondent conditioning	Galvanic skin response	New understanding
Operant conditioning	Electroencephalogram	of autonomic nervous
Behavior cognitive therapy	Pulse monitoring	stress response
Systematic desensitization	Thermistors	patterns related to
Relaxation training	Respiratory monitors	vascular system
Autogenic training	Electrocardiograph	circulatory
Visual imagery	Electromyogram	glandular
Individual personality		neuro-physiology
		homeostatic systems
		drug research
		biomedical technology

Biofeedback (voluntary control of autonomic responses through the monitoring of internal processes via their auditory or visual representation of such techniques as presented in the context of remedial counseling. One young woman comes to mind. She was in one of our senior-level psychology classes and came in for help regarding psychophysiological disorders following a class presentation. She was a straight-A premed student who had suffered from migraine headaches throughout her college career. These headaches were incapacitating and were occurring with increasing frequency and intensity. She was afraid that she would not survive in medical school if something was not done soon. She was under the care of a neurologist who had prescribed several medications without success. We moved quickly into an action approach (relational base was carried over somewhat from previous class contacts and her insights into the problem were quite well developed) directed initially at breaking the stress cycle and increasing her self-control of headache onset and related pain. She was taken through a progressive relaxation procedure paved with visual imagery during the second session (Goldfried and Davison, 1976). The procedure was tape-recorded, and she was instructed to listen to the 15-minute tape twice daily at her own convenience prior to 15 minutes of biofeedback practice, using a thermometer. (This could be done between classes in our biofeedback room.) She was instructed to do a pre- and postsubjective rating (on a 1–100 scale) of each training session and to keep an ongoing daily log of her progress. As she progressed in her relaxation and temperature control skills, both the tape recording and biofeedback device were gradually removed, giving her increasing responsibility. Within a few weeks she had developed remarkable control of her stress response and was actively using it at the earliest onset of migraine symptoms (prodromal cues) to increase external body temperature and preempt the pain phase. She experienced dramatic success in controlling the migraine headaches (reducing incidence from an average of eight episodes per month to only one mild migraine during the 6 months of treatment and follow-up). A tremendous sense of confidence and elation emerged along with her newly found skill. With the stress-pain cycle broken, a variety of other counseling techniques were employed (cognitive restructuring and assertive training became major themes) to help her develop a more permanent low-stress lifestyle. Genuine changes occurred in her perception of and approach to life events during the following 20 hours of counseling and related homework assignments between sessions. What caused the positive change? Certainly the biofeedback training itself played a part, but perhaps the creative application of several interconnected techniques made the difference; or maybe the relational support she felt from her counselor and renewed sense of personal control were the key dimensions.

The popularity of biofeedback training has been accompanied by the increasing acceptance of a variety of related self-control methods ranging from autogenic and relaxation training to meditation. The new fascination with the psychological control of physical functions has even spilled over into the popular media as evidenced by the number of yogis displaying their talents on television. Jencks (1977) suggests that the instruments of biofeedback have only limited purposes with the mind and body serving as the ultimate agents of internal feedback and self-regulation. She points out that biofeedback instruments are expensive, generally provide feedback on only a single physiological function, and present a potential problem with dependency. Furthermore, she argues that most of the purposes of biofeedback (muscle relaxation, changes in heart rate and body temperature, pain relief, and so on) can be accomplished without the use of electronic monitoring and feedback systems. She presents a variety of techniques which can be creatively applied in facilitating the client's efforts at generating increased self-control over physiological functions. Her methodologies are congruent with the notion of personal responsibility in health care and offer the counselor viable alternatives to and supplements for the more rigorously based biofeedback techniques. We are excited about the possibilities and encourage the reader to become well versed in a variety of self-regulatory approaches. Several resources are available to help the interested counselor develop further awareness and expertise regarding these methods (Benson, 1975; Girdano and Everly, 1979; Goldfried and Davison, 1976; Pelletier, 1977). Of course, the critical issue involves developing an individualized program specifically designed for each client.

There is growing support for the psychological impact on all levels of physical functioning and dysfunctioning. Stress appears to be a common denominator in almost all forms of physical anomalies. Seligman (1975) has clearly documented a close relationship between perceived personal helplessness and physical breakdown and death. Laboratory research suggests that stress can deplete body immunities while increasing the incidence of tumors (Raimey, 1975). Physical problems as well as health are being seen as a reflection of lifestyle and personality. This kind of thinking has even extended into the areas of cancer research as investigators look to personality variables as causally related to cell malignancy (Achterberg, Simonton, and Matthews-Simonton, 1976). Practical clinical implications have also been developed and offer some remarkable possibilities (Simonton, Matthews-Simonton, and Creighton, 1978). In reviewing Simonton's work, Scarf (1980) suggests that cancer develops in an atmosphere of emotional despair and that psychological forces can be utilized to defeat or at least delay the course of its spread. Patients are encouraged to take charge of their illness and use positive imaging to produce an inner battlefield where malignant cells are attacked and conquered by healthy cells. Admittedly, this approach is controversial and has reaped considerable criticism from some corners of the medical community. Nevertheless, it represents a growing edge of remedial medicine and affirms our position that physical disorders emerge out of complex interaction of many factors. Pelletier (1977) adds that we might logically view physical disorders as indicators of excessive stress: "A medical symptom may be a useful signal of the need for change in other parts of the person's life." These may serve as early warning signs calling for preventive intervention.

PHYSICAL AVENUE FOR PREVENTING ILLNESS AND MAINTAINING HEALTH

In extending the traditional disease orientation of medicine, the holistic model opens the door for counselor intervention in heading off physical disorders and moving their clients toward optimum health. Traditional medicine has focused on repairing the damages resulting from self-defeating life patterns, and has produced many sophisticated pieces of biomedical technology which can prove dramatically successful in a limited number of cases. At best, however, this kind of technology serves a limited function of repairing damage long enough for the patient to build more constructive support behaviors. Pelletier (1979) espouses a more ecological orientation where "changes in self-destructive life-styles are seen as necessary to prevent the occurrence of severe disorders." He further argues:

> Future directions in health must involve the positive modification of the conditions which lead to disease rather than simple interventions in the mechanisms of a disorder after it has occurred. Health is not the absence of disease but a state of optimum functioning about which we have very little information. Medicine focuses narrowly upon the particular area of acute illness and traumatic injury, but most disorders and health issues far exceed that narrow range of inquiry (p. 5–6).

The counselor, then, can be legitimately involved in helping clientele develop their own systems of preventive medicine based on stress management, dietary, and exercise considerations. Individuals are ultimately responsible for many of their health functions and may be helped immensely by an objective appraisal of destructive patterns and programming for a healthier lifestyle. Unfortunately, too many counselors preempt successful involvement in preventive considerations by allowing their own vascular and respiratory systems to degenerate as they sit in their offices. We have to practice what we preach in order to be a viable resource and model for our clients in any area. The area of physical fitness is no exception. We were struck in a recent luncheon for counselors by the observable level of obesity among many of the participants. When fitness was brought up, one nationally known counselor commented that he "just didn't have time." What a sad piece of irony. No time to take care of ourselves? Perhaps we must be absolutely convinced of our personal worthiness in order to structure the time it takes to maintain physical fitness. And if we are not so convinced, how can we possibly expect to instill a sense of self-worth in our clients (let alone any illusions about building constructive fitness lifestyle programs).

Both authors did some serious self-confrontation several years ago regarding our own levels of physical functioning. We both can vividly recall a backpack fishing trip designed for stress release that turned into a physically grueling experience. As we painfully worked our way out of a steep canyon, we met a man on the trail who was thoroughly enjoying his hike—a man over 70 years old. Both of us resolved to make some changes so that our next outdoor adventure would involve more fun than fatigue. Instead of eating lunch, we set aside that hour every day for an intense physical workout (running, racquetball, or basketball) and have maintained that program faithfully for nearly 6 years. In fact, that daily exercise period (now generally 1 1/2 hours) has become so fixed in our schedules that we maintain our program whether we are on campus, attending conferences, or on vacation. The benefits have gone far beyond the remedial intent of losing weight and our original goal of enabling us to enjoy outdoor and recreational activities more fully. As experienced by our clients, we find that our systematic physical program increases our stamina for personal involvement in all of our activities. Second, a consistent commitment to daily personal and professional activities is extended because of our increased stamina. This stamina-commitment cycle is a positive developmental experience for each author.

We believe that the benefits have been indirectly manifested through many of our clients who we have encouraged to enter individually designed fitness programs. Often the preventive focus comes after initial remedial work with the client as illustrated by a female freshman from one of our psychology classes. Sparked by a class presentation on the psychological benefits of healthy physical functioning, she asked for help in conquering a chronic obesity problem. A goal of reducing 30 pounds over a period of 4 months was set during our initial session, and she was requested to receive the go-ahead from a local physician before our next session while keeping a base-line record of food consumption and related environmental cues. (We incorporated many of the ideas presented by Foreyt, 1977). Keeping records became an important incentive in itself and was maintained throughout the ensuing 4 months of counseling. A 4-week "crisis phase" was initiated in which she lost about 12 pounds on a stringent diet, while we dealt with restructuring related self-defeating patterns. She was elated. As we moved from the remedial focus, she was asked to read an exercise book (Cooper and Cooper, 1973) and consider possible exercise alternatives to replace negative eating habits. She chose to initiate a 1 mile walk-run program during the fifth week of counseling and was asked to read Sheehan's (1975) book to clarify issues regarding appropriate shoes, clothing, and specific steps of program escalation. Incidentally, these outside reading assignments were also written up and used for extra credit in her psychology class. She bought a jogging outfit, structured a daily time for exercise, and continued keeping records. Her calorie intake was increased slightly, and she continued to lose from 1 to 2 pounds per week. Gradually she decreased her time for the mile as her running segments were extended systematically. It is significant to note that she had previously maintained an extremely sedentary lifestyle and that any form of vigorous physical exercise was foreign to her self-image. This image changed. She eventually purchased several exercise outfits and even wore them to class. The concrete steps of increasing exercise and decreasing waistline were tremendously reinforcing—she was ecstatic with her accomplishments. Our sessions became shorter and focused positively on her progress and minor program readjustments. She developed several new friends who were fitness-minded and supported her efforts while she continued to escalate her running way beyond initially perceived limits. The emphasis shifted from weight loss to fitness, and she eventually reached her desired weight. As of 1 year later, she has maintained her weight loss and continues with a sound exercise program. Whereas her need for a therapist is gone, she still stops by quite often to chat as a genuine friendship has emerged in the process.

Building preventive fitness programs with our clients parallels behavior change strategies in the action phase of counseling and many of the same principles apply. As in any behavior modification program, care must be taken to individualize appropriate step gradients (medical consultation may at times be a prerequisite) toward physical activity. The experience of success for the client is paralleled by encouragement and program reevaluation by the counselor. Maintaining the program long enough to receive the positive benefits (moving beyond the pain phase) is critical. It takes time and sustained effort to break down negative patterns or build healthy ones. The fitness area offers no exception. The counselor must build the necessary expertise for developing the fitness program with the client or work on a referral/consultative basis with someone who has the required knowledge. Fortunately, the popularity of fitness programs during the last decade has served as an impetus for the production of numerous excellent resources (Cureton, 1973; Harper, 1978; Sheehan, 1975; Spino, 1977; Spino, 1979). An eclectic blend of several approaches individualized for the client is recommended. Perhaps the most complete and useful system is the aerobics program developed by Cooper and Cooper (1973) which is extremely flexible and conducive to explicit record-keeping (based on a point system) and progress checks. It also identifies numerous activities which are fun and can become integral to the client's fitness program. In keeping with our theme, it also emphasizes that fitness is not merely freedom from disease but promotes cardiovascular-pulmonary fitness which prepares the individual to better cope with daily life stressors. It is based on high-energy output and ironically involves placing your body under periods of intense stress which gradually expand heart and lung capacity and endurance. Thus, it

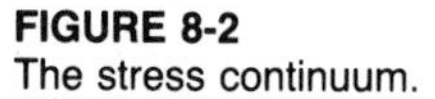

FIGURE 8-2
The stress continuum.

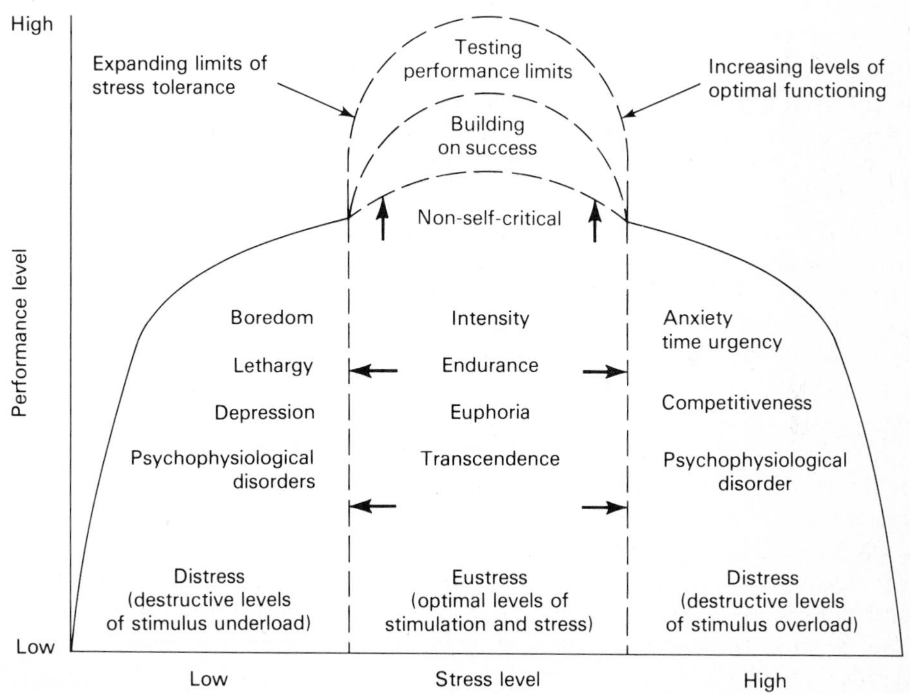

becomes an immunization process for stress management as the limits for stress tolerance are expanded. What was stressful gradually becomes pleasurable, and may transfer into other areas of functioning such as improved self-image and general outlook on life. This notion of expanding self-boundaries in the physical and psychological areas is reminiscent of Selye's (1976) notion of eustress and is illustrated in Figure 8-2.

According to Girdano and Everly (1979), stress is functional only to the extent that it is translated into constructive activity. From a preventive standpoint, the strengths gained from exercise can be transferred into the performance of daily activities. Paradoxically, strenuous physical exercise is generally followed by a period of relaxation. The key to maximizing the personal benefits of the exercise period, then, lies in the learned ability to transfer its benefits back into life situations while learning to move efficiently from stress-producing exercise to feelings of deep relaxation. This requires practice and a regular regime of exercise. It has to assume a high priority so as not to be crowded out by other activities. Counselors will also appreciate that building this kind of pattern may involve external reinforcement initially (their praise or confrontation) until the activities eventually become self-rewarding. There are no real shortcuts. The fun and pleasure benefits come only when a good level of supportive fitness is achieved and maintained. Ultimately, however, the client may develop a powerful preventive agent which allows for daily dissipation of unhealthy levels of stress and corresponding sense of accomplishment.

PERSONAL GROWTH THROUGH PHYSICAL FITNESS

Girdano and Everly (1979) suggest that "the highest purpose of physical exercise is that of well-being." To move beyond remedial and even preventive considerations, high-level physical functioning enhances self-concept, generates positive energy, and can foster a sense of tranquility. Gains in this area tend to promote gains in the psychosocial and even spiritual domains. In moving toward higher-level benefits of physical activity, they recommend that the activity be low on ego involvement. Intense competitive drives can be counterproductive and may increase the stress level built around a vicious cycle of self-doubt and impaired performance. The activity itself is not as critical as the purposes and attitudes with which we enter the activity. Once again, the creative counselor may be in a pivotal position in terms of setting the attitudinal stage for constructive behavioral and physical change.

Glasser (1976) also emphasizes the importance of a noncompetitive approach to activities in achieving the positive addictive state (PA). The PA state is viewed as a transcendent, trancelike state of mind in which creative and pleasurable self-enhancing forces are released. As with the basic theme of our book, creative forces cannot be released until prerequisite skills (and, in this case, physical conditioning) have been developed. Once again, this involves endurance (Glasser suggests an hour per day over a long period of time) which is best supported by a noncritical sort of personal competition. He suggests that you are the only one who needs to measure improvement and that these assessments must be done without self-criticism. Doubt destroys the PA state and blocks the flow of positive energy that might otherwise spill over into other aspects of daily living. Self-competition at controlled levels provides the energy to push you to your limits, but it is easy to go across this fine line. Maintaining a personally effective balance, then, can become a challenge in its own right. We know this from our own daily experience with racquetball as we battle against each other (and ourselves) on the local courts. The more intensely we play, the greater the physical and psychological (often, a genuine feeling of elation) benefits. Unfortunately, self-criticism can destroy the entire process and preempt the truly artful aspects of the game. At its best, however, we experience a transition from intense concentration and effort toward free body movement and creative play.

The fitness gained from regular exercise can also serve as an impetus for transferring physical skills and conditioning into high-risk activities and purely pleasurable types of outdoor adventure. Intense involvement in such activities tends to reduce the impact of external stressors. Success yields exhilaration, whereas failures can serve as a basis for new self-awareness.

SUMMARY

We have built a rationale and practical guideline for a multimodal approach to counseling as a basis for more creative and realistic intervention. This viewpoint moves us beyond the traditional boundaries of psychotherapy (focused on affective, cognitive, and behavioral functioning) toward an expanded involvement in the complex lives of our clients. Counselors simply cannot afford to ignore the clients' spiritual and physical domains of functioning and must expand their role (both attitudinally and in terms of skills) to creatively deal with client concerns in these important areas. Our coverage of counselor involvement in the spiritual arena extends the integrational themes of generating insight into a more usable picture of client strengths and weaknesses. Likewise, dealing with the physical aspects of client concerns was seen as an expansion of the behavior change phase of counseling. Physical considerations in remedial counseling were discussed along with the potential for developing client physical fitness as a resource for preventative and developmental counseling. Once again we promoted our basic theme that creative counseling is based on a continually expanding repertoire of skills and a genuine appreciation of client complexity.

REFERENCES

Achterberg, J., Simonton, O. C., and Matthews-Simonton, S. *Stress, psychological factors, and cancer.* Fort Worth. Tex.: New Medicine, 1976.

Atkinson, R. Physical fitness and headache. *Headache,* 1977, *17,* 189–191.

Beck, A. T. *Cognitive therapy and the emotional disorders.* New York: New American Library, 1976.

Benson, H. *The relaxation response.* New York: Avon, 1975.

Carkhuff, R. R. and Berenson, B. G. *Beyond counseling and therapy*. New York: Holt, 1967.

Carkhuff, R. R. and Berenson, B. G. *Teaching as treatment*. Amherst, Mass.: Human Resource Development Press, 1976.

Carlson, J. Health, wellness, and transpersonal approaches to helping. *Elementary School Guidance and Counseling*, 1979, *14*(2), 85–91.

Collins, G. *How to be a people helper*. Santa Ana, Calif.: Vision House, 1976.

Cooper, K. and Cooper, M. *Aerobics for women*. New York: Bantam, 1973.

Cureton, T. K. *Physical fitness and dynamic health*. New York: Dial, 1973.

Diamond, R. E. and Havens, R. A. Restructuring psychotherapy: Toward a prescriptive eclecticism. *Professional Psychology*, May 1975, 193–200.

Folkins, C. H. Effects of physical training on mood. *Journal of Clinical Psychology*, 1976, *32*, 385–388.

Foreyt, J. P. *Behavioral treatments of obesity*. New York: Pergamon, 1977.

Frankl, V. E. *Man's search for meaning* (Rev. ed.). New York: Washington Square, 1963.

Gatchel, R. J. and Price, K. P. *Clinical applications of biofeedback: Appraisal and status*. New York: Pergamon, 1979.

Girdano, D. and Everly, G. *Controlling stress and tension*. Englewood Cliffs, N.J.: Prentice-Hall, 1979.

Glasser, W. *Positive addiction*. New York: Harper and Row, 1976.

Goldfried, M. R. and Davison, G. C. *Clinical behavior therapy*. New York: Holt, 1976.

Green, E. and Green, A. *Beyond biofeedback*. New York: Delta, 1977.

Gross, S. J. The holistic health movement. *Personnel and Guidance Journal*, 1980, *59*(2), 96–100.

Hammond, D. C. and Stanfield, K. *Multidimensional psychotherapy*. Champaign, Ill.: Institute for Personality and Ability Testing, 1977.

Harper, F. D. Outcomes of jogging: Implications for counseling. *Personnel and Guidance Journal*, 1978, *57*(2), 74–78.

Hilyer, J. C., Jenkins, W. W., Denton, W. L., Dillon, C., Meadows, M. E., and Wilson, G. D. Physical dimensions of counseling: Perspective for helping professions. *Counselor Education and Supervision*, 1980, *20*(2), 101–116.

Jencks, B. Your body biofeedback at its best. Chicago: Nelson-Hall, 1977.

Jones, E. S. *A song of ascents*. New York: Abingdon, 1968.

Judah, R. and Keat, D. B. Multimodal assessment. The classroom ecology. *Elementary School Guidance and Counseling*, 1977, *12*(2), 97–104.

Kaplan, H. S., *The new sex: Active treatment of sexual dysfunction*. New York: Brunner/Mazel, 1974.

Keat, D. B. Multimodal approaches for HELPING children-adolescents. *Counseling and Human Development*, November 1979, 1–10.

Kostrubala, T. *The joy of running*. New York: Pocket Books, 1977.

Lazarus, A. A. Multimodal behavior therapy: Treating the "basic id." *Journal of Nervous and Mental Disease*, 1973, 156, 404–411.

Lazarus, A. A. and Fay, A. *I can if I want to*. New York: Morrow, 1975.

Lazarus, A. A. *Multimodal behavioral therapy*. New York: Springer, 1976.

Mahoney, J. J. *Cognition and behavior modification*. Cambridge, Mass.: Ballinger, 1974.

Marley, W. P. Asthma and exercise, a review. *American Corrective Therapy Journal*, 1977, *31*, 95–102.

Miller, M. J. Cantaloupes, carrots, and counseling: Implications of dietary interventions for counselors. *Personnel and Guidance Journal*, 1980, *58*(6), 421–424.

Mosher, R. L., Carle, R. F., and Kehas, C. D. *Guidance: An examination.* New York: Harcourt, Brace & World, 1965.

Olton, D. C. and Noonberg, A. R. *Biofeedback: Clinical applications in behavioral medicine.* Englewood Cliffs, N.J: Prentice-Hall, 1980.

Pappas, J. P. *Multiple counseling tactics I: Enhancing dating behavior in college males.* Paper presented at the Rocky Mountain Psychological Association meeting, Salt Lake City, 1970.

Pelletier, K. R. *Holistic medicine.* New York: Dell, 1979.

Pelletier, K. R. *Mind as healer mind as slayer.* New York: Dell, 1977.

Raimey, V. Mouse mammary tumors: Alternation of incidence as apparent function of stress. *Science,* 1975, *189,* 465–467.

Rokeach, M. and Regan, J. F. The role of values in the counseling situation. *Personnel and Guidance Journal,* 1980, *58*(9), 576–582.

Scarf, M. Images that heal. *Psychology Today,* September 1980, 32–46.

Seligman, M. E. P., *Helplessness.* San Francisco: Freeman, 1975.

Selye, H. *The stress of life.* New York: McGraw-Hill, 1976.

Shapiro, C. and Surwit, R. S. Learned control of physiological function and disease. In H. Leilenberg (Ed.), *Handbook of behavior modification and behavior therapy.* Englewood Cliffs, N.J.: Prentice-Hall, 1976, pp. 74–123.

Sheehan, G. *On running.* Mountain View, Calif.: World Publications, 1975.

Shostrom, E. L. *Actualizing therapy: Foundations for a scientific ethic.* San Diego: Edits Publishers, 1976.

Simon, S. B. *Meeting yourself halfway.* Niles, Ill.: Argus, 1974.

Simon, S. B., Howe, L. W., and Kirschenbaum, H. *Value clarification. A handbook of practical strategies for teachers and students.* New York: Hart Publishing, 1972.

Simonton, D. C., Matthews-Simonton, S., and Creighton, J. *Getting well again.* Los Angeles: J. P. Tarcher, 1978.

Spino, S. *New age training for fitness and health.* New York: Grove Press, 1979.

Spino, M. *Running home.* Millbrae, Calif.: Celestial Arts, 1977.

Thorne, F. C. *Integrative psychology.* Brandon, Vt.: Clinical Psychology Publishing, 1967.

Tyler, L. The next forty years. *The Counseling Psychologist,* 1980, *8*(4), 19–21.

Wickramasekera, I. (Ed.). *Biofeedback, behavior therapy and hypnosis.* Chicago: Nelson-Hall, 1976.

Wrenn, C. G. *The world of the contemporary counselor.* Boston: Houghton Mifflin, 1973.

Wrenn, C. G. Observations on what counseling psychologists will be doing during the next 20 years. In J. W. Whiteley and B. R. Fretz (Eds.), *From the present and future of counseling psychology.* New York: Wadsworth, 1980.

CHAPTER 9

PERSONAL/PROFESSIONAL SYNERGY: GENERATING COUNSELOR RENEWAL

Maintaining a high level of personal/professional functioning is a goal for both authors. It is basic to offering any creativity in counseling. Unfortunately, burnout has become a growing problem among counselors as reflected in numerous recent publications and workshop themes. However, the focus has tended to be negative which is discrepant to the positive focus necessary to live an effective personal/professional life. We would prefer to view the issue as a challenge—a challenge to apply the principles of creative counseling to our own lives. In this chapter we would like to present concepts which have been important to us as we deal with burnout and try to actively promote an enthused personal/professional lifestyle for ourselves. Each individual reader is encouraged to digest our comments through his or her own personal experience and apply (in good eclectic fashion) the pieces that fit. Some of the cases we have studied have unfortunate outcomes; however, many professionals have dealt with their own personal problems of renewal successfully and have moved on to more productive and creative lives. Our first example deals with the sad results of one of our colleagues. The rest of the chapter presents ideas which have come from persons who have dealt successfully with the challenges of professional renewal.

BURNOUT: A CASE STUDY

Joe started his professional counseling career at about the same time as the authors. He was well liked and demonstrated a successful professional style. He developed confidence and skill which were supported by client successes and professional growth. Personal activities in Joe's life supported the stamina needed for success, and he had a regular pattern of running and a host of other personally rewarding hobbies. He shared these with colleagues and with his clients. The world seemed to open its arms to Joe. Success became an expectancy. He was a support to others and sought out for his ideas. In the last 4 years life has changed for Joe.

Four years ago close friends noticed several subtle changes. Joe began to question evaluations, he was uncomfortable around some of his fellow professionals, and when social gatherings were held among his colleagues, Joe's absence became increasingly noticeable. Discussions with Joe brought out an increasing lack of self-confidence. Joe would state, "I'm not sure I could do that," when before he had been quite successful with the tasks in question. He would also use statements like, "You know I had better check with the boss before I try that," when the task was clearly a part of his responsibility.

Three years ago others began to notice that Joe was isolating himself both socially and professionally in his work. Coffee and personal discussion time were taken up with a personal confidant who was very negative. When others would join the conversation they noticed a larger portion of complaining and negative comments than usual. Family life deteriorated and he started drinking. A divorce ensued. We saw a dramatic change in his physical exercise program. Workout time no longer took a priority and physical activity was erratic. Long hard workouts, no workout, short periods of physical activity. Emotional upheaval. Struggles with work responsibilities. A refocus of energy in work toward avoiding work. Late to work, early to leave, and a general lack of enthusiasm. Little success with the friendship development with others. Alcohol use increased as did the importance of gambling. Sexual involvements became almost random and offered no real sense of worth.

Two years ago Joe felt little success in developing new relationships. He became even more involved with a highly negative colleague. Outbursts in staff meetings where Joe made accusations toward other staff members (particularly those with whom he had had little social contact) became almost routine. Guilt for personally perceived failures alternated from displacing blame on others to intensive self-blame. Work activities which had 60-minute requirements often were shaved to 20 minutes. More isolation. More struggle with personal life. Mounting personal problems increasingly spilled over into his professional life. Professional productivity was nil.

Last year Joe quit. Burnout? Whatever we call it, Joe's situation is a tragic one. Friends and colleagues hurt inside as they watched the deterioration unfold. The very ones who could have helped were the first to be rejected.

BURNOUT SYNDROME

Unfortunately, personal/professional burnout among counselors is a very real phenomenon. A growing body of literature has characterized the end result in terms of loss of esteem, cynicism, psychophysiological disorders, sense of helplessness, and ineffectiveness in our counseling responsibilities. In our initial preparation for this chapter, the burnout focus led both authors to come up with all too many examples. Most of the illustrations we discussed together were painful as they reflected the faces of past colleagues and friends. We both remember the sense of shock we felt as we renewed old graduate school friendships at a national convention for counselors several years ago. Friends that we had gone to school with were disappointed with their professional positions. The enthusiasm we had known had soured into anger and apathy, and we are not talking about a single isolated case or two. Even in discussing our approach to this chapter, it has been all too easy to become hooked on the negativism inherent in the literature surrounding burnout. In order to combat this tendency ourselves, we focus only briefly on the burnout syndrome itself (Freudenberger and Richelson, 1980; Edelwich and Brodsky, 1980; Pines and Aronson, 1980; Truch, 1980). We chose to place our emphasis on a model for alleviating the impact of burnout. Logically, this emphasizes an eclectic approach and incorporates many of the themes presented in other chapters of our book. Finally, we conclude with our highest priority—building enthusiasm and a sense of personal joy back into our professional lives. Counseling can still be fun (and must be reinforcing), and we would like to challenge you to creatively make it that way for yourself.

In a recent review of the current publications on burnout. Chance (1981) offers a consistent definition of burnout as self-depletion through a mismatch between efforts and outcomes. Physical and emotional resources deteriorate as the individual continues to put excessive energy into nonproductive channels set by unrealistic expectations. One of our good friends from Colorado has added to this profile in an article directed at school counselors (Terrill, 1981). He points first to the visionary tendency of counselors to think too big and attempt to be all things to all people. We may carefully help our client break global goals down into manageable units but fail to do so ourselves. Unrealistic goals can set the stage for failure and a sense of despair. Second, he identifies self-criticism as the key to losing a professional perspective on priorities which can lead to trivia involvement and wasted energy. Third, he sees a "failure to be flexible and creative" as putting the counselor in the rut of nonproductivity. Fourth, a lack of an adequate support system can be a critical factor leading to burnout. Ironically, as support dwindles, a cycle is perpetuated in which the professional fails to seek support and becomes less accessible to colleagues who want to offer support. The first line of support ultimately comes from ourselves, but cannot be sustained without outside nurturance. Fifth, a failure to expand and redefine our professional boundaries on an ongoing basis preempts the sense of challenge that vitalizes our counseling functions. Sixth, burnout professionally is directly related to an inattentiveness to our personal needs. We counselors are "givers," but must learn to occasionally (or regularly) take our turn. As Terrill puts it, "There needs to be a balance between initiating and responding activities in our lives or we may feel that someone else is in charge of our lives." He extends this into his final point—that the bottom line of burnout involves a sense of being victimized. A lack of control over our lives can emerge if we yield to the divergent demands and opposing expectations of others without the belief that we offer the central direction for our lives. It is not hectic schedules but our perceived lack of control that is critical. There is almost a direct correlation then between this sense of helplessness and ensuing apathy and depression. In a recent discussion with a leading authority on depression (Seligman, 1981), it was suggested that healthy people attribute a sense of control to most areas of their lives (even if they lack that control in reality)—what is important is the belief of being in charge of our own lives.

This whole dynamic process of burnout appears to have an insidious nature in which the individual may hardly be aware that anything wrong is happening. In fact, people may actively deny the problem and pass off the related symptoms to themselves and colleagues as a temporary reaction to pressures (Shue, 1981). Edelwich and Brodsky (1980) have gone on to identify several predictable stages of professional disillusionment. They identify a sequential flow from enthusiasm to stagnation, frustration, and apathy, and offer suggestions for intervention at each stage. It would appear that this process closely resembles the kind of response to sustained stress that we see all too frequently among our clients. In fact, Daley (1979) has borrowed from earlier works to suggest that professional burnout unfolds in a fashion analogous to Selye's (1976) general adaptation syndrome (the stress reaction pattern presented previously). Environmental stressors interact with the individual's personality to produce a sequence of alarm, resistance, and exhaustion states.

According to the system presented by Daley (1979), the alarm reaction represents the initial stage of responding to stress. As we have mentioned before, this is highly subjective. What stresses one person may challenge another. What once served as an energizing source may eventually produce irreparable damage. Certainly all of us face elements of such stressors (unappreciative clients, red tape, low pay, overwork, incompatible demands), but most of us continue to thrive. At any rate, the alarm reaction is typified by a mobilization of defense mechanisms directed at overcoming perceived obstacles. This is characterized by counselors who increase their striving levels to meet growing demands which may be unrealistically placed upon themselves. Instead of meeting personal needs, extra time is devoted to work demands which may be open-ended: the more accomplished, the more there remains to be accomplished. This is particularly disastrous when the tasks are unclearly defined or unattainable. Our earlier reference to the type A personality comes into new focus here as personal vulnerability mixes with growing pressures. The perfectionistic tendency of some counselors may place them in an impossible situation. Burns (1980) defines the consequences of perfectionism where individuals push themselves compulsively toward impossible goals and measure their own self-worth through their accomplishments. He suggests that these people pay the price in terms of decreased productivity, impaired health, depression, low self-esteem, and dysfunctional interpersonal relations. The counselor must be aware of the difference here between self-defeating perfectionism and the healthy pursuit of excellence. Just as we direct our clients toward realistically established high standards, we too must define our goals in clearly obtainable terms or suffer the consequences. This is particularly difficult in counseling since tangible indices of success are often difficult to establish and challenge the counselor's sensitivity to small increments of success and tolerance for ambiguity.

When stressors persist at an intense and chronic level, the counselor may progress into a resistance stage in which most available energy is directed toward managing stress. As resistance continues, the system deteriorates and high-level functioning becomes impossible. Energies are channeled away from professional responsibilities, and the counselor becomes incapable of offering quality (certainly not creative) involvement with his or her clients. As Carkhuff and Berenson (1967) have suggested, it is illogical to believe that the client can move beyond the level of counselor functioning through their interaction. In fact, if counselors are functioning at a low level, we would expect a related deterioration among the counselors' higher-functioning clients who either break off the relationship or plummet downhill with their counselors. When counselors fail to care anymore, they lose their most basic and potent client resource—themselves. The clients cannot make gains while being treated in a detached and dehumanized manner (Maslock, 1978), but counselors in the resistance stage have little else to offer. They feel helpless, and this feeling is reinforced by professional and personal nonproductivity.

Finally, resistance may give way to even more severe consequences in the exhaustion stage. Some potentially effective counselors are lost here, as they leave the field for less stressful jobs. Some remain at their counseling responsibilities but become functionally dead. Continuation of the nonproductivity of the previous stage is now complemented by cynicism, inflexibility, and withdrawal. This may be further accompanied by more serious manifestations of the earlier warning signs—physical illness, severe depression, or even suicide.

BREAKING THE BURNOUT CYCLE

It should be noted from the onset of this section that not all aspects of burnout are negative. We see this in two respects. First, the burnout signals may reflect more deep-seated personality dysfunctions among some of our colleagues. These counselors may need help themselves and certainly are not in a position to work with others. Unfortunately, our profession has too many unhealthy individuals who continue to counterproductively yield deteriorative outcomes with their clients. Not everyone can function effectively as a counselor, and we have a professional obligation to monitor our own ranks. This kind of screening should be initiated in graduate training programs prior to legitimatizing counselor activities with academic degrees. The authors make no apologies to our graduate students for applying intense pressures. We find that most of the necessary screening comes by the students themselves as we facilitate personal insight in the face of academic and interpersonal stressors. There may also be occasion where we initiate confrontation after watching a student struggle with the pressures. In either case, burnout signs can potentially serve to "weed out" nonproductive counselors. Obviously, our responsibility does not end here as we often are in an excellent position to help individuals rechannel their energies into more constructive professional directions or even into psychotherapy. We might add that this kind of screening not only prevents a lot of misery for the individuals and their would-be clients, but is also an important step in preventing burnout for counselor educators. Second, burnout signals may also serve as early warning signs for the high-functioning counselor. The alarm stage may actually involve increased productivity and does not necessarily reap immediate destructive results. However, it may also herald the potential for serious problems. Early recognition of symptoms is critical and may determine whether subsequent interventions are remedial or preventive in nature. The high-functioning professional who is experiencing the warning signs of burnout will serve as a focus in this section. We will look initially at remedial issues for the high-functioning counselor trapped in the burnout cycle and then shift our emphasis toward prevention and renewal.

In keeping with basic counseling principles, understanding generally precedes constructive steps toward change. Self-assessment is the first step, and yet awareness may be illusive as our defense systems keep warning signals from awareness and may necessitate an appropriate colleague-initiated confrontation. For those who want to take a closer look inside and are interested in building a burnout profile, we have included a self-assessment instrument as Appendix Four. This instrument reflects the organization of this section as it is subdivided into three major areas. Two of the areas can be used to categorize personal (counselor-owned) and professional (client-owned) problems and set the stage for remedial considerations. A third area contains problem-free activities and interactions. This no-problem area can be used to open the door to counselor renewal through creative time management. The following diagram (adapted from Gordon, 1970), thus serves as a conceptual model for organizing strategies to remediate and prevent counselor burnout. Readers may wish to interject the responses from their "burnout profiles" (Appendix Four) into our window diagram as a means of personalizing actual environmental- and personality-related stress factors. As the communication component of our diagram suggests, distress is a highly subjective reflection of our interpretation of stressors. Our screening system (counselor's window) can then be viewed as a critical filter of external events as they interact with our last experiences and basic personalities. As events are perceived as threat and yield distress, the burnout cycle may be set in motion (alarm, resistance, exhaustion). When those same or other potential stressors are dealt with effectively, the result may be increased motivation (eustress) and related productivity. Our perception is pivotal. The window also depicts our personal/professional lives as integrally connected with fluctuations in their respective stress lines as determining the amount of problem-free (revitalization) time that we have available (see Figure 9-1). Distress in one area tends to increase vulnerability to discouragement which can put into motion a vicious cycle of personal/professional problems which virtually preempt any energy that could be invested in no-problem activities. Revitalization potential is squeezed out by a self-perpetuating flow of problems. We will turn our focus on these problem areas first as we develop strategies for opening up more problem-free time toward professional renewal.

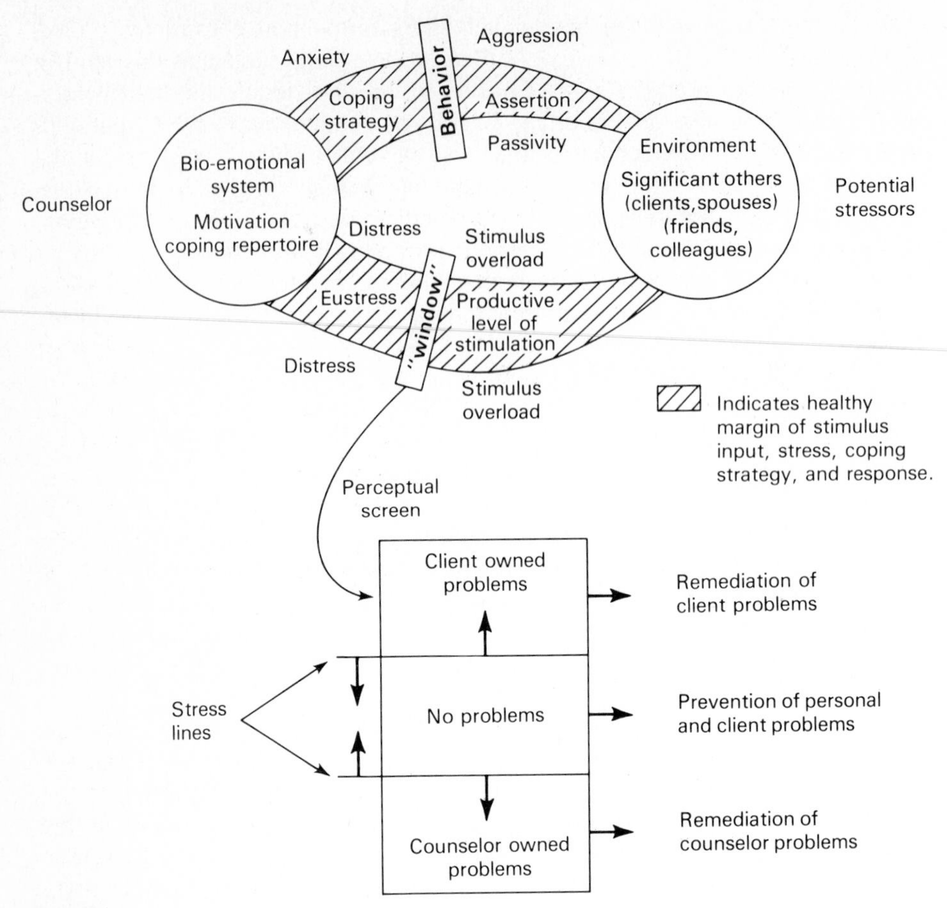

FIGURE 9-1
The stress cycle.

Whereas we laud the counselor role diversity that has emerged in the last decade, a price in terms of external pressures is being paid (Warnath and Shelton, 1976). Outreach themes continue to move (and rightfully so) the high-functioning counselor out of the safety of an office and into the demands that come with increased visibility. The proverbial "rock and a hard place" saying might appear to apply as the counselor struggles to find a viable niche between overdiversity of roles and the impotence that is so often associated with a role that is too narrowly defined. We would like to extend the ideas presented by Boy and Pine (1980) in building guidelines for the counselor facing a professional identity crisis.

Limit Noncounseling Obligations

It is too easy for high-functioning counselors to become enmeshed in noncounseling activities which can gradually pervade their professional involvements.

When this happens, the satisfaction of seeing constructive change in the lives of clients can be preempted. Their sense of contribution may become eroded. We have grown suspect of counselors who continually bemoan the fact that paperwork duties keep them from client contact. Chronic complaining of this nature may more accurately reflect serious deficits in the individual's professional capabilities. This is not to say that all of us are not periodically seduced from our core counseling responsibilities. Some of this may offer a positive diversity, but we must build a personal equation that really fits with our professional needs. We suggest two related strategies. First, a good offense in this case may be the best defense. In other words, we can generally avoid the tedium of unwanted tasks that divert our counseling energies by making our employers a better offer. This is a challenge to create exciting programs that have demonstrably positive benefits to our clients and agencies. Becoming involved with self-defined programs puts us in control of our professional identities and precludes some of the temptations to overextend ourselves in nonproductive pursuits. Second, in good assertion training fashion, it is critical at times that we learn how to say "no." This applies to unrealistic demands from clients and employers. However, we may be our own worst enemies in this respect as we are tempted to move beyond those counseling functions which offer us the greatest rewards.

Prioritize Counseling Involvements

In working in both psychiatric hospital and penitentiary settings, your authors learned some hard lessons about which clients to invest our energies toward. The temptation is to take on all referrals and then find yourself struggling with impossible cases. This can soon evolve into the worst symptoms of burnout. We have seen it over and over again. New helping professionals just out of graduate school who are full of enthusiasm and ready to take on (or even seek out) chronically low-functioning clients and expecting great things are often slapped with the reality that even the smallest changes are unlikely with some clients.

We would suggest the following strategies for increasing the chances of success with clients. First, select your clientele in terms of the potential for success. This is a highly personal formula, but most counselors would do well to balance high-risk clients with those who are relatively well motivated and offer a hopeful prognosis. We are not giving up on the severely disturbed, but simply trying to optimize the potential gain from the expenditure of our limited resources. Chance (1981) suggests a seemingly radical notion that may be worth some consideration: It involves the adoption of tactics used by medical units during times of war. A triage system is used in which treatment is prioritized by the prognosis: Those who can be saved but need immediate attention are treated first, whereas those who can survive without treatment or who have little chance to improve are assigned a lower priority. He points out that this may seem callous, but nevertheless acknowledges the reality of limited resources. Second, we can maximize the success potential by educating our referral sources about our particular skills and interests. This presupposes an honesty with ourselves regarding our limited energy reserves and areas of expertise. Finally, it behooves both client and counselor to carefully delineate expected counseling outcome goals into specific measurable units. This is often the only way that the fine increments of progress can be monitored. This also encourages the counselor to take each session as it comes and to become sensitive to seemingly minute client gains. It also reinforces the reality that change ultimately rests with the clients and that this is directly related to their work outside of the counseling sessions.

"Stack Your Deck" with Healthy Colleagues

Perhaps the best single indicator of our professional viability is found in the level of functioning of our colleagues. It is virtually impossible to remain professionally vital without a healthy positive associational base. Maybe it boils down to the choices that we can choose to make, first in terms of the organization where we work. As Boy and Pine (1980) suggest, some human service organizations become so caught up in funding and political issues that a sense of mission becomes lost. Any counselor is more apt to realize his or her potential in an organizational climate where helping people remains the primary goal while the use of the full range of professional expertise is encouraged and reinforced. Both authors have been exposed to work settings at each extreme and remain happily involved where we are because of the sense of professional enthusiasm at our institutions. However, since no organization, as a whole, is perfect, a second line of choice is critical in "deck stacking." These are the choices we make day by day to spend our time with high- or low-functioning colleagues. In our work setting, the tone of the hour can be set by whom we choose to associate with during breaks or seek out to discuss professional issues. Entering some offices almost guarantees a focus on gossip, low salaries, overwork, and a generally dismal picture. Fortunately, the opposite can readily be found on a consistent basis. The choice is up to us.

Continually Evolve Your Theoretical Framework

We have all been exposed to professors who use the same lecture notes year after year. Obviously, they have lost contact with professional developments. Sadder yet is the loss of enthusiasm that inevitably sets in (first insidiously and eventually persuasively) when we fail to continually expand our professional repertoire. Our clients suffer when the most potent techniques are not being applied, and we suffer a loss of credibility, in their eyes, that is perhaps our most critical resource. We have a responsibility to continue building upon their basic philosophical and theoretical core. This comes only through an openness to new ideas—reading, attending workshops, sharing ideas and cases—and ongoing assessment of our methods of intervention. A decline in the reading of professional literature is a sure warning sign of burnout, especially when paired with a failure to maintain involvement in professional organizations.

Periodic Role Examination

This strategy is an extension of the client priority issue. Just as any effective counseling program structures time to assess progress, the counselor also needs examination periods—a regular time to separate out the trivia and pat ourselves on the back for jobs done well. A periodic check on the realistic limits of our professional energies is essential. We may need to accept limits in some areas and expand boundaries in others. Some things cannot be changed by our efforts—certain clients, organizational power, and even societal factors that spawn burnout—and we need reality checks to head off unnecessary frustration. Once again, it helps to have a colleague with whom you can share successes and areas of needed change. All of us need to "dump the garbage" once in a while or it starts to rot and erode us from inside. We also need to look at areas of achievement and potential growth. Finding the time can be a problem (excuse) so the examination periods themselves must come to be viewed as part of your professional responsibility. Your authors find that frequent fishing and outdoor trips provide an excellent opportunity for us to do much more than relax—we usually talk about our professional directions and help each other keep on track.

PERSONAL RENEWAL

Our diagram of the counselor's window clearly reflects the inseparable interaction between our personal and professional lives. It is just not realistic to think that professionals can simply turn off personal problems as they walk into their counseling offices. Personal problems which are not being handled effectively tend to push the personal stress line up and preclude our effectiveness in helping clients with their concerns. If the personal problem cycle is not broken, it can spill over into our counseling sessions and produce the professional apathy so characteristic of the burnout syndrome. The temptation becomes to say (and may be nonverbally communicated) to our clients, "You think you've got problems, well. . . ." On the other hand, dealing with personal problems effectively lowers the personal stress line and generates more energy to invest in client problems. It also expands the no-problem area opening the door to personal and professional revitalization. Counseling must be a way of life and a direct extension of the effectiveness of our noncounseling relationships. To provide a comprehensive model here for dealing effectively in the area of counselor-owned problems would be beyond our scope. Indeed, all of the theory and techniques that we might blend in helping clients may have some relevance as applied to our own lives. We also choose to limit our concern here to high-functioning individuals who may be experiencing relatively transient encounters with burnout symptoms. We would make no effort to rescue the chronically dysfunctional individual who collects a salary for counseling, but would hope that the burnout symptoms serve as a warning signal for these individuals to seek professional help themselves and perhaps a new career direction. At any rate, here are some ideas to consider as we assess the impact of stressors in our personal lives.

Boy and Pine (1980) point to the necessity of maintaining a personal optimism in order to enrich the condition of our clients. Negativism is a real enemy—the kind of negativism that is fostered by a sense that we are not in control of our own personal direction. We fight this kind of helpless submissiveness in our clients and may need to periodically apply similar strategies to ourselves. Boy and Pine indicate that the roots of optimism and pessimism are within each of us and are unleashed by choices we make. Choice seems to be at the bottom-line. Optimism atrophies like an unused muscle if our ongoing choices do not nourish it. But even more fundamental may be a belief that you deserve to take care of yourself and make self-enhancing choices. After over 40 years of research concerning stress and its impacts, Selye (1978) formulated a "recipe for the best antidote to the stresses of life." We like it. The first ingredient is to seek a level of stress that is optimal for you. Some people can thrive on a racehorse pace and others cannot. Second, he suggests that we choose our own goals. A personal script analysis here might help separate our goals from those imposed on us by significant other people who influence us. Questions surrounding professional direction and life-style are of critical importance in this regard—too many counselors end up in professional positions as a last resort or because of external incentives. The third ingredient is a type of "altruistic egoism"—developing a broad repertoire of competence so as to make ourselves invaluable to others. As Selye puts it, "striving to make yourself even more useful and necessary is an aim you can safely pursue throughout your life, and one that will protect you from the worst of all modern social stresses, purposelessness." We also appreciate the way that Girdano and Everly (1979) have extended these themes into specific strategies for identifying and coping with stress. They provide guidelines for handling a wide range of stressors through relaxation training, diet control, environmental/personality management, and physical exercise. We particularly like their emphasis on stress and its treatment as holistic:

> Stress is environmental and social, it is mental as well as physical; it involves perceptions, thoughts, and anticipation; it is action and the thwarting of action. Stress is caused by many situations—thus, stress cannot be managed, controlled, or reduced via any one technique. Intervention must be holistic—in this context that means you must formulate a program which attacks the problem on several levels (p. 124).

In keeping with this holistic theme we would encourage a highly personalized eclectic approach to counselor renewal which incorporates a wide range of strategies with choice and personal responsibility at the core. In fact, we see problem resolution in our personal lives as involving a sequence of choices and related actions. The extent to which we make these choices on a daily basis will generally be reflected in our own level of personal happiness and related professional productivity. We would invite our readers to "plug in" the faces of people in their lives and everyday situations that create problems as they digest the following guidelines:

Choice Level 1: Resignation or Courage

The most basic choice regarding incoming stressors is whether to attack them or not. Powers and Hahn (1978) present a useful diagram for helping clients with this kind of problem assessment that seems to have considerable usefulness for counselors themselves (see Figure 9-2). As the diagram suggests, it is critical for us to confront environmental and interpersonal stressors where there is a reasonable probability of controlling their destructive impact. Being realistic, however, we cannot control all those things that produce undesirable stress. Some people will not change. We simply have no influence over some of the destructive happenings around us no matter how much we worry. The appropriateness of our choice—to act or not to act—is then a direct reflection of the accuracy of our assessment of the potential outcomes. If you can change something you do not like, do it! If not, then it behooves you to resign yourself to that fact and then move on to invest energy into constructive directions. We are not talking here about "false acceptance" (Gordon, 1970), where the outward appearance of acceptance betrays inward worry and anger that can leave us feeling helpless. We are suggesting that we choose to stand up to those problem areas we can

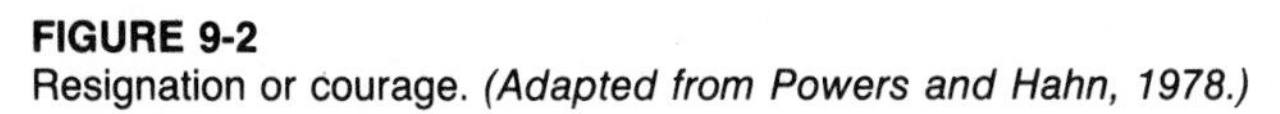

FIGURE 9-2
Resignation or courage. *(Adapted from Powers and Hahn, 1978.)*

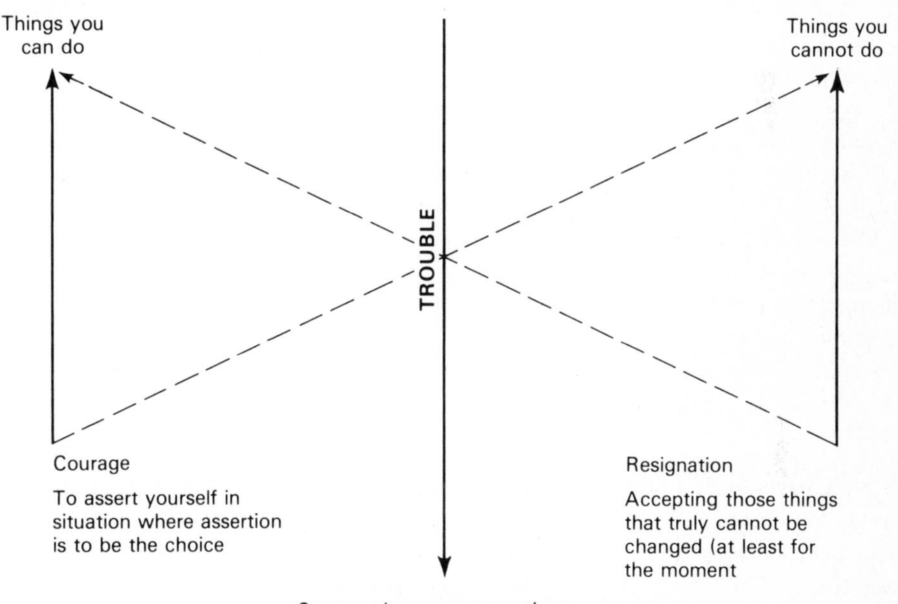

change and truly accept those that cannot be changed. We all know some people who can remain inwardly and outwardly calm in the face of the worst circumstances. Here is a challenge to cultivate this kind of inner peace and to build personal associations with people who will foster this capacity. Ironically, a sense of control often comes when we accept the utter uncontrollability of some things that we have to deal with in our daily lives. Our challenge further encourages the cultivation, through practice, of the wisdom to know when to confront and when to accept our circumstances.

Choice Level 2: Personal Persuasion

There are several second-level choices that follow an initial choice to stand up to an issue or individual creating problems for us. The assertion movement of the past decade has yielded some excellent guidelines (Alberti and Emmons, 1970; Bower and Bower, 1976) for helping us to obtain our needs while minimizing damage to our important support relationships. We would caution that the first choice here involves the level of directness in confrontation. We would go back to the guidelines presented in Chapter 6 and suggest that confrontation should not go beyond the minimal level needed to accomplish the desired result. Never use a harsh direct confrontation when a low-key door-opener will serve the purpose. Overkill generally makes us feel guilty and raises the other person's defenses. This also implies a second choice regarding the timing of the persuasive message and the importance of setting the stage for maximizing success. When is the time right? Hopefully, the confrontation is delivered before undue pressure has built up and precludes our objectivity. It is also desirable to initiate the confrontation when the other person's defenses are low and we are feeling a genuine sense of care for them. Obviously, no confrontation should be delivered unless adequate follow-through time is available. Third, we can choose to preattend the confrontation to maximize our readiness for the possible consequences and reduce our preconfrontation level of stress. Preattending—rehearsing, relaxing, readying yourself—can improve the quality of the confrontation and enhance receptiveness to the other person's responses. A simple persuasive message may accomplish the intended end. If not, the other person's response may herald the need for another choice—retreat to resignation with the belief that nothing can be done at this point in time or move on to more potent tactics (choice level 3).

Choice Level 3: Personal Problem Solving

Responsible assertion is not always the answer—it may end up as an impasse. This issue of choice emerges again—give up, accept, or try another strategy. Scott (1979) says that that problem-solving methods can move conflict situations beyond hopeless deadlocks and into creative, mutually satisfying solutions. In addition to the model for democratic problem solving presented previously (Gordon, 1970), Scott cites a consensus model designed by one of our good friends and colleagues at the University of Colorado. This system (Roark, 1978) outlines five distinct steps that can lead to successful conflict resolution. In the first step, participants define the conflict in mutually understandable terms. Step two moves beyond problem definition into a nonblameful description of the participants' feelings about the conflict. The third step involves agreement on what the situation would look like if a satisfactory resolution was achieved. In step four, participants define the changes necessary to reach the desired solution. Putting this into a written list may help get the job accomplished. Finally, a detailed agenda is generated which includes projected deadlines and follow-up plans. Personal problems can tie up tremendous energy and reduce our professional productivity while preempting efforts at personal/professional revitalization. Successful problem solving not only produces mutually satisfying solutions, but increases the no-problem area as the personal stress line is lowered.

BEYOND RENEWAL: CREATIVE CONTROL OF THE NO-PROBLEM AREA

Up to this point, our focus has been on remediating personal and professional problems in order to break the burnout cycle. In this effort we have extended some of the principles outlined in Part One of our book (basic eclecticism) to promote counselor renewal. To stop here would be incongruent with our more basic theme—moving beyond an eclectic base toward higher levels of creativity. There is much more to being a creative counselor than just getting through the day with a reasonable level of productivity. Consequently, we would like to conclude by moving beyond the basic and extending the concepts presented in Part Two to the personal and professional lives of creative counselors. Dealing effectively with personal and professional issues is only the starting point for creative counselors and absorbs only a fraction of their energies. Large amounts of energy remain to be invested in the revitalizing activities which compose the no-problem area as illustrated in Figure 9-3. Once again, having problem-free time available does not guarantee its successful use. We would encourage counselors to actively plan and structure their problem-free time to maximize its potential for productivity, revitalization, and creative use.

It offers an area of enthusiasm and challenge in its own right, but may also serve as an energy source, when cultivated, for even better handling of personal/professional problems. Effective counselors go beyond the successful management of stress toward creative control of their problem-free time. Creative counselors have a set of positive attitudes toward life which are most clearly reflected in their problem-free-related behavior. They attack life with zest and symbolize the kind of "psychological hardiness" identified by Pines (1980) in her portrayal of people who not only resist the negative impact of stress but thrive on controlled levels of it. The burnout literature may have overstated its point about the hazards of stress in high-stress professions. There is growing evidence that the individual's appraisal of stress situations is perhaps more critical than any objective assessment of it. Stress-resistant people maintain three attitudes which make the critical difference—challenge, commitment, and control. Their profile suggests a proactive

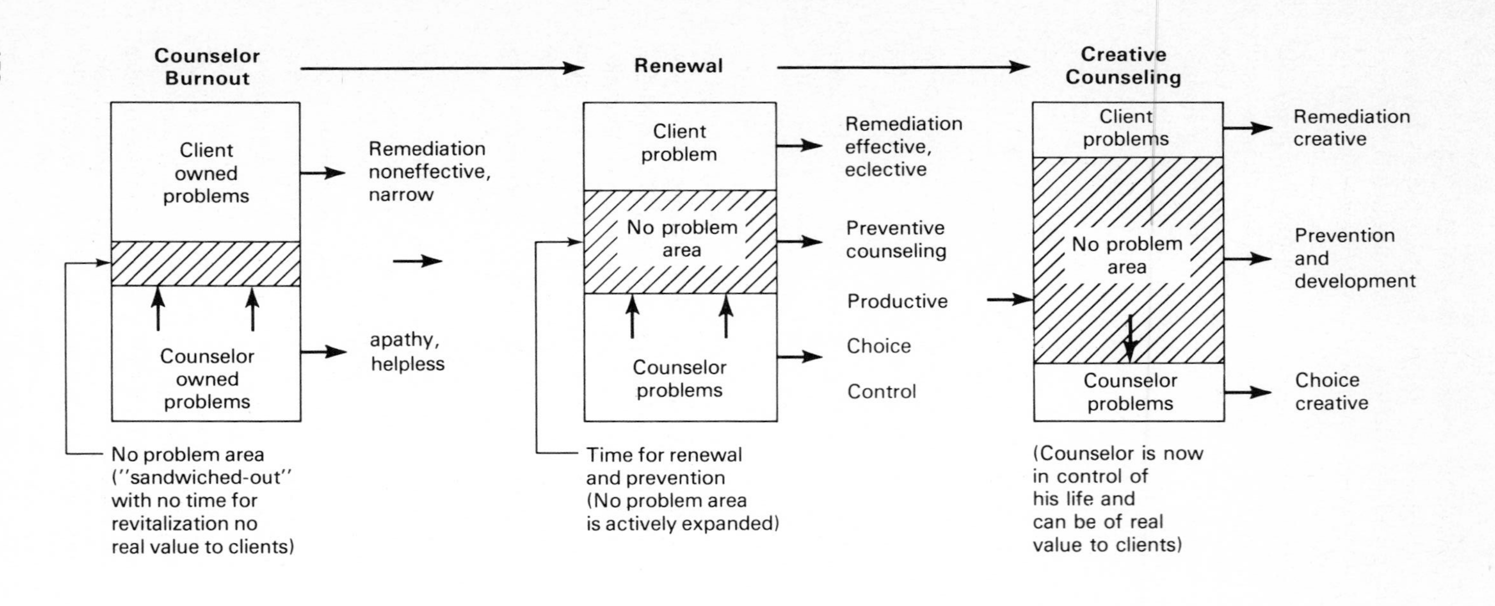

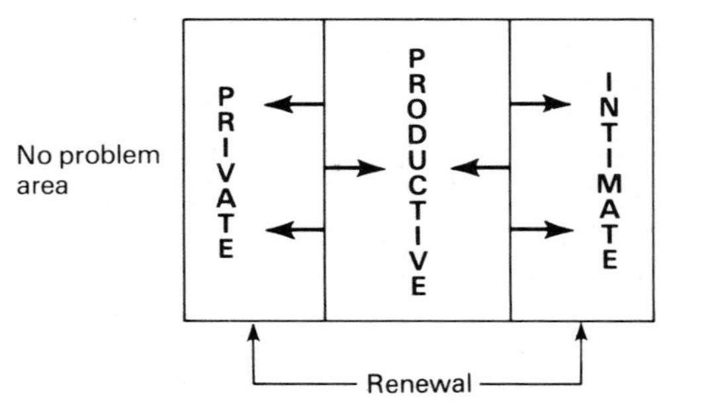

FIGURE 9-3
Counselor burnout, renewal, and creative counseling.

approach in life in which controlled levels of change and challenge are sought out. We would add that these characteristics are best nurtured within the no-problem area, but once established spill over to offer an immunity to serious problems. We may even become so involved in spending our problem-free energies that we forget about previous problems or at least have renewed energy to deal with them. These attitudes can then be actively developed through the creative management of the time available in this area of our daily lives.

CHALLENGE: PRODUCTIVITY TIME

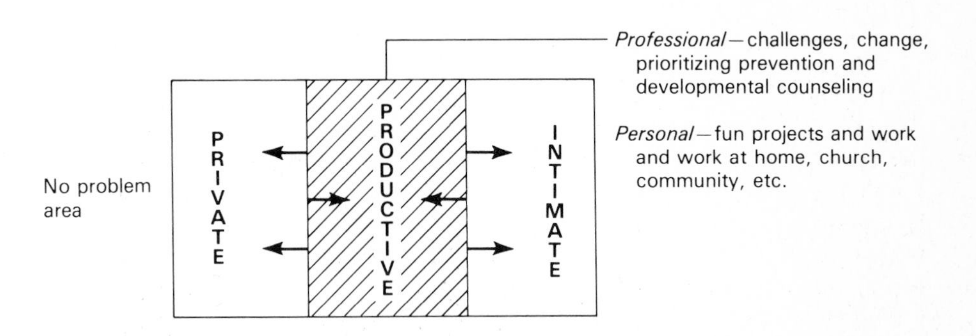

According to the previously mentioned researchers, *psychological hardiness* is characterized by viewing change as challenge rather than as a stressor. We have identified the dramatic changes that have occurred in the last two decades within the helping professions, and have pointed to a decade of continued change. Clearly, the creative counselor of the 1980s must not see change as a threat. We have attempted to suggest some areas of challenge by extending the theme of eclecticism of the preceding decade. The creative counselor will seek out challenge and budget problem-free time according to the importance of pre- and postcreative involvement during the counseling hours. These personal readiness periods maximize the potential for full release of our creative energies and increase our professional productivity. This may be a bit like the conditioning (warm-up and cool-down) process that distance runners go through to enable them to handle the demands of the actual race. An immunity to the stress of peak experiences can be built through our psychological readiness. We have also emphasized the importance of risk in both remedial and preventive counseling. In budgeting the no-problem time we have available, we would strongly encourage counselors to look at the personal benefits gained by prioritizing our client contacts to insure plenty of time with relatively healthy clients. The sense of productivity is enhanced by actively seeking people who are ready for change and motivated to use our help. It is clear that it is also to our advantage to work with clients who will take on much of the responsibility for their desired change. This also means taking a hard look at a professional equation that balances the energies we invest remedially as opposed to preventively. We would prioritize the latter. Both authors have taken on this challenge as we have gradually moved toward a larger investment in healthy people dealing with preventive/developmental issues. We like the benefits and challenge of pushing ourselves beyond our old limits. The challenge of arranging problem-free time to increase our productivity is further extended as we reflect on the issues of multidimensional counseling presented in Chapter 8. The challenges are there—we cannot blame professional stagnation on anyone except ourselves.

A word of caution before we move on. We have to seek a workable balance between increased productivity, both personally and professionally, and resisting the effects of overstress. Productivity of the no-problem time can be seductive in its pull to overextend ourselves. It is too easy sometimes to answer too many challenges and push out our private and intimate time allotments in the process. "I am doing so many things that I just don't have time for myself and family!" Productivity demands a great deal from our resources, and it is wise to be protective of those resources. The best equation has to be unique to each counselor, but always involves a *tempering of challenge with balance*.

COMMITMENT: PRIVATE TIME

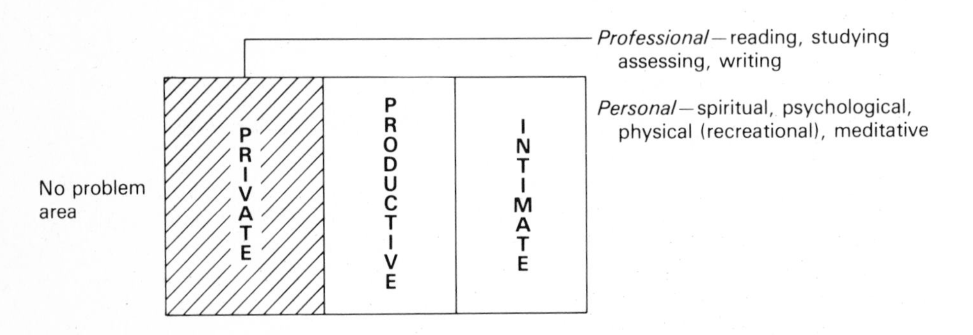

This area offers prime opportunities for personal/professional energizing. Each of us needs time, both personal and professional, to be by ourselves. Obviously, unchecked problems or poor management of the other problem-free areas can rob us of the time we have to ourselves. From a professional standpoint, private (uninterrupted) time is necessary to recharge ourselves, and we strongly recommend that regular structured periods become built into the daily routine. Both authors have special "get-away" corners where we can read, study, and recharge our professional batteries on a regular basis. Private personal time is also vital to keeping the creative counselor in psychological, spiritual, and physical shape. The need for private time may vary considerably from person to person, but all of us need to include some level of it in our revitalization formulas. Interestingly for us, the personal/professional focuses often merge during times set aside to be alone. Long-distance running is an excellent way to buy personal private time, but many of our most creative ideas regarding work (an idea for a lecture or insight into client problems) often emerge during these intensely personal periods. Once again, new energy generated in the personal area carries over into the professional and vice versa. Separating these two interacting parts of our daily lives is important at times, but they can also feed positively off of each other at other times.

Commitment seems to be the key ingredient to maintain private space. This may be the most vulnerable area in the entire window, since it is easily pushed out by the demands for productivity or stresses created by problems. Once again, commitment to structuring time for ourselves is possible to the extent that we are deeply convinced of its importance and our own personal worth. Ideally, of course, a cycle evolves whereby private time reinforces our sense of worth which in turn pries open more private time. Eventually, we can become addicted to the pieces of our busy schedules, where we find time for ourselves and put ourselves high on our priority list. Another aspect of commitment involves a periodic monitoring of balance; that is, balance between the private time spent in revitalizing spiritual, psychological, and physical selves. We are at our best when these areas are in balance, but maintaining that balance takes commitment.

CONTROL: INTIMATE TIME

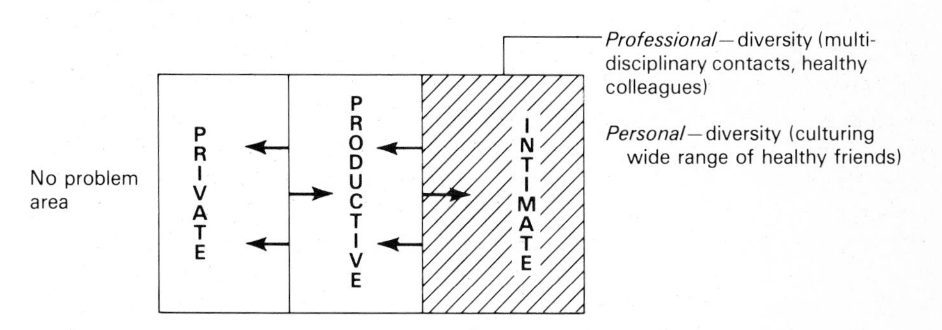

As we have stressed before, it is difficult to rise beyond the functioning level of our immediate support groups, both personal and professional. Maslow (1968) believes that people who transcend ordinary limits not only have periodic needs to be alone but also maintain several nurturing, independent relationships. This is the major ingredient of intimacy which is further characterized by James and Jongeward (1971) as a way to structure time which is free of exploitation and genuinely caring. Intimacy may also survive risk as we become vulnerable in being ourselves. To really excel at anything, be it racquetball or counseling, it helps to line yourself up with the best in that particular activity. One of our clients asked how someone could work with people's problems every day "without letting it get you down." The answer came in several parts, but most important was an active seeking out of a high-level personal and professional support system and the maintenance of intimate contact with those who are part of the system. Particularly for counselors working in clinical settings, it is easy to start seeing everyone in terms of problems. That is dangerous. We have many healthy (potentially maturing) people around us, and we must actively cultivate their support which in turn increases our sense of well-being and control over stressors. Look for the real self-actualizers who can be positive, enthusiastic, and draw out the very best in you. Actively evaluate their vitality and initiate periodic changes when necessary. Strive for diversity in your intimate relationships. In the professional level, we would encourage the extension of the multidisciplinary notion presented in Chapter 8 to spill over into our intimate professional contacts. That means expanding our immediate identity group—psychologists, social workers, or whatever—to include medically trained helpers and high-functioning clergy, among others. The same principle applies to our personal/social lives. Some of the authors' closest personal friends are also professional colleagues, but both of us feel a need to extend this system with a diversity of personal friends who are energetic and supportive. Consequently, our associations in private life include healthy people from diverse interests (mechanics, farmers, business people). This intricate system then serves as base for keeping us tuned up and creative in our counseling contacts.

Certainly, the core of your authors' support lies in family relationships. Both of us found it sad and ironic to see graduate school friends gaining counseling degrees while divorcing their spouses in the process. Unfortunately, this did not end with graduate school as we have witnessed several of our colleagues go through major family breakdowns. It is too easy to leave this most important area of intimacy to last as we push up career ladders, and fill the no-problem area with time for productivity and privacy. Our themes here of challenge, commitment, and control all must come into play in nurturing our most critical support resource.

In concluding this section on a positive note, we would like to share another case example to illustrate the principles we have presented. Our initial case study of Joe reflects the too frequently observed consequences of burnout. Fortunately, we have many examples of high-functioning counselors who actively build burnout prevention measures into their daily lives. Burnout is not only handled successfully, but these effective counselors have learned to thrive (and teach others to thrive by example) on the intensity that is inherent in creative counseling. Jake is a very close counselor/friend of ours and serves as an excellent example of what renewal is all about (see Appendix One: Part E, Jake: Breaking the Burnout Cycle).

KEEPING COUNSELING CREATIVE

We feel privileged to be in a position to enter meaningfully into the lives of our clients and students on a daily basis. Entering deeply into the lives of others and impacting their life course can be a source of tremendous gratification for both participants. There may be a tendency to play down the benefits of counseling, but both authors are continually awed by the gains that some of our clients make as we help them reach for untapped resources. In the process, a part of us is also touched that few people in other professions even begin to comprehend.

This book has emphasized a foundation for counseling in eclectic theorizing, a diversity of technique, and continual reassessment. It sounds like hard work. It is at times, but it also offers a challenge to personal limits not equaled in other professions. It is not the place for the partially committed or complacent. Certainly, not everyone meets the basic prerequisites, and many in our profession do a disservice to our title. But for those who have their own lives in basic order and are willing to develop the basic foundations for effective helping, it is possible to consistently move beyond the limits of textbook models—to become a creative counselor. To see our system of counseling evolve is exciting in itself, but it rarely matches the experience of seeing your own creative energies unleashed in the midst of your efforts to help another human being.

SUMMARY

Chapter 9 is a personal summary of the concepts presented in *The Creative Counselor.* Three major themes surfaced: (1) the process of achieving acceptable control in our lives; (2) commitment as a central issue in life success and in personal growth; and (3) challenge as a perceptual outlook necessary to bridge the gap between life's risks and the process of personal growth. The processes of growth as they relate to control, commitment, and challenge were summarized as concepts which counselors can apply to themselves in order to overcome burnout and to experience life as an enthusiastic, positive, involved, personal challenge.

Control in one's life is seen as related directly to the decisions individuals make and to the way we manage choices in our lives. We validate ourselves by providing for personal, individual private time. We grow professionally by blocking out time to learn professionally as well as maintaining time for making a professional contribution. We generate a personal feeling of support and develop individual energy by ensuring that we have time with the intimate people in our lives. Friends—our spouses, our children, other people close to us—are a major source of the close support needed as a base from which we take the risks necessary for growth. This three-part program of time management and choice management (balancing private, professional, and intimate time) is the key to establishing the feeling of control in our lives which is necessary for growth and development.

Commitment to people, to our personal beliefs, to our personal/professional purpose, and to ourselves provides the energy to extend individual growth in difficult situations and during successful experiences. Stamina is developed as a direct result of personal contact with individual commitment. The authors believe that commitment is the pivotal key to longtime service and that our personal commitment is directly influenced by a dynamic relationship of the personal stamina we have developed (stamina is directly influenced by our physical condition) and of the personal contact we maintain with our life purpose (contact with purpose is directly influenced by our spiritual condition).

Challenge as an approach to life is reflected in a personal ongoing process of growth. An important relationship of challenge is that of risk and growth. Utilizing rational risk taking to stimulate and open personal doors which makes life a journey of joy is the result of viewing life as a challenge. The specific process includes utilizing the flower model to analyze skills, designing steps to growth in each area of the flower model, and successfully maintaining a personal commitment to these specific areas of life which we have decided to change and develop. Contact with the specific areas of the flower model—social, physical, emotional, behavioral, spiritual, and cognitive and with activities, experiences, and people who stimulate growth—provides for ongoing growth and for consistent contact with our own uniqueness.

The model we provide individuals around us as we strive to utilize the *creative counseling* process in our own lives is a most conclusive test of the skills we offer as creative counselors. Creatively achieving control in our lives, creatively maintaining commitment, and creatively attacking life as a challenge is the essence of creative counseling.

REFERENCES

Alberti, R. E. and Emmons, M. L. *Your perfect right: A guide to behavior.* San Luis Obispo, Calif.: Impact, 1970.

Bower, S. A. and Bower, G. H. *Asserting yourself.* Reading, Mass.: Addison-Wesley, 1976.

Boy, A. V. and Pine, G. J. Avoiding counseling burnout through role renewal. *Personnel and Guidance Journal,* 1980, *59,* 161–163.

Burns, D. C. The perfectionist's script for self-defeat. *Psychology Today,* November 1980, 34–52.

Carkhuff, R. and Berenson, B. *Beyond counseling and therapy.* New York: Holt, 1967.

Chance, P. That drained-out used-up feeling. *Psychology Today,* January 1981, 88–95.

Daley, M. R. Burnout: Smoldering problem in protective services. *Social Work,* September 1979, 375–379.

Edelwich, J. and Brodsky, A. *Burn-out: Stages of disillusionment in the helping profession.* New York: Human Sciences, 1980.

Freudenberger, H. and Richelson, G. *Burnout: The melancholia of high achievement.* New York: Anchor/Doubleday, 1980.

Girdano, D. A. and Everly, G. S. *Controlling stress and tension: A holistic approach.* Englewood Cliffs, N.J.: Prentice-Hall, 1979.

Gordon, T. *Parent effectiveness training.* New York: Wyden, 1970.

James, M. and Jongeward, D. *Born to win: Transactional analysis with Gestalt experiments.* Reading, Mass.: Addison-Wesley, 1971.

Maslock, C. The client role in staff burnout. *Journal of Social Issues,* 1978, *34*(4), 111–123.

Maslow, A. H., *Toward a psychology of being.* New York: Van Nostrand, 1968.

Pines, M. Psychological hardiness: The role of challenge in health. *Psychology Today,* 1980, *14*(7), 34–98.

Pines, H. and Aronson, E. *Burnout: From tedium to personal growth.* New York: Free Press, 1980.

Powers, R. L. and Hahn, J. M. Resignation or courage: The wisdom to see the difference. *Personnel and Guidance Journal,* 1978, *57*(4), 219–220.

Roark, A. E. Interpersonal conflict management. *Personnel and Guidance Journal,* 1978, *56*(7), 400–402.

Scott, N. Beyond assertiveness training: A problem-solving approach. *Personnel and Guidance Journal,* 1979, *57*(9), 450–452.

Seligman, M. E. Personal communication, June 1981.

Selye, H. *The stress of life.* New York: McGraw-Hill, 1976.

Selye, H. On the real benefits of eustress. *Psychology Today,* March 1978, 60–70.

Shue, J. C. Staff burnout prevention programming in a residential treatment facility. Unpublished masters thesis, Adams State College, Alamosa, Co., 1981.

Terrill, J."Burnout"—A problem arising from many factors. *ASCA Newsletter,* 1981, *18*(3), 4–5.

Truch, S. *Teacher burnout and what to do about it.* Novato, Calif.: Academic Therapy Publications, 1980.

Warmath, C. and Shelton, J. The ultimate disappointment: The burned-out counselor. *Personnel and Guidance Journal.* 1976, *55,* 172–195.

APPENDIX ONE

CASE STUDIES

PART A: MARTY AND THE DOWNWARD SPIRAL

It became clear during our first session that Marty's aggressive behavior toward guards and fellow inmates was only the tip of the iceberg. A lifelong cumulative process of negative experiences had left him angry and disgusted with himself and his situation. The spiral started early in life. His parents, who had low self-esteem, were uneducated and openly aggressive in their child-rearing practices. Early aggressive attempts for attention were reinforced with angry words or beatings. Hundreds of preschool communications from mom, dad, and siblings evolved into building an unhealthy self-picture and an expectancy for more of the same. Even potentially constructive efforts by teachers would be met with resistance since anything positive was inconsistent with Marty's self-picture.

Add to this picture the impact of poverty and parents who did not care about Marty's growing sense of failure. Once the label "stupid" was attached at school, a secondary self-fulfilling prophecy began to support the primary one of self-degradation. His family was transient, moving every few months, so any real peer or teacher relationships during his first few years of school were impossible. The picture solidified further as he became labeled a "nonreader," first by a teacher and then by himself. The embarrassment related to school failure was overwhelming. Unfortunately, he was clever enough and transient enough to avoid any real efforts at remediation. He began to make a lifestyle of avoiding academic work as he more consistently defined himself in terms of inadequacy. What little support he had from his family was transferred onto a negative peer group at age nine when he was placed by the courts in a home for delinquent boys. School attendance continued, but Marty had psychologically dropped out. His only reinforcement system was attached to an increasingly criminal peer group. The downward spiral continued to feed off on itself: held back in school → increased hardening to positive efforts by adults → more negative peer models → ingraining negative self-image → physically dropping out of school → failure at any meaningful employment → more boys' homes. The story is all too familiar to most of us and becomes a stereotype of the personality disorders so often seen in adult reformatories across the country.

The criminal lifestyle had solidified by early adolescence. Still struggling for some kind of love and acceptance, the odds of successful involvement with any high-functioning girls became increasingly poor. Consequently, a string of destructive relationships were interwoven between more job failures and more serious criminal patterns. By the time he was twenty, Marty had gone through two adult terms of incarceration, a divorce, and numerous arrests. Back on the streets, the cycle was further reinforced by the labels he had accumulated. He found it nearly impossible to get a job and could not keep the few menial ones he had found. Recall that he was still functionally illiterate and actively resisted any efforts at change. The few people who might be of help gave up before anything constructive could take place. Clearly, the odds were against even the smallest therapeutic gains should he become involved with an effective counselor. The downward spiral, which he was directing, had left Marty angry, frustrated, and short-fused. He continued to bury himself deeper. Unfortunately, this picture was quite typical in the prison setting where I worked for 2 years as the only psychologist for 750 inmates. Sadder yet is the reality that this kind of destructive pattern (the downward spiral) is not limited to personality disorders and penitentiaries. The basic principles are lived out by the clients who come to us with the entire range of debilitating problems. Self-defeating behaviors are often reinforced and become the core of destructive approaches to life.

Marty was referred to me following an incident in the auto mechanics shop where he had attacked a guard. He had been working (during his third adult prison term) in the laundry for the past 6 months. He hated it. He had heard about an opening in the auto mechanics shop and had gone over to apply. What he got was an application that he could not read and the usual abrasive treatment typically dished out by the guards. It was hot, he was angry, and. . . .

Was Marty too deeply ingrained to be helped (even a little bit) by anyone, let alone a counselor whom he saw as part of the prison administration? Maybe so. I only had so much time and energy, and I was not inclined to waste it on people who did not want to change. I had to be selective when it came to counseling, or I would reap little more than frustration myself. Nevertheless, I decided to give it my best shot and set out to break down some of the barriers that separated me from my client. It would involve some risk, but I sensed that it might pay off. The first step was a concrete one—helping Marty get a reduced penalty for his fight with the guard and later to have him transferred out of the laundry unit into the auto mechanics shop. This opened the risk of being manipulated by Marty, but also the possibility of establishing my credibility. These actions seemed to open the door to a more basic part of his problem—Marty's inability to read, which had compounded his difficulties for over 20 years. In eclectic fashion, I borrowed reading materials and some good advice from a reading specialist and went to work. He had been through several remedial efforts, but usually lost interest and became overwhelmed with a sense of helplessness. This time seemed to be different as rapid progress toward building reading skills was made. The dramatic improvement surprised Marty and opened the door for us to deal with related interpersonal problems. No miracles took place, but small successive gains seemed to feed on each other. Long-ingrained patterns remained, but some alternative coping mechanisms began to be established in several areas. My brief (6-month) encounter with Marty led to at least a temporary reversal.

Unfortunately, the downward spiral holds an insidious grip. He still had many things going against him, and any realistic appraisal of potential had to be one of guarded optimism. At least he had managed to prove himself in the auto shop, had learned some reading and social skills, and had basically stayed out of trouble for several months. I was not overly optimistic about basic changes, but at least a temporary reversal had occurred. The door was open for a more constructive future. A more definitive conclusion cannot be offered since I have not heard from Marty since I left the prison setting.

PART B: ALICE AND THE CARKHUFFIAN MODEL

In discussing the basic Carkhuffian model in Chapter 4, three major components were presented: first, the structural framework for counseling involving three major phases (relational, integrational, and action); second, the core dimensions (empathy, respect, genuineness, concreteness, self-disclosure, interpretation of immediacy) which unfold within the three phases and reflect the personal functioning level of the counselor; and third, specific moment-by-moment interventions which reflect the core dimensions and are borrowed from a wide range of resources (the eclectic emphasis of the model). These components (general process to specific verbal and nonverbal exchanges) unfold in a unique way for each client, but remain basic to every counseling process. Obviously, our example cannot adequately capture the intensity and complexity of these ingredients as they emerge in actual counseling, but it may capture a small part of the model's usefulness. A session-by-session summary hopefully will illustrate the essence of the model and its three basic components.

Background Alice was a twenty-two-year-old senior who had been attending one of my classes for about 2 months prior to our counseling involvement. She spoke very little in class and had never stopped to chat as many of my students tend to do. I had pictured her as being quite shy, but she had performed quite well on exams and written assignments.

First Session While I often find myself looking through student messages to detect need for help, Alice came to me directly to say that she needed help with a personal problem. She had approached me after class, and I set up an appointment for later that morning, which gave me time to preattend our first session. She was prepared to talk when she came in but spoke in a soft and guarded tone. There was virtually no eye contact. According to the Carkhuffian model, the major focus was on phase I relational concerns (conveying acceptance) and on drawing out some meaningful client exploration of the problem. The core dimensions of empathy, positive regard, and concreteness were conveyed (nonverbally and with basic listening skills—silence, simple acknowledgment, summaries, "door-openers," and reflection). As is often the case with students, she had already sized up the professor and saw me as someone she could trust. Consequently, the groundwork for this phase had previously been laid, and we moved quickly toward building a picture of the problem. Sharing was difficult, but a minimum of support and encouragement enabled her to get the problem out where we might have a chance to resolve it. The major presenting problem focused on an unwanted pregnancy, rejection from her boyfriend, and a desperate sense of being unable to handle the situation. She was 2 months pregnant but had kept this secret to herself where it had evolved into overwhelming proportions. I brought closure to our session and asked her to see me again that afternoon to pursue the problem further. As usual, my summary closure statement reflected the basic Carkhuffian model as I laid out the steps—exploration, integration, action—that are ultimately involved in any problem-solving process and set the tone for hope in resolving the crisis.

Comments There were at least three reasons for setting an appointment for later that same day, which meant cancelling some scheduled commitments and making her concern a top priority. First, the limited time frame of the first session (approximately 35 minutes sandwiched between other appointments) did not allow for an adequate closure. There was not time to lead into a relevant homework assignment or to process relational issues related to our first session. Second, there had been a considerable amount of high-intensity catharsis during our brief session, and the session ended with far too many loose ends. I anticipated an emotional reaction on her part to having shared this personal material and felt a need to provide an immediate follow-up. Finally, while some obviously long-term themes had emerged, I needed to respond quickly to the presenting crisis—decisions regarding a course of action needed to be made within the next few weeks. The timing of the second appointment might also reflect my genuine concern for her dilemma and the intensity of her problem.

Second Session I took out 10 to 15 minutes of my schedule to *preattend* this next session. This effort at analyzing the pieces presented in the first session brings the *integrative* phase into play and increases the potential of accurate interpretation for the next session. This presession time also allowed me to formulate a strategy and possible homework assignment for the next session. I concluded that there were probably some chronic relational/nonassertive issues that fed into the immediate pregnancy-related problem, but these issues would have to wait until the presenting crisis had been handled. With these considerations in mind, I finished my preattending period with some self-talk related to phase I attitudes (empathy, regard, concreteness, and related skills). I tend to move too quickly at times, so a brief reminder to slow down set the tone for my upcoming session. She appeared to be in better control, so I started the session with a summary of what had been presented earlier, and then presented a picture of my approach. (Pregnancy-related crisis first, with more chronic issues at a later date.) We moved on to define the steps needed to resolve the crisis issue which would involve a closer look at the alternatives and a plan of action to be developed within the next 3 weeks. We also agreed to meet twice each week until a workable plan could be implemented. These considerations reflect phase II (integration) efforts at piecing together the major therapeutic themes and helping the client see the bigger picture as an alternative way of viewing the problem. Hopefully, Alice's sense of overwhelming helplessness was being gradually replaced by a more realistic and constructive frame of reference and sense of direction. She responded well to my problem-solving approach, so I shifted back to listening skills to help generate a list of alternatives. She presented the pieces of the puzzle and we translated them into the concrete steps necessary to resolve the problem. The following areas needed to be explored: carry the fetus full term and then give the baby up for adoption; carry the fetus full term and then keep the baby; have an abortion. Each area involved many facets and a great deal of information needed to be gathered and organized so that a sound decision could be made. A potential list of resource contacts was drawn up (a physician, priest, adoption agency, etc.) which would eventually be translated into information-gathering homework assignments.

Our next step was to prioritize our list and start to work. Since we were running out of time again, this became a logical homework assignment. An appointment was set for the following afternoon (again responding to the immediacy of the situation), and I asked Alice to revise her list into a rank ordering and further identify strategies for obtaining the information related to each item. This assignment was seen as part of the *integrative phase II* concerns directed toward reorganizing the overwhelming problem into manageable units. Further clarification of our overall direction was made by defining the basic steps in problem solving and providing her with a related handout (adapted from Gordon, 1970). She appeared to understand the assignment and logic behind it and agreed to set aside an hour that night to read the handout and prioritize our list. While Alice had again shared some emotionally laden material, the process had clearly shifted from an affective (the first session being almost exclusively cathartic) to a cognitive focus, and the foundation was laid for action (doing something concrete about her dilemma).

Comments Some new information had solidified my hypothesis regarding the chronicity of self-defeating patterns. While dealing with the pregnancy-related crisis was an essential focus, it was clearly symptomatic of long-term relational problems. She had a history of destructive involvements with noneffectual males and a related poor self-image. She also presented a picture of low-esteem-related depression which could be traced back to early adolescence and had been punctuated by two suicide gestures during the last 3 years in college. Depression at this point had both reactive (to the unwanted pregnancy) and endogenous components related to years of perceived inadequacy. Whereas the broader picture was becoming clear to me, I chose to put these issues aside until more progress had been made with the crisis situation. In terms of the Carkhuffian model, the empathy level had increased as expressed by a transition from reflection (level 3) to several interpretive reflections (level 4)—I knew her better now and could give her more insightful responses. Most of the interpretation centered around the boyfriend involved with her pregnancy and her unwillingness to deal directly with him. Self-disclosure on my part was used here relating to a past difficulty I had overcome regarding the avoidance of a particularly threatening issue with a close friend. My confrontation (borrowing from Eisenberg and Delaney, 1977) had been low-level (a "door-opener" asking about the potential of reestablishing her relationship with the boyfriend), and she responded with resistance. I stored this response and put the issue aside temporarily.

Third Session A great deal of information had been generated during nearly 2 hours of counseling, and I needed extra preattending time to sort it out in preparation for our critical third session. I saw it as critical in the sense of moving her toward the first steps of the action phase of counseling—translating insights into change. Several risks were involved. I took the risk of testing our relationship and her motivation level by asking her to do something—the written homework. Failure at this minor task would lead to a reassessment of her willingness to resolve the problem and/or her confidence in me and our strategy. I also preattended our third session by further developing my plan of approach. I wanted to focus on the boyfriend issue but decided to wait until she had successfully dealt with some less threatening areas related to the problem. I also sensed that a direct confrontive approach would be needed on the boyfriend issue so decided to let our relational support system develop further before opening this touchy area.

Alice came in with her homework completed in a thoughtful and detailed manner. The mood was somewhat elevated, and we went to work on tuning up the priority listing she presented. This is what I was looking for—a visible index of her motivational level and her confidence in our approach. It also provided an organizational scheme for the problem and subdivided the basic goal (resolving the crises) into more manageable steps. These subgoals could then be translated into the concrete steps of the action phase. I let her know that I appreciated her effort and shared my optimism in reaching a tolerable solution to a bad situation. She arranged the list in the following manner: *physical* (information on the physical realities of pregnancy and abortion); *moral* (she was from a conservative Catholic background and needed to sort out issues surrounding the church's view of her problem); *financial* (realistically assess the economic consequences of her choice regarding the pregnancy); *academic* (she was a good student and needed a plan of action regarding the completion of the semester and future plans related to the pregnancy decision). I added a *personal* area as a first step in opening the boyfriend issue and informed her that we would approach this after dealing with the areas she had listed. I also let her know that I saw the immediate steps in reaction to crisis, but that long-term issues regarding her self-defeating patterns would have to be confronted when the time became appropriate. It should be noted that my hidden agenda was also to expand her support base and deal with her feeling of alienation. The information-gathering process also put the problem in clearer perspective and reduced her sense of being overwhelmed. For the present, however, we would focus on defining a course of direction for handling the pregnancy. In our rural setting this would involve information gathering from several sources. It was my job to direct her to these resources and coach her on what information to obtain.

We continued our problem-solving efforts by focusing on the top-priority item—*physical concerns*. We discussed in detail the questions that needed answers (types of abortion, timing, etc.), and I gave her the name of a physician who I knew personally as competent and sensitive. She was to be responsible for setting up an appointment with him for later in the week. Her appointment with him would be her "ticket" to our next session. We also discussed the kind of information (physical and financial) that she could get from a local adoption agency which offers assistance in these cases. I contacted (during our session) a female friend at the agency and set up an appointment for Alice. This would give her a chance to gain a female perspective on the problem and further process alternatives to abortion and hopefully put an apparently impossible financial barrier into perspective.

Action Facilitation Phase III proceeded according to the model (Egan, 1975) by incorporating all of the dimensions (empathy, self-disclosure, immediacy, confrontation, alternative frames of reference) and adding an elaboration of action programs and direct support. The closure focused on further clarification of the steps to be taken and the offering of support for the risks of seeing these people. She left prepared to carry out her assignments and meet with me again in 3 days. It should be noted that our efforts were collaborative as we defined the steps needed to be taken. She was more in control, more rational, and more capable of using her own resources than in our earlier sessions, and I pushed her toward that end. This is not always the case, as some higher-functioning clients take over the responsibility for change at this point whereas lower-functioning ones need to be led step by step.

Fourth Session Less preattending time was needed since we had initiated a sequence of steps that could cut across several sessions. I did, however, preattend by reminding myself not to get locked into the sequence so as to be insensitive to other concerns. (I generally start my sessions by chatting so the client has the opportunity to offer redirection. I also reminded myself to be sensitive to possible failures in her homework assignments and to reward her successes.) I had also reviewed her list and knew that the morality and academic issues needed to be approached in the next few sessions. I would look for the right time to introduce them.

Once again she had followed through on her assignment—making an appointment with the physician and talking with my friend at the adoption agency. She shared the information with me, and we discussed the implications. I cautioned her about reaching any decisions before more information was collected. It should be apparent here that the action and integration phases must work together, as each feeds into the other. Insights are translated into goals, goals into specific steps, and action leads back into new insights, which evolve into an expanded picture of the problem.

Next we discussed the morality issue. It came up in the context of our discussion about the abortion alternative. This alternative had an appeal (ridding herself of the problem), but obvious religious ramifications. I cautioned her not to take this lightly and suggested that she discuss it further with a Catholic priest; not just any priest, but one I knew personally who was very sensitive and could give her a chance to sort through her beliefs. Her ticket to the next session would be an appointment with this priest. There was some resistance here, but I insisted that she see him. I also wanted to initiate an action component related to her academic problems. She was a good student and her recent neglect of classwork had magnified her sense of self-reproach and dissatisfaction. There was also a realistic chance of losing her scholarship if she failed to pull her classwork together before finals.

I suggested a second part to her homework—a list of all the work remaining to be completed prior to finals. We drew up a rough outline of a work calendar, and I asked her to fill in tentative completion dates for each task. As suggested in the Egan (1975) version of the Carkhuffian model, our interactions had become more directional, and I had been able to self-disclose regarding my success in using a scheduling system similar to the one I had proposed. Furthermore, Carkhuff and Berenson's (1967) notion of immediacy came into play toward the end of this session as we took a brief but direct look at our relationship and how it evolved. This not only solidified the relational progress we had made but would set the stage for evaluating other relationships in later sessions. We ended, as usual, with a brief review of her assignment and a pep talk to increase the chance of her successfully completing the tasks.

Fifth Session Alice had again completed her assignments as she continued to compile more information to support her decision regarding the pregnancy. The priest had been particularly helpful in clarifying her religious beliefs, and it appeared more likely that she would cancel the abortion alternative. My friend at the adoption agency had further supported the option of keeping the baby and had made a commitment regarding the medical expenses. Alice was gaining control. She had also completed the academic schedule, and the primary focus of this session became the refinement of a plan of attack for getting her schoolwork back in order. The calendar of completion dates was translated into more specific subunits, and we used my class as an example. She had a good history of academic success so the primary function here was motivational as she tied herself down to an almost hour-by-hour schedule. She had done poorly on my last exam and had a major paper due in 3 weeks. We subdivided studying and writing into specific units and specified the completion of a paper outline as her ticket to our next session. She had two classes from one of my colleagues, and I encouraged her to make an appointment to clarify her standing in these classes. The chronic issue of Alice's overly stringent expectancies could be dealt with later, but we were still trying to make it through the crisis.

Now she was ready to approach the issue we had avoided—her boyfriend. This was an important piece of the puzzle, and we needed some answers before reaching any final decisions. She perceived him as having used her and had not spoken with him for several weeks. I suggested that she contact him by phone and set up a time for them to discuss the role he played in her problem. We rehearsed what she was to say, and she agreed to call him. Our next appointment would be in 3 days.

Sixth Session This session focused on the boyfriend issue. She had not followed through as promised, and I responded with some gentle confrontation and a much more detailed rehearsal of her next assignment—try again. The discussion made it quite clear that she had a long history of problems with the opposite sex related to her passive/subservient approach to relationships. This opened the door to a discussion of long-term counseling before shifting back to focus on the pregnancy issue again. I still felt that she needed to talk with him and insisted that she call him that evening.

Seventh Session Alice had completed her assignment. It was scary, but she had taken the risk to make the phone call. It had resulted in a lengthy face-to-face meeting in which a great deal of insight was generated. He had, in fact, expressed a surprising degree of sensitivity to the situation and offered to help in any way she deemed appropriate. At this point, Alice rejected his offer and made it clear that she would take care of the problem herself. At any rate, the issue was now somewhat clearer, and she was at a decision point. The decision involved the following components.

1 Have the child and then give it up for adoption through the agency we had contacted. Specific arrangement would be made as part of her next assignment.

2 Inform her parents and her roommate about her pregnancy and related decision. We would determine the exact approach together during our next session. She had kept this pretty much to herself and needed to let these key people know.

3 Continue the progress made on her academic strategy. Grades remained important to her, and now she had some renewed energy to invest in that direction.

4 Initiate long-term counseling regarding some of the chronic problem areas that had been touched upon during our sessions. We would use the time before the end of the semester to further define these concerns.

Eighth through Tenth Sessions Three areas were dealt with during these sessions that took us to the end of the semester: monitor and redefine approach to school work, help devise a plan to present her pregnancy-related problem to her parents, and further define the long-term issues that we would work on for the next several months. The sense of crisis was over so we shifted from two to one session per week.

Before leaving for Christmas vacation, we were able to clarify some of the areas that had been bothersome for a long time and had made her vulnerable for the crisis problem we had partially resolved. It should be noted that our success with the crisis situation (moving from relational to integrational to action phases) had set the stage for a more long-term in-depth look at herself. I had gained her confidence, and our relationship would withstand a considerable amount of pushing toward more basic lifestyle changes. The central theme evolved around chronic depression related to a very low self-esteem. When asked how she would rate herself on a 10-point scale, Alice replied, "Zero." We later defined progress in terms of that 10-point scale and climbed to a 6 as her own subjective self-rating. As a homework assignment during these sessions, I asked her to list the major components of this picture of degradation. She came up with the following list: shyness, frequently used by others, lonely (no really close friends), sexually exploited by many of her male acquaintances, physical unattractiveness (she described herself as being 50 pounds overweight). We spent a considerable amount of time over these weeks prioritizing these components and redefining them into specific subgoals to be systematically attacked.

Eleventh through Twenty-Eighth Sessions Our weekly sessions carried us through the end of the spring semester. She returned after Christmas vacation relieved over her parents' surprisingly supportive attitude regarding the pregnancy and committed to the goals we had established. I will summarize our approach briefly. It primarily focused on action steps toward improving Alice's self-concept, but integrative efforts occurred at each junction. Carkhuff and Berenson's (1967) notion of "preferred modes of treatment" emerged throughout the process as we borrowed bits of strategies from a wide range of resources. The following will illustrate a few of these resources that came into play.

Integration Phase We continued to revise the list of problem components and reestablish specific subgoals for implementation in the action phase. Each success and failure in the action phase was also dealt with in terms of generating insights and incorporating behavior change into attitude and belief systems. Her belief system supported the lifestyle problems and was gradually reshaped through interpretation, confrontation, and my own self-disclosures regarding my beliefs. In the process, I borrowed heavily from the following techniques: direct instruction (I use paper and pencil frequently to diagram problems and strategies), and bibliotherapy (actually a reading assignment geared toward new self-appraisal—Ellis and Harper, 1973; James and Jongeward, 1971). I also had her read an article by Beck and Young (1978) which proved to be quite insightful regarding her problem with loneliness and set the stage for a related behavior change approach that was somewhat successful. I should mention my use of a wide range of techniques borrowed from Beck (1976) in our attack of the cognitive base of her esteem problems. These techniques ("experimental method," rule changing, altered self-talk) emerged throughout the process and supported behavior change efforts.

Action Phase The format for this phase of our long-term counseling was set by our extensive use of homework assignments related to the key issues. The basic job was to translate insights regarding the chronic concerns into tangible change strategies to be carried out between sessions. This format remained fairly constant, but a wide range of strategies ("perferred modes of treatment") were brought into play as we generally moved from the areas where success probabilities were high into high-risk concerns. It was critical at several junctures to work on bringing her skill level up to meet tasks successfully, and a variety of role-playing and rehearsal techniques were employed. She kept an ongoing log as a way to focus on change and monitor her progress. Assertion training became a major theme that seemed to tie together several of the esteem-related issues, and we also initiated a weight control and exercise program at the seventeenth session which had some success. Alice's involvement at that point with an aerobic dance class was a considerable boost physically and provided an opening for several good social contacts.

Whereas we worked directly on overcoming her tendency toward social withdrawal (and related sexual vulnerability), we also created an opportunity for her to act as a helping role herself. She was encouraged to take on a tutoring job through our basic skills program, and found herself in a position to apply some of the helping skills that I had modeled during our sessions. I will never forget the sense of elation she expressed over the progress of one of her students and the kind of confidence that she generated for herself in this process.

SUMMARY

I do not want to paint an overly glowing picture. This was a highly successful case, but with many ups and downs. Alice will continue to struggle in many areas, but she has replaced some areas of weakness with a new sense of control. She has also learned a process of problem solving that can be applied to future problems. Most importantly, Alice has developed some social skills that enable her to gain a more constructive and dependable support system. She had even developed several dating relationships in which she had maintained a sense of control and appropriate distance. A great deal of constructive change had occurred. Even though my illustration has become quite lengthy, it does not begin to reflect the intensity, energy, and pieces of creative counseling that went into this effort.

REFERENCES

Beck, A. T. *Cognitive therapy*. New York: Meridian, 1976.

Beck, A. T., and Young, J. E. College blues. *Psychology Today*, September 1978, 80–92.

Carkhuff, R. R., and Berenson, B. G. *Beyond counseling and therapy*. New York: Holt, 1967.

Egan, G. *The skilled helper*. Monterey, Calif: Brooks/Cole, 1975.

Eisenberg, S., and Delaney, D. J. *The counseling process* (2nd ed.). Chicago: Rand McNally, 1977.

Ellis, A., and Harper, R. A. *A guide to rational living*. Hollywood: Wilshire, 1973.

Gordon, T. *Parent effectiveness training*. New York: Wyden, 1971.

James, M., and Jongeward, D. *Born to win*. Reading, Mass.: Addison-Wesley, 197l.

PART C: MIKE: WHEN WE FAIL TO PREATTEND: AN ILLUSTRATION OF THE WINDOW CONCEPT

Mike had taken an incomplete in my fall research class and needed to change this into a grade in order to graduate at summer commencement. The paper was the last remaining ingredient in his graduate program. He had been in other classes, and we had become rather good friends. At any rate, I had spent many hours helping him with his research project, but he continued to procrastinate on the final draft. The final manuscript was 2 weeks overdue, and graduation was only a few days away. I had made an appointment with him for Monday at 10:00 A.M. following my two early classes. He had promised to turn in his paper at our meeting. The following will illustrate the dynamics of the acceptance line as it operates within my window and sets the tone for my interaction with Mike.

I had been up very late the night before because of an out-of-town swimming meet in which my daughters were participants. It was too late to adequately prepare for my morning classes at 7:00 and 8:30 A.M.. So Monday morning rolled around all too soon, and I dragged myself out of bed, too late to ride my bicycle as planned. I hopped into my truck just in time to make it to class. It seems that my three-year-old son had been playing with my truck radio, and the battery was dead (see Figure A-1 and follow the flow of my acceptance line). Frustration was building as I dashed into the house to get the keys for my wife's car. She was not particularly pleased since this messed up her plans, and she let me know it. My line continued to go up as my tolerance became less and less.

Now I was on my way to work, and trying to think through the lecture material that had been neglected over the weekend. As I came around a curve, I saw an old man struggling to put a spare tire onto his truck. He needed help, and I normally would have stopped. My stress level increased. I hope that you are getting the picture. Your normally calm and relaxed author was becoming very uptight with increasingly less tolerance for other people's problems. I would like to say that I stopped this nonsense and preattended my class and 10:00 A.M. appointment with Mike. Unfortunately, these situations tend to feed on themselves, and I found myself fumbling through my first class. My second class was even worse, and I should have quit early to get myself together for my upcoming session with Mike. I did not, and found myself coming out of class wishing that

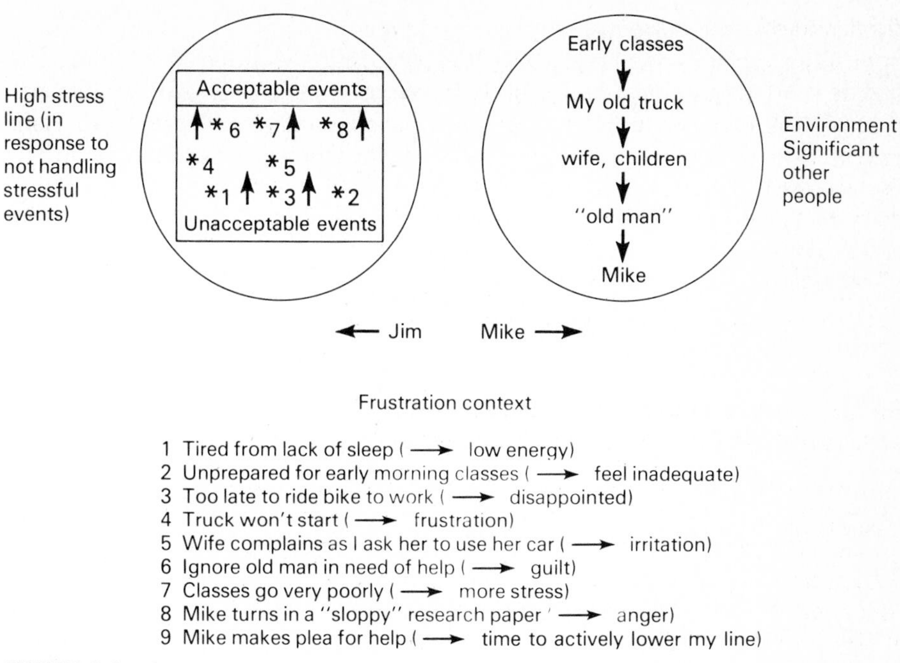

FIGURE A-1
Failure to preattend a counseling session.

I did not have to see Mike about his incomplete paper. I should add that with graduation approaching, papers and exams were already stacked a foot deep on my desk.

Down the hall I went, feeling more and more irritated at Mike for putting off his paper this long. "Why do students do this to me?" I mumbled to myself as I brushed past Mike and motioned for him to come into my office. He laid his research paper on my desk as we both sat down. A cursory glance is all it took to see that the paper was inadequate in every respect—totally unacceptable. I threw it down on the table in disgust and began to let Mike have a very clear picture of what I thought of his paper (what I may have thought was "clear" was really a clouded reflection of my high level of overall stress). My loud critical voice stimulated a response that I will never forget—tears started to stream down Mike's face. This was no stranger I was yelling at—Mike had been in several of my classes, and I had come to know him as a friend. His tears shook me and forced a momentary look at my acceptance level and a little effort at getting a hold of myself. Things had gotten out of hand.

As I backed off and apologized (not for the assessment of his paper but for my harsh approach), the real reason for the tears was presented. Mike began by reminding me that his father had been quite ill, and then informed me that he had died the night before. My level of intolerance was suddenly put into perspective. Mike had stayed up all night working on his paper in an effort to keep from going to pieces. He indicated that his graduation was one of the things that had kept his father going. Mike felt tremendous guilt, anger, and loss, but apparently had no one to turn to except me at that point in time. All the little irritants that had set the tone of my day up to that point seemed pretty trite within this new context. My previous concerns seemed small. Fortunately, I was able to push my line down enough to be of some help to my friend as we put aside the issues of his paper and my nonacceptance.

Although this incident occurred several years ago, it still comes to mind. It is a reminder of my own personal vulnerability to stress buildup, and the close tie between my personal life (and ability to handle small frustrations) and my professional effectiveness with students and clients. I never know when I will have to deal with crises in other people, but I do know that I need to keep my stress line down so that I can intervene effectively when needed.

PART D: SHERRY AND JOYCE: PUTTING INSIGHTS INTO ACTION

Sherry was a fifteen-year-old girl referred to Gordon and me by a local minister. Actually, the referral was the result of a series of counseling classes we had taught for the local clergy. Her minister was quite concerned as she had experienced a dramatic weight loss during the past few months and medical interventions had made no impact. He asked us to see her about the weight-loss problem and her parents regarding the related stress they were experiencing. We decided that I would see the daughter initially, whereas Gordon would deal with the parents. We would decide on an overall strategy after our first sessions.

First Sessions

Jim's Session with Sherry The phrase "shy and withdrawn" would understate my initial impression—she was scared to death as her parents let her off at my office. Initial efforts at warming up to our session were fruitless—I was completely shut out (verbally and nonverbally) for the first 15 minutes of our session. Then the floodgates burst, and I saw an angry girl unleash a series of self-abusive statements such as I seldom hear (and I hear a lot of it). She hated herself; everything about herself. With some gentle probing, she was later able to verbalize the anger she also felt toward her parents (particularly her mother) and her younger sister—an anger that had apparently turned inward and was vented only through her controlling abuse of food intake. She had lost 30 pounds in the past 3 months and presented a preanorexic picture with some of the classic characteristics—refusal to eat, self-induced vomiting, history of obesity, overactivity, and distortion of body image (American Psychiatric Association, 1980). She had been given physical examinations on two occasions without any apparent organic basis for the dramatic weight loss being uncovered.

Gordon's Session with the Parents Two key themes emerged from Gordon's first contact with Sherry's parents. First, a sense of frustration and utter helplessness in dealing with Sherry's weight loss and related issues surrounding it. They "had tried everything" and were very aware of the potential health hazards should the pattern persist. Second, and a chronic issue—the intense achievement needs of the mother which had been transferred onto her oldest daughter. It was critically important to Sherry's mother (Joyce) that Sherry achieve in areas (social, academic, sports) that had been thwarted in her life. Gordon saw the mother as domineering and authoritarian in her approach to Sherry. He suspected that Joyce had cut off any means for Sherry to communicate her needs. The father appeared to be quite passive and was physically removed from family life most of the time because of the nature of his work.

Our Assessment

Gordon and I got together following our first sessions to compare notes and develop a strategy. We conceptualized the situation as involving chronic and crisis components. The chronic problems centered around the mother's displacement of intense achievement needs and her harsh approach toward Sherry. The communication system between mother and daughter was deteriorated, and alternative approaches to dealing with each other would have to be developed.

The crisis considerations evolved around the dramatic weight loss itself. Whereas Sherry presented many of the classic anorexic symptoms along with the characteristic shyness, anxiety, and dependency (Smart, Beumont, and George, 1976), we saw it as a case of conscious manipulation on Sherry's part. She had found a powerful way to control her mother and the rest of the family. In doing our homework we found an excellent supporting resource (Walen, Hauserman, and Lavin, 1977), which made some important diagnostic distinctions between anorexia nervosa and oppositional noneating. In the latter case, food has not reached phobic magnitude, and the refusal to eat is supported by considerable attention from significant other people in the environment. They further suggest that attention withdrawal will eventually lead to the resumption of eating. We saw a need to replace poor communication skills with a more assertive means of resolving mother/daughter conflicts rather than a simplistic extinction approach.

Our Strategy

A strategy package was formalized. We would continue to meet separately until the stage became ready for dealing with the chronic communication problems. The plan for me was to deal directly with Sherry regarding her weight-loss manipulation. I would confront her gently and move on to prepare her to deal with the communication issue. I would be careful not to add to the attention-getting problem, but firmly push toward building the support and skills necessary for her to approach her mother in a more constructive manner. I would develop a picture with her of the problem in terms of her manipulation with the weight loss as a self-defeating symptom of chronic conflict and her sense of desperation in dealing with her mother. The skill focus would combine elements of assertion training and desensitization but would lead to building a problem-solving system to be used between Sherry and her mother. Hopefully, the attitudes and skills would transfer to other important but less destructive relationships.

Gordon would continue meeting with the parents. The focus would be on Sherry's mother, but her father, who paralleled Sherry's passivity, would be brought into the picture as much as possible. It appeared at this early stage that Sherry had modeled her father's passivity and that he might need to develop a more assertive approach to both Sherry and her mother.

The emphasis would be twofold: development of a supportive context in which insight could be built regarding their role in Sherry's problem; and, development of problem-solving skills to be applied with Sherry in later sessions and between-session problem-solving efforts. Gordon would also ask Joyce to obtain the medical evaluations that had been done on her daughter and grant us permission to discuss the case with their primary physician. The projected goal was to bring our clients together as soon as they were ready to try out an alternative means of communicating. We would coach them separately on problem-solving skills (active listing, confrontation, and a step-by-step process) before trying a joint session.

Second through Fourth Sessions These sessions progressed very well. Both Gordon and I were able to establish a good supportive context for our respective clients (relational phase in the Carkhuffian model). The integration phase (generating a conceptual picture of the problem) evolved quite differently for each of us.

Sherry actually preempted my interpretations about the manipulation component of the weight loss. She admitted to this during our session (actually through her homework assignment which was to express the problem in her own words in writing). Her withdrawal from food initially may not have been a conscious attention-seeking controlling effort, but it had soon developed to that point. She had found a powerful means of controlling her mother and was very aware of it. She also (to my relief) agreed to drop this tactical device if she could just get her mother to listen. The medical reports revealed no apparent organic basis for the weight loss. I was relieved because it simplified our goals, reduced the family stress level, and cut off a potential dangerous pattern which very well could have progressed into a more ingrained habit. Our energies were free now to prepare Sherry to deal more effectively with her mother. An orientation to problem-solving strategies was given during the second session, and our plan was put into action through a second homework assignment—read through a handout on democratic problem solving abstracted from Gordon, 1972 (see Table A-1). Our third session focused on clarifying an image of how Sherry wanted the communication between her and her mother to become, and a review of the six-step problem-solving process. We discussed problem areas that she might present to her mother and

TABLE A-1
SIX STEPS TO PROBLEM SOLVING AND CONFLICT RESOLUTION (DGEFIF)

Step I.	*D:* Define the problem in terms of needs a. State your side of the problem as accurately as you can in a way that does not communicate blame or judgment. b. Try to verbalize the other person's side of the problem after he or she has had an opportunity to state it. Do not be in a hurry to get to Step II. Be sure that both sides have been stated and that the conflict or problem is defined accurately. Frequently, a problem will be redefined with the initial problem turning out to be a superficial one. Before moving to step II, be sure that both of you accept the definition of the problem. Are both sets of needs stated accurately? The problem, not the solution you want.
Step II.	*G:* Generate all possible solutions No evaluation is allowed until step III. All ideas are accepted during this creative step in the process. Have someone write down each suggestion. If things get bogged down, state the problem again.
Step III.	*E:* Evaluate the various solutions Primary ingredients here are critical thinking and honesty. Do a verbal preliminary test of each solution to increase chances of the final solution working out. Are there any flaws? Will it be too difficult to implement with the time limits? Is it really fair to all concerned? Do not permit the solution to stand if it is not acceptable to you.
Step IV.	*D:* Deciding on a mutually acceptable solution A mutual commitment to one solution must be made. The solution may have many components. Work toward *consensus*. Do not accept a solution until everyone agrees to try it. Write down the agreed-upon solution and prepare a copy for everyone involved. Do not push the solution on the others.
Step V.	*I:* Implementing the solution *Who* does *what* by *when* is determined (write it down). Do not talk about penalties for failure to implement solution at this time. Let all involved assume the total responsibility for his or her part in the solution (do not nag).
Step VI.	*F:* Follow-up Evaluation of the success of the solution to discover weaknesses and possibly return to the problem-solving process. Decision is always open to revision (may from initial enthusiasm set a specific time to check the effectiveness of the solution).

Source: Abstracted from Gordon, *Parent Effectiveness Training: Parent Notebook,* 1972.

gave another homework assignment—exercises on confrontation and active listening adopted from *Parent Effectiveness Training* (Gordon, 1970). I also asked for a list of problem areas that would later provide the focus for problem-solving sessions with her mother. Sherry was serious and did her assignments with considerable enthusiasm. (I was quite surprised and very pleased.) Our fourth session gave us a chance for review, rehearsal, and further clarification of the issues that she wanted to present to her mother. I believed that the time was right for a joint meeting so the stage was set to meet with Gordon and Sherry's mother next time.

In the meantime, Gordon had worked through a considerable amount of resistance with Sherry's mother. Her role in creating the weight problem (her authoritarian and domineering style coupled with high-achievement demands for her daughter) was difficult to accept and became a recurring theme throughout the counseling process. This, perhaps, was intensified by the fact that Sherry's father dropped out of counseling after the first session. Gordon's primary focus was on what could be done to improve communication rather than reunifying past problems. Instead of dwelling on blame and deep-seated problems, he focused positively on communication skill training. He started with an overview of conflict resolution meetings as a means of establishing better communication between Joyce and her daughter. Excerpts from a parenting manual (Dinkmeyer and McKay, 1976) were assigned to be read initially and followed up with a series of training exercises from another manual (Gordon, 1972). The main direction of their sessions shifted toward instruction in communication skills and coaching on specific techniques of problem solving. They also developed a list of issues that presented barriers between them.

We saw a dramatic shift in attitudes with both of our clients during these initial sessions. Our insight into the problem appeared to be accurate, and our related action program was working. A good level of support had been built between us and our respective clients, both of our clients accomplishing their homework assignments and acquiring the prerequisite skills for our problem-solving approach (skill development was rudimentary, but there was clear evidence of progress). Sherry had returned to more normal eating patterns which relieved pressures on all sides. Both clients had gained insight into themselves and the role each played in their chronic conflict. They were eager for change and fairly optimistic about the potentials for an improved relationship. Gordon and I believed that they were ready to work directly together on our problem-solving approach to conflict resolution.

Session Five The four of us met together in a lengthy session. We concentrated on preparing them for the first of a long series of weekly at-home problem-solving sessions. The following list identifies the basic steps taken in this session:

1 Issue identification: Both clients shared their issue lists, and we reviewed them together. We explained that we needed to start from issues that would be relatively easy to resolve. When successful with less loaded issues, we would move on to more intense and chronic problems. The focus was placed on the importance of developing a better way of communicating rather than on the issues themselves. In addition to generating a hierarchy, we also pulled out the major underlying themes (achievement drive, rigidity of thinking, inability to express affection) and discussed the interrelatedness of the problem areas.

2 Ground rules: We established a list of ground rules for their up-coming at-home sessions. We set up times, places, and a series of do's and don'ts.

3 Modeling: After identifying our target issue for the next week's at-home session, we played a taped conflict-resolution session we had obtained from a similar case. This gave us a concrete example, and we went through it step by step pointing out good points and pitfalls.

4 Rehearsal: Gordon and I felt like a couple of coaches preparing our respective athletes for the "big game" with a last minute pep talk and brief discussion of realistic expectancies for their problem-solving efforts.

Sixth through Twelfth Sessions A great deal of time was spent here monitoring their progress and reviewing the taped sessions they were making at home each week. We took on a teaching, coaching, and supportive role as a backdrop to the implementation of their action program. Ups and downs were expected and vividly reflected on the tapes we critiqued, but the overall direction was positive. Most importantly, an alternative to the strictly autocratic approach had been established along with a renewed sense of caring and mutual respect. They were learning a process that could maintain an improved relationship long after Gordon and I ended our involvement. They also have developed skills which could be transferred into other significant relationships, and we defined those extensions before bringing our weekly joint sessions to a close. The following reflects our plan for follow-up.

1 Sherry: I would continue to work with her on building a more assertive approach to other areas of her life, i.e., her teachers, track coach, and a boyfriend.

2 Joyce: Gordon would see her at 1-month intervals to check on progress. He also referred her to an ongoing parent training class to further support the gains she had made and provide an opportunity to share her accomplishments with a peer group of parents.

3 Sherry and Joyce: Both clients agreed to continue their weekly tape-recorded sessions at home. Obviously, not all the problems were resolved, but they would continue to work on them. We also generated a list of positive topics which could be developed in their weekly sessions and hopefully evolve into some healthy mother/daughter activities. We introduced the concept of time management and the importance of balancing the amount of time they spent together, alone, and with activities.

Follow-Up

I met with Sherry for five more formal sessions and have seen her since on several occasions (see Figure A-2 for a summary). She is presently a sophomore at one of our state universities and is active in sports, school organizations, and dating. She has maintained a 3.5 grade-point average and has become an exceptionally charming young lady. The weight problem has never reemerged.

Gordon's follow-up became a bit more complicated than planned. Joyce's husband decided to join her for the parenting classes, and their relationship underwent some significant changes. Several months after termination, Gordon started a marriage counseling program with Joyce and her husband. There was a lot of work to be done, and Gordon continued with them for nearly 6 months. We have both been in their home since that time and believe that the constructive changes have been maintained.

Sherry (15 y.o. client)		Jim with Sherry
Jim (Sherry's counselor) Initial support establishment Problem assessment Decide on problem focus Defining our approach	Preparation and implementation of our plans, refine strategies, further goal refinement, "issue hierarchy," Problem-solving focus Joint sessions	(5 additional sessions and informal follow-up) Continuation of assertion training and application to other people and settings
RELATIONAL ⟶ INTEGRATIONAL (INSIGHT)	PUTTING INSIGHT INTO ACTION	FOLLOW UP
Skill development Homework assignments Practice Rehearsal Joyce (Sherry's mother)	Jim and Gordon with Sherry and Joyce Continue with support for their efforts at change, coaching and teaching continued (use of taped sessions, modeling, strategy building, critiquing, role playing, rehearsal, etc.)	Continue with parent skill training (referral to parent group) Initiate and follow through with extensive marriage counseling Gordon with Joyce + Joyce's husband
Gordon (Joyce's counselor)		(Marriage counseling, 6 months Parent group instructor (8 week course)
Session #1 2 ______ 4	5 ______ 12	13 ______

FIGURE A-2
Summary of case with Sherry and Joyce.

REFERENCES

American Psychiatric Association. *Diagnostic and statistical manual of mental disorders* (3rd ed.). Washington, D.C.: American Psychiatric Association, 1980.

Dinkmeyer, D., and McKay, G. D. *Systematic training for effective parenting: Parent's handbook.* Circle Pines, Minn.: American Guidance Service, 1976.

Gordon, T. *Parent effectiveness training.* New York: Wyden, 1971.

Gordon, T. *Parent effectiveness training: Parent notebook.* Solana Beach, Calif.: Effectiveness Training, 1972.

Smart, D. E., Beumont, P. J., and George, G. C. Some personality characteristics of patients with anorexia nervosa. *British Journal of Psychiatry,* 1976, *128*(13), 57–60.

Walen, S., Hauserman, N. H., and Lavin, P. J. *Clinical guide to behavior therapy.* Baltimore, Md.: Williams and Wilkins, 1977.

PART E: JAKE: BREAKING THE BURNOUT CYCLE

One of the most rewarding things that Gordon and I have done together involved the development of a postgraduate renewal workshop. We have run this weeklong program for several summers and have a growing list of participants that come from a wide variety of counseling backgrounds. We spend the week sharing new directions in counseling, but also take out plenty of time for fun, i.e., backpacking, raft trips, etc. Two years ago we spent one of our information sessions focusing on burnout in much the same way as we did in Chapter 9. This session was followed by an afternoon raft trip, and one of the men in my raft (call him Jake) really unloaded. He was fed up with his job and said that he was becoming a good example of the burnout profile we had presented that morning. Jake was a high school guidance counselor in a large school system and had been at the same job for 12 years. He had felt a growing sense of professional impotence over the past several years and sensed a need for change. Unfortunately, he had hung on to the same old patterns that brought him more into administrative work and further away from the children he had been trained to help. Even his involvement with students had become misdirected as Jake became everything (scheduler, disciplinarian, etc.) except counselor to them. He felt alienated from his students, and found himself tied more and more to an office full of paperwork. Colleague relationships had become more superficial, and professional involvement with our state organization had become nonexistent.

We talked again on several occasions that week, and Jake left with a renewed sense of potential and commitment to work his way out of the rut. Lots of people do this periodically without any real change, but I was optimistic in this case, partly because Jake had begun to lay out a very sensible course of action. Let us take a look at the report I received (first in a series of letters and finally in the full-blown version at the retreat we recently completed this past summer). As a creative counselor, preattenting set the stage for what was to be a year of genuine renewal for my friend Jake. He met with his principal shortly after attending our workshop and presented a plan for reorganizing his counseling job. The plan paralleled the outline for renewal that I had given him (an outline that gradually evolved into the final chapter of our book). The key to reversing this cycle was in limiting his noncounseling obligations. It is all too easy to get caught up in tangential responsibilities that drain time and personal energy away from client involvement. I know quite a number of formerly productive teachers and counselors who have become unfulfilled and overstressed by taking on too many administrative roles. This was the case with Jake. Rather than continue to complain, Jake had taken the offensive, and his proposed plan replaced many of his former duties with reinvolvement with students, faculty, and parents. It offered a creative blend of remedial and preventative approaches and was designed to get him out from under the paperwork and into a visible place in the school. This had its risks, but any new constructive direction of change always contains that element. At any rate, the principal was supportive, and Jake spent his year creating a new professional image. Much of the desired change really did occur, and Jake found himself caught in a positive cycle. Keep in mind at this point that Jake was a basically high-functioning person to begin with and had a wide repertoire of skills to fall back on, and a work situation that had not deteriorated beyond repair. It was salvageable, and the awareness for needed change and a plan of action were enough in this case.

This renewal cycle had many ingredients that had begun to feed into one another. It had become clear in our discussions that one of the core ingredients of the problem had been a particularly negative colleague that he had spent an increasingly large amount of time with over the last few years. He was a drain on Jake's enthusiasm. The strategy was to identify and cultivate healthier professional contacts rather than confront the colleague directly. This shift proved quite successful as Jake became reinvolved with our state counselor's association and found less and less time to spend with this negative influence. A secondary benefit of this involvement came as proposal for a presentation (regarding his school's peer counseling program) which he and two of his more positive colleagues are scheduled to deliver at a state convention.

In addition to the efforts directly geared toward breaking the burnout cycle, Jake had begun to work on the positive side of the equation. Although he was even busier than in previous years, he seemed to have more private time for himself and intimate time with family and friends. An exercise program that he has promised for years to develop was initiated on a regular basis. This not only became a reenergizing source, but made him physically fit enough to enjoy some of the sports involvement, i.e., playing church league basketball and participating in several racquetball tournaments that he had let slide. The loss of an extra 20 pounds did not hurt the positive cycle either. In terms of intimate time, Jake said that he was enjoying his family much more and had something positive to share with his wife after work for a change. Friendships had been renewed out of his sports involvement, and he had even taken a raft trip with several of these men.

I should emphasize that Jake had been a highly successful counselor who became trapped in administrative duties and paperwork. The joy of counseling had returned—he was productive (and probably creative) in his approach to his clients once again. His report at our summer workshop took on an almost evangelistic quality. He had recruited two of his colleagues to attend with him, and his enthusiasm set the tone for our entire workshop.

APPENDIX **TWO**

THE CARKHUFFIAN MODEL: AN ANNOTATED BIBLIOGRAPHY—A SAMPLE OF THE MAJOR CONTRIBUTIONS

Carkhuff, R. R., and Berenson, B. G. *Beyond counseling and therapy*. New York: Holt, 1967. This is the original and most thorough presentation of the Carkhuffian model. It presents a philosophical foundation for eclecticism and a structure for the counseling process and techniques to go along with it. The core conditions are introduced and the major contributions of the various schools of therapy critiqued. This text, which is a classic on eclecticism, has been updated in a 1976 revision.

Carkhuff, R. R. *Helping and human relations (Vols. I and II)*. New York: Holt, 1969. This scholarly two-volume work brings together Carkhuff's major findings regarding theory, research, and practice of his model. It is a thorough presentation of the eclectic viewpoint and also offers specific guidelines for the selection and training of people in the helping profession.

Carkhuff, R. R. *The art of helping*. Amherst, Mass.: Human Resource Development Press, 1972. Written in simple language, this book presents the basic Carkhuffian view in clear and readable fashion. It is focused on skill training and is a very practical guide for the layperson or professional helpers. The emphasis is on application rather than theory.

Carkhuff, R. R., and Berenson, B. G. *Teaching and treatment*. Amherst, Mass.: Human Resource Development Press, 1976. A translation of the basic model into prevention. Carkhuff introduces the theme of "moving upstream" as we go beyond remedial applications of his model. It contains the processes and skills necessary in moving the helping profession into a proactive stance that can make a difference in the lives of our clients.

Egan, G. *The skilled helper.* Belmont, Calif: Wadsworth, 1975. A three-stage model of helping is presented as an extension of earlier work by Carkhuff. It integrates both theory and skill training. It provides a very thorough orientation to the basic stages and illustrates their practical application through examples. It is supplemented by a training manual (Egan, G. *Exercises in helping skills.* Belmont, Calif.: Wadsworth, 1975) which serves as an excellent practicum guide for skill training. It consists of exercises designed to put the concepts and techniques presented in *The Skilled Helper* into practice.

Sisenberg, S., and Delaney, D. *The counseling process* (2nd ed.). Chicago: Rand McNally, 1977. This book defines the basic helping process in terms similar to Carkhuff and then explores a variety of application issues. It provides some excellent guidelines concerning confrontation, reluctant clients, goal identification, termination, and specific action strategies.

Other related references by Carkhuff and his associates:

Berenson, B. G. *Sources of gain in counseling and psychotherapy.* New York: Holt, 1967.

Berenson, B. G. *Belly-to-belly and back-to-back: The militant humanism of Robert R. Carkhuff.* Amherst, Mass.: Human Resources Development Press, 1976.

Berenson, B. G. *Introduction to human technology.* Amherst, Mass.: Human Resource Development Press, 1977.

Carkhuff, R. R. *The development of human resources.* New York: Holt, 1971.

Carkhuff, R. R. *The art of problem-solving.* Amherst, Mass.: Human Resource Development Press, 1973.

Carkhuff, R. R. *How to help yourself: The art of program development.* Amherst, Mass.: Human Resource Development Press, 1974.

Carkhuff, R. R., and Friel, T. W. *The career skills series.* Amherst, Mass.: Human Resource Development Press, 1974.

Truax, C. B., and Carkhuff, R. R. *Toward effective counseling and psychotherapy.* Chicago: Aldine, 1967.

APPENDIX

THREE

RISK WORKSHOPS: AN OUTLINE

Our risk workshops provide an opportunity for individuals to experience increased risk in their lives within a supportive group context. The authors have designed opportunities for involvement by participants in situations which are generally perceived as high risk by participants and which foster an intense level of personal challenge.

The important focus of any of these experiences should be on: (1) providing as much information as possible to the participant about each activity; (2) experiencing the importance of *individual* choice; (3) experiencing rational risk taking; (4) generating alternate choices for action to enhance problem solving; (5) affirming individual action; (6) providing for a series of time-out periods for the specified purpose of processing group experience; (8) transferring activity-related insights back into the individual's everyday life patterns; and (9) stimulating awareness of the importance of building challenges into the person's approach to life.

Participation in high-risk activities should be based on an evaluation of personal skills. When an individual either perceives risk inappropriately or evaluates personal skill inaccurately, the chance of physical injury is increased. This same perception process is true of other areas of life. Our job is to encourage a rational assessment of each activity in order to maximize challenge while minimizing the actual physical dangers. Growth occurs in the context of confronting risk squarely. Whether the activity is actually attempted or the participant drops out, the emphasis is placed on personal choice and the decision-making process. Processing individual and group participation, personal skill evaluation, risk perception, and the resulting activity choices allow participants to make more effective choices.

As mentioned in Chapter 7, lifelong friendships and intimate relationships which provide personal support are side benefits of the experience. Both are necessary conditions for effective risk taking in any life experience. The following outline illustrates a workshop led by the authors to accomplish these tasks.

ACTIVITY OUTLINE

Day 1:

1 Ride to the mountains while getting acquainted informally.

2 Hike to the top of a cliff. "Human knot" exercise to get acquainted and build support (cold wind and snow seem to enhance this exercise).

3 Basic instruction on the use of ropes and on safety procedures. Demonstration by leaders.

4 *Repel.* Participants who choose to repel receive constant instruction and support from instructors with experienced people below doing the same. Repel course is set up ahead of time under skilled supervision.

5 Process the experience during and after repel with each individual.

6 *Travolean traverse.* Walk to traverse site which has been set up ahead of time across a narrow canyon.

7 Demonstration of traverse and instruction of technique. Leaders should emphasize the importance of individual choice during each outing activity.

8 Ride back to base camp to process the resulting "high" which follows these two unique experiences.

9 Cook supper together on a campfire. Allow the high of high risk to flow into relaxed peace around a campfire.

10 Camp. Sleep in small groups with leaders in each group to facilitate discussion.

(An additional activity we have used quite successfully is a midnight raft trip in the dark—a gentle stretch of water is recommended with an instructor in each raft.)

Day 2:

1 Meet as group and have individuals share thoughts. Individual strengths from each person can be identified based upon their contribution. Actions from the day before as well as ideas currently being shared should be identified so that individual contributors begin to see their strengths more clearly.

2 Utilize a ropes course (a premountaineering training facility) to develop individual skills and further develop group cohesion. Our rope course was built near the mountains in a rugged setting, and consisted of a series of obstacles, barriers, and climbing structures. Similar courses can be erected inexpensively almost anywhere. *Caution!* These activities are attempted only under expert instruction and supervision. All activities involving actual physical risk use balay ropes for safety.

a A variety of group problem-solving tasks are used prior to actual course activities (paddle spinning, blind rope square, etc.)
b *Slanted wall barrier.* Task is to somehow get each participant over the slanted barrier, down the 90° drop 12 feet to the ground, and back over the barrier.
c *Trust fall.* Backward or forward free fall into the group from a 5-foot post or table.
d Process group and individual insights.
e *The vertical wall.* Individuals climb a 25-foot wall (straight up) through use of small foot holes.
f *The high rope.* A tightrope walk at 20 feet above ground with balance support rope and balay.
g *Individual activities.* A series of rope activities (fidget bridge, jungle ropes, swinging log, high log, etc.) may be approached after appropriate instruction and demonstration by the leaders. These activities are all potentially dangerous, and every precaution must be taken. Several hundred participants have gone through our course without any serious injury (lots of scrapes and bruises, however).
h *Blind walk.* Using verbal instructions but no contact. This activity is done on a half-mile course in rugged terrain.
i Process the experiences (group pressure, fears, exhilaration, failure) at each juncture.

Day 3:
1 Journey to river setting. It is important to focus on a low-key small group interaction. An informal appreciation of each participant should develop.
2 Set up camp. Complete this task as a unit.
3 A day of rafting.
a It is important that leaders teach skills of handling rafts and demonstrate the skills needed by participants in emergencies.
b As skills are learned and confidence develops, the authors believe that classes 1 and 2 water are appropriate for new groups so that they can relax and enjoy other participants as well as the rafting experience. More dangerous water can be arranged for advanced groups.
4 Camp music and a relaxed campfire supper is enjoyed. This time is important for group success and cohesion building.
5 *The night hike.* The challenge should be difficult enough so that individuals evaluate whether staying by the campfire is more appropriate than taking the hike. Select a mountain and hike the group to the top and back without the aid of flashlights. Groups discover the importance of helping each individual with this activity. At night, walking ability and eyesight vary drastically, and participants learn the importance of being helped. The processing of this activity has been one of the major highlights of the risking workshops. Profes-

sional helpers (counselors, teachers, social workers) who have participated in our workshops have often had difficulty asking others to help them.

Please note this day extends from early morning to around midnight.

Day 4:

1 Participants build fire and cook breakfast together. It is important for the facilitators of the workshop to encourage every participant to take part in this task. Day 3 is exhausting and participation in this morning activity helps participants internalize previously unrealized stamina.

2 *Raft trip.* A short trip on higher-risk water to extend risk and skills from the previous day.

3 Camp clean up.

4 The authors have used a variety of activities at this point—the time immediately prior to beginning the trip home. The goal has been a calm time with one intimate friend to recap personal feelings at this point. The second part of the activity is directed at providing an activity in which participants can share specific points of appreciation they have developed for each other. These two steps seem to confirm new friendships.

5 The trip back. Participants take this opportunity to reiterate the enthusiasm of day 3 and the closeness confirmed in the morning activities of day 4.

6 After reaching home, equipment cleanup and a formal closure takes place. An overview of theory relating recreational risk to everyday life is presented. The goals and insights of participants are placed on paper. Participants review and modify these goals during established follow-up dates.

APPENDIX FOUR

ASSESSING COUNSELOR BURNOUT

1 EXPLORATION: SELF-RATING INVENTORY

Assess each of the following areas. Subjectively rate yourself in terms of your general level of functioning in each area. A 5 rating reflects optimal functioning in that area, and the need to continue what you are already doing. A 1 rating denotes serious problem and should lead to further assessment and strategy building for related change. Ratings should reflect typical patterns for the target area and can be made by placing an X in the appropriate space.

	Low 1	2	Minimal 3	4	High 5
A Behavioral					
1 I have control over my behavior.	___	___	___	___	___
2 I am punctual in carrying out my responsibilities.	___	___	___	___	___
3 I am relatively free from self-defeating habits.	___	___	___	___	___
4 I am satisfied with my management of time and money.	___	___	___	___	___
5 I am flexible in my approach to problem solving.	___	___	___	___	___
6 I maintain a healthy activity level.	___	___	___	___	___

Sum of Ratings ________
Average ________

	Low 1	2	Minimal 3	4	High 5
B Cognitive					
1 I have an active imagination that I use constructively.	____	____	____	____	____
2 My interpretation of people and events is sensitive and accurate.	____	____	____	____	____
3 I rarely engage in dichotomous thinking or overgeneralization.	____	____	____	____	____
4 I have control over my patterns of thought.	____	____	____	____	____
5 My level of intellectual functioning is consistent with my personal and professional goals.	____	____	____	____	____
6 My self-expectancies are positive, flexible, and realistic.	____	____	____	____	____

Sum of Ratings ________

Average ________

	Low 1	2	Minimal 3	4	High 5
C Affective					
1 I am spontaneous and expressive in my emotional responses.	____	____	____	____	____
2 My prevailing mood is positive and optimistic.	____	____	____	____	____
3 I am rarely depressed or overanxious.	____	____	____	____	____
4 My motivational level is optimal for meeting my personal and professional goals.	____	____	____	____	____
5 I frequently experience genuine care and love for others.	____	____	____	____	____
6 My mood swings are maintained within a constructive balance.	____	____	____	____	____

Sum of Ratings ________

Average ________

	Low 1	2	Minimal 3	4	High 5
D Physical					
1 I have regular periods of strenuous physical exercise.	____	____	____	____	____
2 My physical fitness is at a level consistent with my personal and professional goals.	____	____	____	____	____
3 I see myself as physically attractive.	____	____	____	____	____
4 I have high levels of energy, stamina, and strength.	____	____	____	____	____
5 My nutritional needs are supported by a sensible diet.	____	____	____	____	____
6 I do not experience physical symptoms related to stress (cardiovascular, gastrointestinal, etc.).	____	____	____	____	____

Sum of Ratings ____________

Average ____________

	Low 1	2	Minimal 3	4	High 5
E Spiritual					
1 I have a system of beliefs that is positive and helps me understand my world.	____	____	____	____	____
2 I have peak experiences in which I experience an intense sense of joy.	____	____	____	____	____
3 I sense being a part of a larger scheme of living.	____	____	____	____	____
4 I have a strong sense of purpose in life.	____	____	____	____	____
5 I have a spiritual basis for life which serves a powerful organizational function upon which I can build.	____	____	____	____	____
6 I am striving to grow spiritually and convey this development to others.	____	____	____	____	____

Sum of Ratings ____________

Average ____________

	Low 1	2	Minimal 3	4	High 5
F Social/Environmental					
1 I have a well-developed and positive support system of friends and family.	___	___	___	___	___
2 I actively seek out high-functioning people to relate to on a daily basis.	___	___	___	___	___
3 I am assertive in my relationships with others as I attempt to meet my needs without infringing on the rights of people around me.	___	___	___	___	___
4 I am effective at implementing constructive changes in my environment.	___	___	___	___	___
5 I can accept those negative aspects of my environment which honestly cannot be changed.	___	___	___	___	___
6 I give a considerable amount of my skill and energy to promoting positive change in my environment and the people in it.	___	___	___	___	___

Sum of Ratings ________

Average ________

2 INTEGRATION: DEVELOPING A PICTURE

The preceding inventory was designed to help you generate some raw data to be assessed in this section. There are no established nouns for comparison. The key here is your own honest assessment of patterns of strengths and potential problem areas (burnout symptoms). The following steps are designed to lead you into a clear picture of yourself as related to personal and professional burnout patterns.

Step 1: Key Items Scan your self-rating inventory for extremely high- (strengths) and low- (burnout symptoms) scored items. Pull out the key items on both extremes and rewrite them in your own terms to add personal meaning.

Step 2: Pattern Analysis Sum the ratings on each of the six dimensions and then compute an average for each. Plot your average scores on the following assessment form to generate a personal/professional burnout profile.

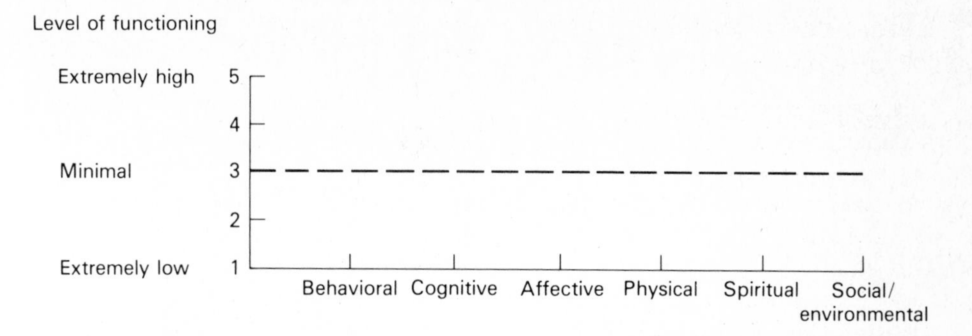

Scan your profile for signs of strength and areas of burnout potential. Redefine dimensions that are at the extremes in terms of specific behaviors that support both good and bad trends. State in specific operational terms, i.e., #1 Behavior: "I have control over my behavior"—rating of 1 or 2 becomes translated into self-defeating behaviors that have become habits, such as watching too much TV, overeating, inability to say "no" to demands, etc. We are looking for recurring themes which can be subdivided into specific patterns and ultimately into strategies for change. It may help to monitor target patterns and keep a daily record in order to establish their actual frequency and intensity. Now identify the burnout-related patterns by ranking them in order of severity (see hierarchy #1 below). Make another ranking in order of the highest potential for change and place list into hierarchy #1. Finally, search your hierarchies for a reasonable starting place—one that has a high probability for success. Additional guidelines for further assessment are described in several excellent resources (Hammond and Stanfield, 1977; Kazdin, 1980; Walker, Hedberg, Clement, and Wright, 1981).

Hierarchy #1 (burnout symptoms)		Hierarchy #2 (potential for constructive change)	
Most severe	1. ______	Highest change potential	1. ______
	2. ______		2. ______
	3. ______		3. ______
	4. ______		4. ______
	5. ______		5. ______
	6. ______		6. ______
Less severe	7. ______	Least likely to change	7. ______

Step 3. Creating a Visual Picture The next step involves building a mental image of the profile you have been developing. This should put the pieces of your puzzle together and serve as an organization structure to filter additional bits of data and monitor related changes. It should be creative, dynamic, and uniquely your own picture.

Using the data and integrated information developed to this point, create a visual representation of the patterns that have emerged. It should reflect strengths, weaknesses, burnout areas, and the degree of balance (or imbalance) in your personal/professional life. There are many possibilities:

a Draw your own window which reflects the patterns you have been pulling together. This conceptual scheme comes from Gordon, 1970 and appears throughout our final chapter on burnout. Each line in the window is dynamic and may move slowly or rapidly depending on your personality, your environment, and how you deal with it. A high stress line reflects serious burnout potential and very little constructive energy for yourself and others. We would suggest that you draw your window as you typically find it (reflecting relative time spent in each area), and then insert specific areas of strength and weakness. This is your chance to be creative so do not be limited by our diagram.

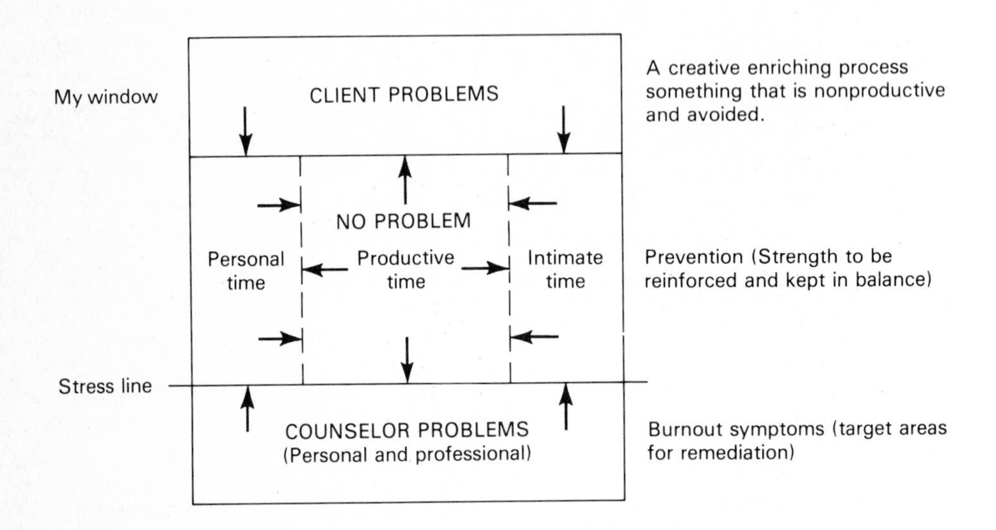

The Ideal Window Now draw a second window that reflects an ideal. A low stress line and wide no-problem area would seem to be characteristic of most high-functioning creative counselors. Now compare the two windows and look for target areas around which to build strategies for improvement.

b There are many ways to visually represent ourselves. The following offer possibilities that may fit you. Once again, we would challenge you to be creative and draw a visual portrait that is personally meaningful. We frequently ask (and help) our clients design similar self-profile pictures and find it extremely useful in our own lives. Colored and three-dimensional drawing may add considerably to our ability to understand ourselves. Other possibilities are limitless. Every major school of counseling from psychoanalytic to Gestalt to transactional analysis has developed visual conceptualizations to help their clients gain a clearer image of themselves and identify areas of needed change. Spirals, pyramids, concentric circles, free-style drawing—use whatever it takes to formulate an image that can be translated into action.

The Wheel

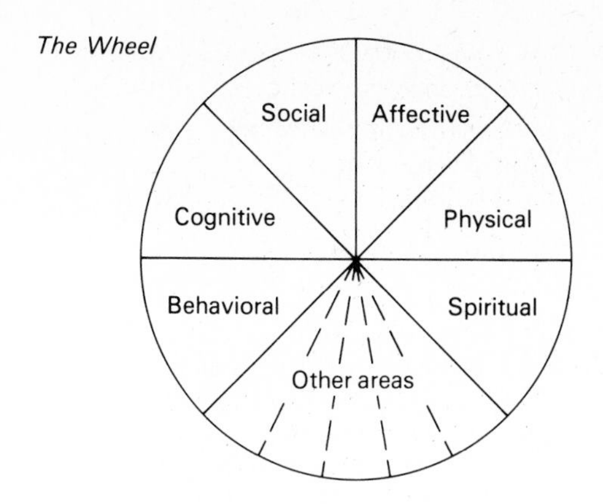

The Flower

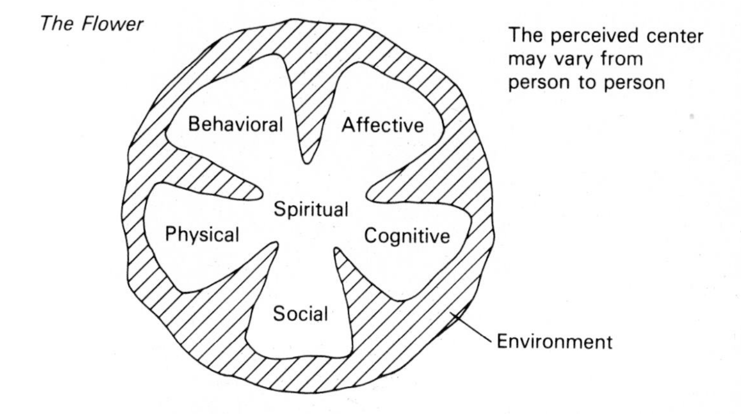

CHANGE: PUTTING INSIGHT INTO ACTION

Following the basic model (Carkhuff and Berenson, 1967), it becomes imperative that we translate insights into goals and strategies for constructive change. The direction and amount of change will depend on your assessed level of functioning overall and in the areas you have evaluated. The following might serve as a rough guideline for equating your profile with a plan of action.

Serious Burnout Pattern (Levels 1 and 2) Serious interventions may be called for at this time. We suggest that you seek out professional help. We counselors are not always very good at practicing what we preach to our clients about taking care of ourselves. When caught in a burnout cycle, we can become our own worst enemy, and there are times when we just cannot break out by ourselves. Perhaps this is why the suicide rate is so high among helping professionals. Depending upon the pervasiveness and chronicity, the intervention may be short- or long-term, but do not put it off if you need help.

High Functioning (Levels 4 and 5) Our entire book was written with you in mind. You are in a good place to take risks and push yourself beyond perceived limits. You have a high potential for creative counseling, and we hope that our suggestions will help you realize the use of this potential as frequently as possible. We would further hope that you would be proactive in identifying and helping fellow professionals who have burnout problems. We have to support each other, and the strong are the only ones in a position to help other professionals function at a higher level.

REFERENCES

Carkhuff, R. R., and Berenson, B. G. *Beyond counseling and therapy*. New York: Holt, 1967.

Gordon T. *Parent effectiveness training*. New York: Wyden, 1970.

Hammond, D. C., and Stanfield, K. *Multidimensional psychotherapy*. Champaign, Ill.: Institute for Personality and Ability Testing, 1977.

Kazdin, A. E. *Behavior modification in applied settings* (2nd ed.). Homewood, Ill.: Dorsey, 1980.

Walker, C. E., Hedberg, A., Clement, P. W., and Wright, L. *Clinical procedures for behavior therapy*. Englewood Cliffs, N.J.: Prentice-Hall, 1981.

INDEX